# The
# Collector's
# Guide to
# eBay®

## The Ultimate Resource for *Buying, Selling,* and *Valuing* Collectibles

# The Collector's Guide to eBay®

## The Ultimate Resource for *Buying, Selling,* and *Valuing* Collectibles

Greg Holden

**McGraw-Hill**/Osborne

New York  Chicago  San Francisco  Lisbon
London  Madrid  Mexico City  Milan  New Delhi
San Juan  Seoul  Singapore  Sydney  Toronto

The *McGraw·Hill* Companies

**McGraw-Hill**/Osborne
2100 Powell Street, 10th Floor
Emeryville, California 94608
U.S.A.

To arrange bulk purchase discounts for sales promotions, premiums, or fund-raisers, please
contact **McGraw-Hill**/Osborne at the above address. For information on translations or
book distributors outside the U.S.A., please see the International Contact Information page
immediately following the index of this book.

**The Collector's Guide to eBay®:**
**The Ultimate Resource for Buying, Selling, and Valuing Collectibles**

1234567890 FGR FGR 0198765

ISBN 0-07-225766-0

| | |
|---|---|
| **Vice President & Group Publisher** | Philip Ruppel |
| **Vice President & Publisher** | Jeffrey Krames |
| **Acquisitions Editor** | Marjorie McAneny |
| **Project Editor** | Beatrice Wikander |
| **Acquisitions Coordinator** | Agatha Kim |
| **Technical Editor** | David T. Alexander |
| **Copy Editor** | Leslie Tilley |
| **Proofreader** | Paul Tyler |
| **Indexer** | Claire Splan |
| **Composition** | Lucie Ericksen, Peter F. Hancik |
| **Illustrators** | Kathleen Edwards, Melinda Lytle |
| **Series Design** | Mickey Galicia |
| **Cover Design** | Jeff Weeks |

This book was composed with Corel VENTURA™ Publisher.

# Dedication

To my mother and father, and to the fun we've had finding,
restoring, and selling treasures of all sorts.

## About the Author

For much of his adult life, Greg Holden has been hunting down and reselling collectibles, oddball items, and antiques of all sorts. In his younger days, he assembled an old sports car from pieces of three different sports cars. He bought and restored a century-old townhouse. Now, he hunts down fountain pens, watches, and other items online. Greg has written more than 25 books on computers and the Internet, including *How to Do Everything with Your eBay Business* and *How to Do Everything with eBay*, also by McGraw-Hill/Osborne, and *Cliff's Notes Guide to Buying and Selling on eBay* and *Internet Auctions for Dummies*, both published by Wiley. His lifelong interests in literature and writing and the history of Chicago recently culminated in the book *Literary Chicago: A Book Lover's Tour of the Windy City*, published by Lake Claremont Press. He lives in Chicago in the house he restored along with his two daughters and an assortment of pets.

## About the Technical Reviewer

David T. Alexander has been involved in a lifelong quest to locate weird, rare, and unusual collectors' items including comic books, movie posters, pulp magazines, and original art. In the late 1960s David set up his first mail-order operation, and since that time he has devoted all of his professional efforts to buying and selling collectibles. He has been an editor, publisher, or advisor for many well-known and respected publications in the collectibles market, including *The Overstreet Comic Book Price Guide*, *The Baseball and Sports Publications Price Guide*, *The Old Magazines Price Guide*, and the *Poster Price Almanac*. Since 1999 David has been buying and selling on eBay. He is a PowerSeller who has achieved more than $100,000 in one month's selling on eBay. He currently runs his collectibles web site, CultureandThrills.com, from Tampa, Florida.

# Contents at a Glance

# Contents

# Acknowledgments

Collecting on eBay seems like something you do yourself. But the truth is that you're never really alone. You ask other collectors for appraisals, you scour other web sites for information on special brands and models, and you communicate with the sellers from whom you purchase the items you seek so eagerly. Any transaction sale on eBay depends on help and cooperation from a community of collectors and other members.

In the same way, writing a book about eBay depends on a community of individuals you might never meet face to face. First, I want to thank the eBay sellers who took the time to share their knowledge with me either on the phone or by e-mail. Thanks go to Nancee Belshaw, Paula Amato, Jo Stavig, and Wayne McKenzie. Also thanks to Emily Sabako and Scott Wills.

I have been impressed with the enthusiasm and encouragement I have received from all the folks at McGraw-Hill/Osborne, starting with Margie McAneny, who got the ball rolling (and kept it rolling smoothly); Agatha Kim, who kept everything on track as acquisitions coordinator; Beatrice Wikander, who served as my project editor; technical editor David T. Alexander, an experienced collector in his own right; copy editor Leslie Tilley; and publicity manager Bettina Faltermeier.

Thanks also to my agent Neil Salkind and everyone at Studio B Productions. Also thanks to Ann Lindner, my intrepid assistant, who helped me with this and many other projects (including my own collecting excursions). Last but not least, thanks to my mother and father, who instilled the love of giving new life to someone else's castoffs—a practice that carries over perfectly to the new electronic flea market, eBay. Bargain hunting is an art I'm now passing down to my two daughters, Zosia and Lucy, as their sharp eyes are becoming ever more skilled at finding just what they're looking for at thrift shops and garage sales. Sharing so many adventures with them puts fun in my life, especially when they allow me to share their ever-widening circle of loving friends and pets.

# Introduction

From the start, eBay has been a collectors' paradise. Among the first items put up for sale on eBay in the fall of 1995 were a Hubley toy dump truck and a Rolls Royce Silver Shadow motor car. In the ensuing decade, amateurs, antiques dealers, and entrepreneurs have all seized upon eBay as a way to make money and find buyers for their wares. These days, eBay is very much part of mainstream society. Buyers are learning to turn to eBay for household goods, clothing, and everyday items of all sorts. But it's still the ideal place for collectors to buy, sell, and appraise their wares.

If you haven't started buying on eBay yet, this book will give you a user-friendly introduction to the world's most popular marketplace. Even if you've already done a few searches on eBay for long-lost toys from your childhood, you'll learn how to round out your collection and locate scarce, rare items that are in most cases no longer manufactured. You'll also learn how to get a competitive price for such rarities and not get cheated by sellers who aren't trustworthy. And, whether you need to clear out your shelves and get rid of part of your collection or want a new source of regular income, this book will provide the know-how so you can sell successfully on eBay.

You don't have to take just my word for any of it, either. Along with my own sage advice, drawn from my 30-plus years as an obsessed collector, *The Collector's Guide to eBay* also includes tips and advice from folks who have successfully used eBay—both as buyers and sellers. Together, my fellow collectors and I will show you how to access eBay's database of completed auctions to determine how much your own possessions are worth in the real world. You'll also learn how to use other web sites to learn about what you collect. For example, the Elgin Watches web site compares different methods of valuing its collectible watches at http://elginwatches.org/help/watch_values_accurate.html. It also suggests that eBay may provide the most accurate method of determining worth: "It's worth what someone will pay for it," as the saying goes.

Unfortunately, not every resident of eBay is a good citizen. There are a few who get distracted and don't follow through with transactions, and even some who actively try to swindle other people. Accordingly, the experienced members who are featured in this book's Trade Talk and other sidebars will tell you how to stay out of trouble, too.

But most of the aspects of the free market that eBay has inherited are good. And over the years it has become more reliable and easier to use. So, whether you're a casual computer user or have been surfing the Internet for a while, this book will have you buying and selling on eBay in no time.

# How This Book Is Organized

The only assumptions this book makes about you, the reader, are that you have some familiarity with the Web and the Internet and that you want to use eBay successfully. Part I, "Collecting: Basic Information," starts at the beginning—explaining how eBay differs from traditional auctions as a place to buy and sell collectibles. You'll discover how to find your way around the site and how to find and research collectibles. You also get suggestions for how to sell off some of your collection: how to create sales descriptions, how to take good digital images, and how to take advantage of the eBay collectors' community if you need help and advice.

Part II, "Shopping and Collecting," seeks to take you beyond being a casual eBay user. In Chapter 5, you learn how to be an eBay "power searcher" by creating complex searches, saving favorite searches, and scouring parts of eBay's voluminous web site that you might have otherwise overlooked. In Chapter 6, you get some tips on shopping and bidding on overseas auctions. In Chapter 7, you learn about eBay Live Auctions, which enable you to compete with collectors in some of the world's great auction houses and place bids in a matter of seconds.

Part III, "Selling Collectibles," focuses on how to start selling and generating some income on eBay. In Chapter 8, you explore the ins and outs of one of the most important ways to attract bids: providing good images of your merchandise. Chapter 9 focuses on ways to find bargains and discover what's desirable on eBay so that you can maximize your chances of success. In Chapter 10, you learn some advanced strategies for selling collectibles on eBay. These include eBay's Live Auctions, the Trading Assistants Program, becoming a PowerSeller, and opening an eBay store. Chapter 11 examines how to exchange payments safely on eBay, whether by accepting traditional paper checks or taking credit card payments.

Part IV, "Advanced Collectors' Options," takes a look at the "back end"— indispensable business operations that can transform your collecting hobby into a successful eBay business. Chapter 12 focuses on using eBay as a tool for appraising collectibles and merchandise of all sorts. Chapter 13 encourages you to build volume and increase sales by automating your sale listings. Chapter 14 shows you how to reach out to other collectors and become a player in the community by starting your own eBay group. Finally, Chapter 15 covers accounting, tracking sales and inventory, and other financial details of interest to anyone who buys and sells collectibles for a living. You'll learn how to save records that are sure to come in handy at tax time.

# How to Use This Book

I didn't write this book with the expectation that you would read it from beginning to end like a story. As on the Web itself, you should feel free to skip around from chapter to chapter to find the information you need to get down to business immediately. Here are some special elements that will help you get the most out of the book:

- **Collecting Step-by-Step** These boxes explain, in a nutshell, how to accomplish essential tasks. Read them to focus on key points covered in each chapter.

- **Trade Talk** These short sections provide you with extra information so that you can better understand eBay or a particular way you might want to use the site.

- **Collector's Note** These notes spotlight basics that will give you an immediate grasp of a particular topic.

- **Tip** Tips tell you how to do something smarter or faster.

- **Watch Out!** These notes point out potential pitfalls that you need to steer around so you can keep operating smoothly.

- **Sidebars** Here, I address topics that are related to the subject at hand and that illuminate it in a new way.

- **Voices from the Community** These are profiles of eBay collectors who buy and sell regularly and who have volunteered to tell their stories to help you be a smarter eBay collector.

- **Links for Collectors** Each chapter ends with a set of links to resources on eBay and other web sites that will help you save time and buy and sell more effectively.

Within the text, you also find words in special formatting. New terms appear in italics, while specific commands you need to choose or type yourself are in boldface.

Along the way, you'll read comments and tips from individuals who sell on eBay on a daily basis and who have been generous enough to share their expertise with you. The information in this book has been compiled by me with the help of other online "experts." Don't be surprised if a web page or a piece of software isn't exactly where it's described in the book: eBay's site changes all the time, as does the rest of the Web. A quick Google search should enable you to find any of the resources covered in this book. That's just part of the fun of doing business online.

I wish you happy buying and selling on eBay. Relax, have fun, and enjoy being a member of the community. And why not keep the ball rolling by telling me about your own experiences and whether this book has helped you? Please drop me a line at greg@gregholden.com. Either on eBay or via e-mail, I look forward to seeing you around.

# Part I

## Collecting: Basic Information

# Chapter 1

# Exploring the New Collectors' Paradise: eBay!

## In This Chapter You'll Learn...

- Why eBay is replacing many traditional collectors' marketplaces

- How you can use eBay to build up your collection

- How to trade smart and avoid common mistakes

- Ways to become a more knowledgeable collector with eBay

- How to find buyers for your collectibles on eBay

When eBay started as AuctionWeb in the fall of 1995, it had only two categories, and one of them was Collectibles (the other was Computers). eBay has always been an ideal place for collectors: after spending years scouring flea markets and stores for hard-to-find treasures, you go on eBay, and suddenly you find often obscure and rare variations on what you collect. You can shop in the comfort of your own home anytime of the day or night, and you don't have to accommodate the hours kept by antique stores or the distance you have to drive to get to flea markets.

This chapter introduces you to eBay as a marketplace for collectors. You learn about the countless varieties of collectibles you can find for sale, both at auction and at fixed price. Buyers learn how eBay can help them build up a collection; sellers learn how they can make some extra money by selling what they already know, love, and collect. You learn how eBay and its knowledgeable communities of collectors can help you become an expert in your area of interest. You learn how to avoid some common pitfalls and be a smarter trader, too.

# Changing the Playing Field for Collectors

The first visit to eBay's home page (http://ebay.com) can be mind-boggling for collectors. Consider one time-honored collectors' item, the comic book. Even the most dedicated collectors might go years without seeing famous issues like Action Comics No. 1, Batman No. 1, and the like. Such items will probably turn up at collectors' conventions but, depending on where you live, you might have to drive hours to reach the event, only to find that these rarities are priced at tens of thousands of dollars each. The moment I did a search on eBay in June 2004, I turned up these scarce issues:

- Three copies of Batman No. 1 for fixed prices of $6400, $5995, and $5499 respectively. (The second of these three examples is shown in Figure 1-1.)

- Variations on Batman No. 1, such as Batman Cult No. 1, Robin No. 1, and Batgirl No. 1

- Many 1976 reissues of Action Comics No. 1, which was produced in a limited edition

- Superman No. 1, dating from 1939, for $8899

- Superboy No. 1, from 1949, selling for $1999

Thanks to eBay, your challenge as a collector has shifted. The problem is not simply finding these items but being selective about them. You have the luxury of being able to pick the issue in the best quality or the seller who has the best

**FIGURE 1-1**    Thanks to eBay, the challenge is no longer finding rarities like this but choosing between various offerings.

reputation in the form of feedback left by other eBay members. The higher the feedback rating, the better the seller's experience and reputation. For instance, Table 1-1 compares the three Batman No. 1 copies mentioned earlier.

The sellers all have fairly similar feedback ratings; the seller of copy 2 has a slight edge, perhaps, because of the high feedback number. But at nearly a thousand dollars less than copy 1, copy 3 looks like a fairly good buy. The point is that eBay gives you the power to choose; if you shop long enough and have the patience to wait weeks or even months, you're sure to find a copy that's just as good, possibly at an even better price—or one that prospective buyers can bid on at auction rather than being available only at a fixed price.

## What Can You Collect on eBay?

In spring 2004, eBay held its first annual Crazy for Collecting contest—a contest held to locate eBay collectors with outstanding collections. The winners won a free trip to eBay Live, eBay's annual gathering of members, which was held that year in New Orleans. Winners included:

- Kathryn Nuttall, who has an extensive collection of sports photos

- Cindy Miller, who has a collection of Nascar models

- Rachel Armstrong, who collects pottery

- Margaret Rosack, who collects antique trivets

- Bill Cawlfield, who has an amazing collection of radios (see Figure 1-2)

| Item | Price | Seller Feedback Number | Feedback Rating | Condition |
|---|---|---|---|---|
| 1 | $6,400 | 195 | 100% positive | The copy is restored and graded 6.0 by the well-respected Comics Guaranty Corp. (CGC) |
| 2 | $5,995 | 360 | 99.3% positive | Graded only 1.5 by CGC because cover and centerfold are detached and copy is unrestored |
| 3 | $5,499 | 164 | 96.6% positive | Restored copy, graded 3.0, with white pages rather than worn, off-white ones |

TABLE 1-1　Choosing between high-quality collectibles on eBay

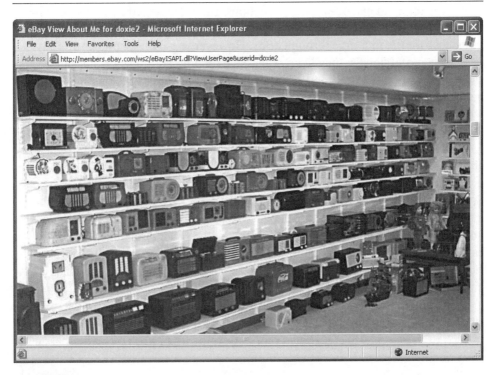

**FIGURE 1-2**    eBay collectors are passionate about anything and everything, and some carry their passion to great lengths.

These kinds of collectibles are more or less "normal" when compared with other objects seen on eBay, including Band-Aid memorabilia, anything having to do with the processed meat product called Spam, rolling pins, egg cups, or telephone pole insulators.

## Comparing eBay and Traditional Auctions

eBay is best-known for its auctions, even though fixed-price sales called Buy It Now are also popular options on the site, as are web sites called eBay stores, where members can put up large quantities of fixed-price items for sale.

If you are at all familiar with the kinds of traditional auctions held by antiques dealers, liquidation sellers, and others, you can understand eBay better by comparing how traditional auctions work to how virtual auctions work on eBay. eBay auctions have some similarities to traditional auction sales, but the big difference is the seller.

eBay specializes in person-to-person auctions: sales conducted by amateurs who are either trying to raise money on eBay in their spare time or trying to start up a business for the first time through eBay. However, a growing number of eBay sellers are professionals: they have experience running antique stores or other shops housed in brick-and-mortar storefronts, and they are expanding to eBay to boost their income and stay in business. eBay, after all, represents a significant source of competition to traditional vendors of antiques and collectibles.

The other big difference between eBay sales and those in the real world is timing. eBay sales last for a fixed period of time—1, 3, 5, 7, or 10 days. The seller chooses how long the auction can last. The auction's ending time is determined by the time it appears on eBay: if a sale goes on eBay at 10:05 A.M. Pacific time on a Sunday and the seller chooses a length of 7 days, the sale will end at 10:05 A.M. the following Sunday. The seller can choose to end the sale early, but this does not happen often, because doing so can damage the seller's reputation. The sale can also end before the specified time if the seller has added a Buy It Now price. If a Buy It Now price is available, a buyer can click the Buy It Now button and purchase the item immediately.

Within this general framework, eBay auctions fall into one of three categories: standard, reserve, and Dutch auctions. See Chapter 2 for more detailed explanations of each of these types of sales and a more in-depth comparison of traditional and eBay auctions.

## Attracting a Worldwide Audience

Numbers increase the odds for collectors that they'll find that special something, or find a buyer for the special something they hope to sell. When you attend a flea market that has several thousand sellers, you're more likely to find something than at a flea market with 100 sellers, for instance.

The "numbers" principle works on eBay, too. Every day, an estimated 16 million new items are being offered for sale either on the main eBay site in the United States or in other versions of eBay around the globe. eBay has said that it has as many as 69 million members. Every day, 2 million new sales items are placed online. With that kind of volume, shoppers are bound to find just about anything up for sale on eBay sooner or later. If you are a seller, you gain the ability to place your sales items before the eyes of prospective customers around the world. If you are a buyer, you can shop eBay not only in your own country but also in special international versions of the site located around the globe. For instance, you can find travel bargains and regional specialties in overseas eBays like the UK version shown in Figure 1-3.

**FIGURE 1-3**  eBay's U.S. auction listings include sales in other countries, but you can also find travel and ticket bargains by visiting international versions of the site.

**COLLECTOR'S NOTE**  *The figures about eBay's membership are taken from an eBay Radio show conducted in early 2004 and an interview with an eBay spokesman on the WebTalk Radio site in summer 2003 (http://www.webtalkguys.com/ article-ebay.shtml). eBay Radio is a weekly show presented on the Internet live every Tuesday. You can read instructions on how to listen in at http:// www.wsradio.com/ebayradio.*

## Moving Beyond Price Guides

For many years, we collectors had to depend on printed price guides to tell us what was rare and special and give us an idea what constitutes a reasonable price for something. When I collected records, I remember poring over the Record Collectors' Price Guide for hours at a time, eagerly looking for the rarest and most unusual variations on records by the Beatles or other groups—things I would never even know about otherwise. I have four or five different price guides on fountain pens and one especially thick one on watches.

Price guides are updated regularly (usually every year), so collectors are forced to make an annual purchase in order to stay on top of the latest changes in the market. Every year, for instance, my mother comes up with a short list of Christmas gifts, and every year the latest edition of the same antiques price guide is on the list. I don't think eBay is going to completely replace price guides, because they are so convenient and portable, and they often include photos of rare items that are of higher quality than you typically see online. But when it comes to convenient shopping and real-world values of collectibles, you can't beat eBay. eBay's database of completed auctions provides you with accurate records of what buyers in the real world have paid for antiques and collectibles in the recent past.

 *See Chapter 5 for more about searching eBay, and Chapter 12 for tips on using eBay to assess the value of collectibles you want to buy or sell.*

# Building Your Collection on eBay

People collect on eBay for many different reasons. Some are trying to make an investment in the future. Many follow the age-old advice that you should buy what you love, not just because you're hoping to make a profit. Others just want to have fun. eBay's wide-open marketplace is big enough to accommodate all your collecting dreams and goals. But it's important to be a smart collector. Some suggestions for avoiding trouble are described in the following sections.

## Setting Goals for Acquiring Your Collectibles

It's so easy to start acquiring and accumulating on eBay that you can quickly end up with rooms full of things you don't have room for. Plus, it's easy to go into debt quickly as a result of an eBay "addiction." (I personally know people who've been in both situations.) Buying on eBay works best when you set goals and parameters for your collecting. Limit the scope of what you search for, and be selective about what you buy. Also set limits on how much you spend, keeping in mind that, no matter how unusual it seems, you're likely to see it again on eBay at some time in the near future.

TIP *You can configure a special page called My eBay to "watch" for items. When items turn up with the qualities you are looking for, you'll automatically receive an e-mail notification about them. See "Watching Sales" in Chapter 5 for instructions on how to have eBay watch so that you don't have to keep visiting the site continually (unless you want to, of course).*

You can organize your collecting activities by focusing on a particular area of interest and limiting your purchases according to one or more of the following criteria:

- **Era**   Lots of collectibles can be organized by decade, century, or even individual years. By searching for and purchasing objects that were manufactured and distributed in a particular period you make your hunt more manageable, and you can save money, too. You might like shoes, but you might focus only on those from the 1950s, for instance. Or you might collect items from a particular era or period, like the Roaring Twenties or the World War II years.

- **Manufacturer, designer, or artist**   Many collectors focus on a single artist or designer they like, or a special brand name or manufacturer. I'm partial to fountain pens made by the Waterman company and watches made by the Elgin National Watch Company of Elgin, Illinois, for instance. If you take the time to acquire pieces that fall into a series or a complete line made by a single manufacturer, you can come to a detailed understanding of the materials used, the design elements, and the manufacturing process. In the world of fountain pens, you learn that some colors are rare because they were experiments; others (like yellow) are hard to find because they were fragile and cracked easily.

- **Special features**   If you focus only on first-edition books or only on books with dust jackets, you'll have a more manageable collection.

- **Price**   This is the most obvious way to keep yourself from getting carried off to an eBay "12-step program." Setting a spending limit is always a sensible idea. You'll get flexibility if you don't stick to a firm ceiling for a maximum price but set a median price you're willing to pay and keep track of purchases that go under and above that amount. For example, you might set a median price of $35 but find a rare item you've always wanted for $50. You can pay the higher amount, but keep in mind that your next purchase price needs to be $20 to stay at your desired median.

It's easy to pile up dozens of purchases on eBay. It's harder when you set limits and try to be discerning about what you buy. It takes longer to build up a collection this way, but each item you add to your collection is more exciting and memorable.

**WATCH OUT!** *When you collect, give some thought to whether value is likely to increase or drop in the future. Collectors who bought Beanie Baby plush toys during the height of the craze in the late 1990s haven't seen great appreciation in that area. On the other hand, the release of the DVD of* Star Wars *increased interest and made that film's collectibles even more valuable. If you know the anniversary of a famous person's death or other significant historical event is coming up, consider buying memorabilia in the hope that it will grow in value as the anniversary approaches.*

## Collecting for Kids and Parents

Kids make great collectors, and collecting can be a rewarding family activity. My own kids have collected the state quarters that are being released each year, as well as other coins like the Sacajawea gold dollar and the Susan B. Anthony dollar. One of my daughters has rock and marble collections as well.

In order to actually bid on and purchase on eBay, however, you have to be 18 years old. So collecting for kids on eBay *needs* to be a family affair: you should log on and shop with your kids, sharing your knowledge of what constitutes a good buy and what makes a reputable seller. (See Chapters 2 and 5 to brush up on these subjects.) When it comes time to bid, place bids and make purchases using your own account, and keep track of just how much your children spend.

**WATCH OUT!** *In my book* How to Do Everything with eBay *(McGraw-Hill Osborne; 2004), I interviewed one teenager who was obviously too young to bid on eBay, but who told me his parents approved of his buying and selling online because it was bringing in extra money. Keep your own user ID and password private, and change your password periodically for greater security.*

## Evaluating Condition

It's easy to take digital photos and post them online. But many digital photos, when viewed through a web browser, have serious limitations. The limitations don't necessarily come from digital cameras, which now have the capacity to capture many megabytes' worth of digital information. The problem is that many digital photos are too big in file size, and most computer monitors have a limited capacity to display that amount of information.

The important thing for you, as a collector, to remember is that you need to be absolutely sure about any cracks, stains, or other flaws that might detract from the value of what you want to buy. If the seller's description does not show the item from many different angles and does not show clear close-ups, ask that more photos be taken and posted online or sent to you by e-mail. Or just ask the seller for assurances about the condition of what is being sold. For high-end collectibles such as works of art, you can even get an appraisal from an authority in the field (see Chapter 12 for suggestions).

 *Many eBay sellers (especially the more successful ones) have a return policy: buyers can return items if they are not satisfied and get a refund. Many buyers look for such sellers, because they know their satisfaction is guaranteed.*

# Avoiding Beginners' Pitfalls

Failing to be aware of the condition of what you purchase on eBay is only one of the potential problems you can run into. When you make a purchase online, your biggest challenge is the lack of personal contact with the people with whom you do business. You can't always inspect an item personally before you buy it, unless you are considering something offered by a seller who lives in your own immediate area. For sellers, you can't inspect the buyer's credit card or other information before he or she hands over payment. Problems do arise when items are lost in shipment, arrive damaged, or don't arrive at all. Buyers who win an auction don't always pay for what they've won; checks sometimes bounce, and credit cards can turn out to be stolen. But such problems only occur in a small percentage of transactions; most sales on eBay go smoothly—so smoothly that buyer and seller occasionally strike up a friendship, and buyers decide to revisit the same seller on a regular basis. If you avoid a few common pitfalls, your eBay collecting experience will be smooth sailing, too.

## Bid with Your Head, Not Your Heart

eBay is far more exciting than I can hope to describe in the pages of this book. Nothing can match the heart-pounding excitement as a sale winds down to its final seconds and you wait to see if your high bid will be outdone. If you are a seller, it can be astonishing and rewarding to see something you put up for sale attract bids and counterbids that are far higher than you could ever have hoped.

But remember not to bid so high that you can't afford what you have purchased. If you have to walk away from a sale, or if someone outbids you at the last second, it's a safe bet that you'll see something similar later on. Time and again, I've tried to win a certain Waterman fountain pen on eBay, and time and again I've been outbid. But nearly every time I revisit the site, there's another one for sale. As I write this, in fact, there's another one for sale and the auction is ending in a few hours (see Figure 1-4). But the price is a little above my budget.

**COLLECTOR'S NOTE** *What happens if you make a Buy It Now purchase or win an auction and have second thoughts? This has happened to me: I purchased a birdcage on eBay, and later discovered a better and less expensive cage at a local store. I followed through with the original eBay purchase. Why? I didn't want to incur negative feedback by backing out of a sale. I'm also fairly confident I can resell the cage for the amount I paid for it. There isn't any provision for backing out of sales you make on eBay; you can ask a seller for mercy, but technically, you are obligated to follow through with a sale because a purchase is considered a binding contract.*

**FIGURE 1-4**    Stick to a budget and don't overbid; you're likely to see another item in the future among eBay's millions of sales.

# Don't Bid at the Wrong Time

Sometimes, *when* you place your bid is as important as how much you bid. Because eBay auction sales end at a fixed time that is often announced as much as a week in advance, they attract bids placed in the last few minutes, or even the last few seconds. These are called *snipe bids.* They occur so late in the sale that they prevent other bidders from placing a counterbid. If the snipe bid turns out to be the high one when the sale ends, that bid is the winner.

The problem is that you can't always be present at the end of a sale. In that case, you can place a proxy bid: you tell eBay the maximum amount you are willing to pay, and eBay automatically places bids on your behalf until your maximum amount is reached. If a snipe bid is placed that isn't as large as your proxy bid, your proxy bid wins.

# Make Sure You Read the Fine Print

Sometimes, buyers are surprised when they unpack what they have purchased, and not in a good way. As a collector who wants to buy on eBay, your goal should be to have no surprises. You should know exactly what you are willing to pay, how long before it will be shipped, when it is shipped, and approximately when it will arrive at your door. When you open the box, you shouldn't get any surprises in the form of flaws or color differences.

Don't be in a hurry to read through a sales listing on eBay. Take your time; write down the important points; click the Ask Seller a Question link on the sales page, and send the seller a message through eBay's message system. In particular, make sure you are aware of the following points, which are sometimes missing from eBay descriptions:

- Shipping charges
- Handling charges
- Sales tax requirements
- Return policy
- Whether the item comes with original packaging
- Whether the item has been repaired or restored
- Where the item comes from (collectors and appraisers call this *provenance*)

*Asking the seller questions is a great way to get an idea of the level of customer service you are likely to get from that individual. If the seller responds quickly, is courteous, and answers your questions completely, you can tell that person ranks customer service as an important consideration. If the seller doesn't respond for several days (and hasn't provided notice in the description that he or she will be out of town while the sale is going on) or doesn't respond clearly to your questions, you might think twice about clicking the Place Bid or Buy It Now button.*

## Research Your Seller

People who run brick-and-mortar storefronts seem reputable. They are listed in the phone book; they pay rent for their store; they may be listed in the local Chamber of Commerce or be known to the Better Business Bureau. On eBay, sellers also have different ways to let prospective customers know that they are reputable and trustworthy individuals. But it's up to you to do the research that makes you aware of that fact. The PowerSeller icon that appears next to sellers who have met eBay's requirements for that coveted designation is definitely a sign that the seller is committed to good customer service.

On eBay, the primary way of evaluating buyers and sellers is through feedback: comments left on eBay by individuals who have previously done business with that same person. By reading such comments, you get an idea whether the person can be trusted. If the seller has a feedback rating of 0, it's not a definitive sign that you shouldn't do business with that person, but only that you should be careful. If the seller or buyer has a negative rating, that *is* a warning sign, however. See Chapter 2 for more on taking advantage of eBay's feedback system, which rewards good behavior and encourages all members to act in a trustworthy way.

# Using eBay to Become an Expert in Your Field

eBay isn't just a place for buying and selling. Thanks to the discussion boards where its members have congregated for years and where they share tips and advice, eBay is a great place to learn. Plenty of eBay buyers and sellers have learned from other members how to take photos, how to post them for sale, how to handle shipping, and how to iron out disagreements with buyers. Not only that, but you can use eBay to learn more about the very items you want to collect, so you can be a smarter collector.

# Learning from Other Experts

Margaret Rosack, one of the collectors recognized in eBay's first Crazy for Collecting contest, runs several eBay Groups, and has written a book about collecting trivets (see Figure 1-5). She's a great example of someone who shares her knowledge and reaches out to eBay's community for support.

You'll find Margaret in the eBay Groups area of eBay's community venues. eBay Groups are discussion areas created by members themselves and moderated by other members; they bring collectors together based on the area where they live or the type of objects they collect. You'll also find her on her About Me page: http://members.ebay.com/ws2/eBayISAPI.dll?ViewUserPage&userid=tornado-lynn. An About Me page is a web page that eBay lets each of its members create about themselves so they can tell other members about their interests and background.

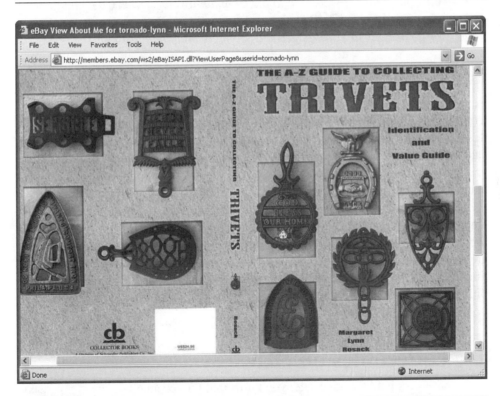

**FIGURE 1-5**   eBay collectors are often knowledgeable in their field and willing to share tips and advice with "newbies."

 *You'll find more about eBay Groups in Chapter 14. To browse groups to learn about those in your own area or find out whether a group already exists for what you collect, go to http://groups.ebay.com/index.jspa.*

## Turning to the Community

Whenever you have a question about whether one of your own objects is valuable, or simply about what an object is or where it comes from, turn to one of the eBay community venues. The Answer Center, in particular, is a place to turn when you have a question about something you collect. You can post photos along with your question and ask other members for an identification or evaluation.

 *The eBay Community area is among the most valuable resources on the site; it's the place where you can make lasting friendships and learn about eBay from the "inside." Go to the Community area (click Community in the navigation bar that appears at the top of nearly every page on eBay, or go directly to http://pages.ebay.com/community/index.html).*

## Researching Sales Descriptions

Research is all-important on eBay, for both buyers and sellers. eBay is fast becoming a good place to do research on collectibles simply because so many photos and descriptions are available. As long as you keep in mind that the person making statements about a particular collectible is not necessarily an authority in the field and that you need to take what eBay members say with a grain of salt, you can still learn a lot about what you collect.

I'm not saying that you have to take a course and study up on something like Chinese porcelain or Early American folk art and become a know-it-all on the topic. I am saying that you need to find out a few important facts about what you are selling that will help attract interest. Many collectors depend on dates, model numbers, and identifying trademarks or other attributes to decide if they want to bid. The more such information you can provide up front, the fewer questions you'll have to field later on.

# Selling Collectibles on eBay

If you have ever held a garage sale, you know that the revenue you get is not "easy money." You have to do all the organizing, advertising, arranging, and displaying.

Then, either you or a trusted relative needs to be available during the sale to greet and accept money from customers (and make sure no one walks off with anything). Afterwards, as a reward for your hard work, you get to clean up.

eBay isn't easy money, but it's far superior in many respects to holding a garage or estate sale: You can sell at your convenience. You don't have to be present while the sale is going on. You can attract buyers from around the country rather than around the block. You can ship and pack on your own schedule. And you don't have to clean up the house or garage afterwards. The last several chapters of this book address issues associated with selling collectibles on eBay; the following overview summarizes some of the advantages of turning to eBay for unloading all or part of your collection.

## Finding Customers—and Friends—Around the World

Nancee Belshaw (eBay user ID: nanceestar), who is profiled in Chapter 3, is a perfect example of a collector who has broadened her reach on eBay. She's used eBay to make friends, collect more of what she loves—postcards—and change her life by starting up an online business.

Nancee, who lives in Los Angeles, regularly travels to Europe to meet a friend she encountered on eBay, and the two of them travel to postcard shows, buying up stock that she couldn't find at home. Nancee sells through eBay auctions, through her own eBay Store, and on her web site, EyeDeal Postcards (http://www.eyedealpostcards.com), shown in Figure 1-6.

## Opening an eBay Store

An eBay store is a web site that eBay lets you establish where you can sell items at a fixed price. Stores help you get maximum exposure for your merchandise. eBay claims that sellers who open eBay stores see their sales increase substantially. That statement is substantiated by the PowerSellers I've interviewed for previous books on eBay—provided you promote the store on a regular basis by making links to it in your auction listings. One of those sellers, Jennifer Karpin-Hobbs, promotes her bed and breakfast as well as her collectibles in her store (see Figure 1-7).

There's also no guarantee you'll get enough business to make the store worthwhile, and it takes work, time, and commitment. If you're already spending 10, 20, or 30 hours a week on your auctions, expect to add several hours more for your store. You've got to put new items up for sale regularly and ship items out quickly, just as you do with auctions. But if you want to be a full-time seller on

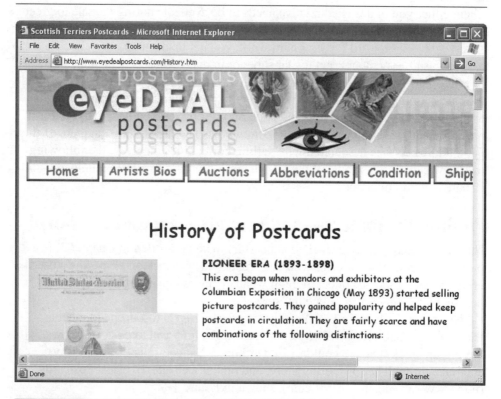

**FIGURE 1-6**   eBay sales can bring you new friends and help you start up a new online business.

eBay and are thinking of depending on eBay for all or part of your income, an eBay store can help you reach your goals.

  *You need a minimum feedback of 20 and an ID Verify listing to open an eBay store. The fees include the $9.95 per month charge, a 2-cent-per-item listing fee, and a "final value fee" of 5.25% for items priced at $25 or less.*

## Diversifying What You Sell

Longtime eBay sellers know that rare and old items are good when you can find them, but for long term, year-round sales it's a good idea to diversify.

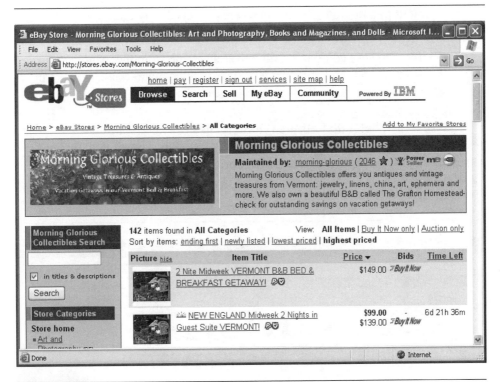

**FIGURE 1-7**    Many sellers agree that eBay Stores boost overall sales.

Don't overlook items that are created for the sole purpose of being "collectibles." I'm talking about the recent lines of dolls, figurines, collectors' plates, holiday items, and plush animals that have taken the collecting world by storm. Many sellers find wholesale suppliers of such collectibles, buy large quantities at bargain prices, and sell them gradually on eBay. The sales can be spread throughout the whole year in order to provide a steady source of income at all times—not just the busy end-of-year holidays, when there is always a sales rush.

Often, these collectibles are sold as limited editions. Not all "limited editions" are created equal, however. They include the following types:

■ **Original**    These limited edition items are signed by the artist.

■ **Limited number**    These numbers are reproduced in a limited quantity, and each piece is usually (although not always) numbered.

■ **Limited production**   Some items are produced only once a year or for a fixed period of time.

■ **Retired**   These editions are no longer available from the manufacturer because they are no longer made and will not be made again. (This term is widely associated with Beanie Babies.)

eBay's own Wholesale Lots area (http://pages.ebay.com/catindex/catwholesale.html) is a good place for sellers to find large quantities (or *lots*) of supplies or other items, often at bargain prices (see Figure 1-8).

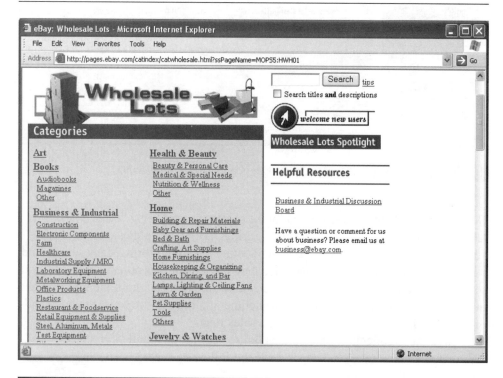

**FIGURE 1-8**   Wholesale Lots can be a good source of collectibles you can sell year-round.

## Links for Collectors

| Web Site | Address | What's There |
|---|---|---|
| eBay's home page | http://ebay.com | Links to categories on eBay as well as links to international eBay sites. |
| eBay UK home page | http://ebay.co.uk | One of a number of eBay sites around the world; check out the Travels & Tickets category for travel bargains and tickets to concerts in the UK. |
| eBay Radio | http://www.wsradio.com/ebayradio | eBay's own weekly radio show. |
| eBay Groups | http://groups.ebay.com/index.jspa | Groups created by eBay members, including regional and collectors' groups. |
| eBay Community Hub overview | http://pages.ebay.com/community/index.html | eBay's main community page, with links to discussion areas, chat rooms, workshops, and the Answer Center. |
| Wholesale Lots | http://pages.ebay.com/catindex/catwholesale.html | A category where sellers list lots of supplies and other cut-rate materials. |

# Chapter 2

# eBay for Buyers: A One-Hour Primer

## In This Chapter You'll Learn...

- How to find collectibles and collectors' resources on eBay's web site

- How to evaluate the condition, authenticity, and value of what you find

- How to bid at auction or buy at fixed price

- How to pay for what you have purchased and make sure you receive it

- How to use the feedback system to research collectors with whom you want to trade

As a collector, you already know the importance of being able to find what you want, no matter how or where it turns up. Sometimes, it's fun to leisurely explore all the nooks and crannies of an antique mall or flea market. Other days, you need to make the most of the time that's available to you: You ask a store's proprietor to point you to any items you collect. You plan exactly which garage sales you're going to visit early in the morning. You map out a path through buildings or areas in a huge outdoor flea market.

eBay is able to accommodate both styles of shopping, the leisurely browsing and the directed searching. This chapter is designed to give you a quick overview of the entire process of buying collectibles on eBay. Yes, shopping on eBay is dramatically different than going to flea markets, antique malls, collectors' shows, or even catalog stores that sell collectibles. But that doesn't mean it's hard to learn. Plus the benefits in time, convenience, and the range of objects you view is something you just won't find anywhere else. You may also strike up friendships that last for years and discover rarities that you have only seen depicted in collectors' price guides. eBay is a paradise for collectors, and you'll find out how to start exploring that paradise in the sections that follow.

# eBay's Web Site: A Collector's Paradise

What do collectors want? That's a hard question to answer, especially if you are focusing on the psychology of collecting. As you probably know, collecting isn't always a rational activity. Sometimes, it doesn't make financial sense, either. However, no matter what their inner motivation, virtually all collectors can describe what they want when it comes to searching for, locating, and buying items in a marketplace. They want to have plenty of things to look through. They want to be able to inspect what they find so they can get a good idea of its condition, color, and other distinguishing features. Finally, they want to be able to buy something easily and quickly.

eBay fits all of these requirements, and gives collectors a few additional features besides. You may never get to personally meet the person who has put something up for sale in an antique mall. But you can approach eBay sellers and ask them questions by e-mail. If they have created an About Me web page, you can find out something about the seller's own hobbies and the kinds of things he or she sells on eBay. As you'll learn later in this chapter, you can review feedback comments others have left about the individual, too. And, because of their shared interests, it's not unusual for collectors to end up befriending the people with whom they do business.

COLLECTOR'S NOTE    *Some collectors have published essays on the Web describing their hobbies in detail. A Westerner who became obsessed with posters published during the Chinese Communist era describes his difficulties locating posters and then bringing them home at http://www.iisg.nl/ exhibitions/chairman/landsberger.html. A collector who visits labor union meetings hoping to find union badges describes his adventures at http:// workers.labor.net.au/features/200304/c_historicalfeature_muse.html.*

Studies have shown that eBay remains one of the "stickiest" sites on the Web. In other words, once people go online and get to eBay, they tend to spend a half-hour to an hour or more, rather than just a few minutes, on the site. What do they do with all that time spent on eBay? They don't just end up searching for items and reading auction descriptions. Much of the time is spent on eBay's message boards and chat rooms, comparing notes and visiting with people who share the same interests. If you have ever joined a collectors' group or attended a show that features the sort of things you love to accumulate, you know how your own hobby is enriched by personal contacts. You learn more about your interest than ever before. You see models and varieties you never knew existed. You can do the same thing on eBay. It's a marketplace where people chat, haggle, ask for advice, gossip, and share what they know. The many options for beginning to find your way around that marketplace are described in the sections that follow.

## eBay's Front Door: The Home Page

The first thing you notice about eBay is that it is highly organized. The site has systematized the process of buying and selling in a way that contrasts dramatically with flea markets, malls, or other shopping venues in the real world. When you start up your browser and go to the home page (http://www.ebay.com), you notice the organization right away. But the version of the home page that you actually see depends on whether or not you are a registered user. Let's assume you haven't registered as yet and you are visiting the site for the first (or almost the first) time. You see the version of the home page shown in Figure 2-1.

As the home page for new users, entitled Welcome to eBay, implies, the process of finding and obtaining a collectible, a household item, a car, or anything else on the site can be broken into three steps:

**1.** You shop for what you want.

**2.** You buy it, or place the winning bid at an auction.

**3.** You pay for it.

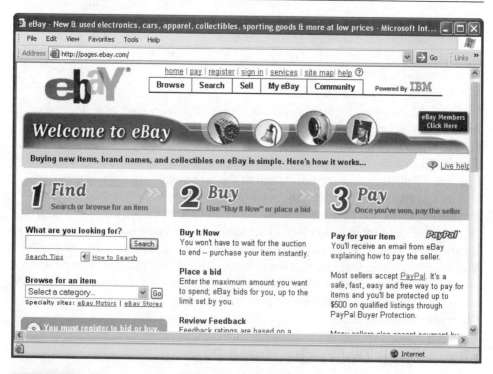

**FIGURE 2-1**    eBay's home page for new users breaks the trading process into easy-to-follow steps.

Along the way, there are other important activities, such as checking feedback, comparing prices, and asking questions that increase your chances of completing a transaction in a satisfying way. But the three steps I've just described are the main ones, and they'll be the primary focus of this chapter.

You can move from the Welcome to eBay page to the "regular" eBay home page—the one that registered users see—by clicking the inconspicuous Home link at the left end of the eBay navigation bar (the row of links at the top of the page) or the blue eBay Members Click Here button. If you click either of these links, or if you are a registered user and your browser is set to accept cookies (which are described in more detail in the Table Talk feature that follows) you see eBay's U.S. version of the home page, shown in Figure 2-2.

**FIGURE 2-2**   This version of eBay's home page is one of the most popular locations on the Web.

## Trade Talk

You might be wondering why you see the Welcome to eBay version of the home page before you register and the "regular" version of eBay's home page after registration. The Welcome to eBay version enables you to search the site but do little else. The page's primary purpose is to encourage visitors to become registered users. In fact, it's important to register with eBay if you want to do just about anything beyond shop. After you register, if your browser has been configured properly, you don't connect to Welcome to eBay anymore when you connect to the address http://www.ebay.com. Instead, you go to the other home page.

Why? It has to do with small bits of digital information called *cookies*. Normally, when you connect to a web site, information comes to your browser in the form of image files and HTML (HyperText Markup Language) documents. A cookie is something extra—a small file that a web site sends to your browser. If your browser accepts the cookie, it is stored on your hard disk. The cookie contains some information that identifies you as someone who has visited the site in the past. When you revisit the site, it checks to see if a cookie is available. If it is, you view content that is reserved for returning users.

Some sites (like the well-known online bookstore Amazon.com) use cookies to greet you by name and to make book recommendations. eBay uses cookies to send you to the regular home page rather than Welcome to eBay. Cookies are also used to remember your registration information when you are on the site; you can configure eBay's Sign In page so that you don't have to enter your user ID and password every time you want to place a bid, post a discussion group comment, or view a completed auction record, for instance.

Cookies do enhance your experience of eBay, and they don't really invade your privacy the way some intrusive e-mail messages and software programs called spyware do. You should make sure your browser can accept them. In Microsoft Internet Explorer, you choose Tools | Options. When the Internet Options dialog box appears, click the Privacy tab. Move the slider to Low or Accept All Cookies; then click OK. If you use Netscape, choose Edit | Preferences, click Privacy & Security, click Cookies, and make sure one of the "Enable cookies" options is selected. Then click OK.

eBay's regular home page is the gateway to virtually all the important areas of its site. Some of the links are more helpful than others. The best starting points for navigating eBay from the home page are described in the following sections.

# eBay's Global Positioning Tool: The Navigation Bar

In any marketplace, you need a way to find where you are and where you want to go. eBay's navigation bar provides such a tool. The navigation bar is a set of buttons that appears at the top of almost every page on eBay's web site. The fact that the navigation bar is virtually omnipresent and has a consistent appearance from page to page helps you find your way around eBay no matter where you are. You see the same row of underlined links at the very top of the page and the same set of five buttons, outlined in black, as shown here.

home | pay | register | sign out | services | site map | help

| Browse | Search | Sell | My eBay | Community |

Some of the seven links at the top of the navigation bar help you with activities related to buying and selling collectibles. Others are there to help you learn how to use the site or find specific resources and services you need. The seven links are:

- **Home**    This link enables you to get back to eBay's home page at any time.

- **Pay**    If you have won an auction or purchased something using Buy It Now, you can go here to pay for it or leave feedback for sellers.

- **Register**    Click here to sign up for an account so you can start bidding and buying on eBay.

- **Sign In/Sign Out**    If you see Sign In, it means you haven't logged in to eBay with your User ID and password. If you see Sign Out, it means you are logged in, but you can click this link if you want to sign in with a second user ID and password, if you have one.

- **Services**    Click here, and you connect to a page full of services for buyers and sellers. Many of the services help you resolve problems and improve your safety.

- **Site Map**    This link takes you to a page containing a long series of links. The links take you to all the top-level categories on eBay and connect you to almost all the services on the site. Go here if you can't find something elsewhere.

- **Help**    If you need a definition or a quick answer to a question about how to use eBay, and you can't find what you want in this book, click here to access eBay's own Help Center. Register.

When you are actually cruising through eBay's web site looking for collectibles, you are more likely to use the five buttons in the navigation bar:

- **Browse**    This link takes you to the Buy Everything on eBay page, so you can look for items by category and subcategory. See "Browsing for Treasures" later in this chapter for more.

- **Search**    Click here, and you go to the Basic Search page, where you can enter keywords and do searches by an item's name, model number, or a word or phrase in its description. See "Searching for Collectibles" later in this chapter for more.

- **Sell**    This takes you to the Sell Your Item form, which enables you to put collectibles or other not-so-collectible items up for sale on eBay. See Chapter 3 for an overview of the selling process.

- **My eBay**    This takes you to a page that eBay provides you for free that collects information about items you want to bid on, purchases you have made, and preferences you can change for how to use eBay's site.

- **Community**    This link takes you to eBay's Community Hub Overview page. This page contains links to the many forums and chat rooms where you can meet other collectors, share notes, listen to complaints and gripes, ask questions, and make friends. See Chapter 4 for more on this invaluable resource.

## Trade Talk

When you click some of the five main buttons in the navigation bar (the ones enclosed in boxes), you see a new set of buttons appear beneath the one you just clicked. For instance, if you click Search, your browser goes to the Basic Search page, but you also see the subcategories Find Items, Find Members, and Favorite Searches. The Find Members option is described in Chapter 4, and the Favorite Searches option is described in Chapter 5.

## eBay's Table of Contents: The Site Map

Those printed price guides with which you are probably familiar make it easy for you to find the kinds of things you collect. You look up models, brands, and varieties in the book's table of contents. eBay's own table of contents is its site map. If you are used to scanning a long list in a price range and trying to pick out just the item you want, you'll have no problem getting used to the site map. It's a page full of links to the main areas of eBay's voluminous web site. You can't be expected to remember the URLs of eBay web pages you visit frequently, and only a few pages have direct links in the eBay navigation bar. When you can't find a resource easily, the site map is the place to go. You'll find links to pages that are hard to locate otherwise (unless you bookmark them or add them to your browser's toolbar, as described in Chapter 5) such as:

- The home page for eBay Groups, eBay's place where users can create or join groups related to what they collect, where they live, or any shared cause or interest.

- Special pages that collect items currently being sold, such as Big Ticket (which presents high-priced items), New Today (which collects newly listed items), and Ending First (which lists sales that are about to end.

- Seller Central, a place that collects articles, statistics, and tips of interest to sellers.

- About Me, the place to go if you want to create a web page about yourself and your interests that you can share with other eBay members.

Site maps, in general, are supposed to contain links to all the main areas of a web site. I can assure you that eBay's site map doesn't include direct links to every last subcategory or specific page on eBay. But it does contain links that will lead you to those pages. The site map (part of which is shown in Figure 2-3) contains so many links that, if you are looking for something in particular, you should use your browser's Find menu option to find a page or category name, as described in "Browsing for Treasures," later in this chapter.

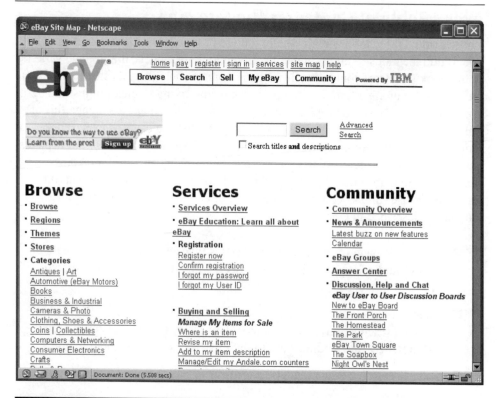

**FIGURE 2-3**    The site map is rich with links that lead to all parts of eBay.

> **TIP**    *Another place to find links to many areas of eBay's web site, including its sales categories, is the eBay Toolbar. This is a toolbar you install and add to Microsoft Internet Explorer's set of default toolbars. Once you have the toolbar installed, you can use its built-in menus and buttons to quickly find categories, access your My eBay page, and connect to other parts of the site. Find out more in Chapter 5.*

## Searching for Collectibles

When you are on the hunt, you want quick results. You don't want to wait days to hit that estate sale or even to drive to a new Disney store or other retail outlet. eBay gives collectors instant results: with a few keystrokes and mouse clicks, they can learn whether that 1959 Radio Flyer wagon or that piece of pottery they've been looking for is up for sale on eBay.

Every few weeks, for instance, I turn to eBay to see if a particular kind of Waterman fountain pen is for sale. It's called a Patrician, and it's one I've been pursuing for years. I've never seen one for sale in a store—only at pen shows, and on eBay. Remarkably, such pens (which date from the early 1930s) come up fairly frequently on eBay. Because I know the specific model number I am looking for, I don't have to browse through categories for it. I only have to enter a word that describes the pen I want. In a matter of seconds, I can see if a pen is being offered, when the sale ends, and make a decision whether or not to place a bid.

*If you have a collectible you are seeking and you don't see it on eBay (or if you place a bid but don't turn up the winner) you can configure your My eBay page to "watch" the item.*

## The Search Box

If you have surfed the Web and used search services such as Google, you probably understand the concept of a search box. This is a box into which you type a keyword or phrase and submit it to a web site. A search program on the server that runs the site scours the site's contents and returns a list of any pages whose title or contents match those keywords. Such boxes can be found near the top of most pages on eBay, from the home page on—even pages like eBay Groups and the archive page for the eBay Life newsletter have a search box at the top. It's pretty easy to use search boxes. But the ones on eBay have some features you may not know about:

- Most of the search boxes have a limit to the number of characters you can enter. However, the limit is pretty big: 250 characters for the search box on the eBay home page, and 100 characters for boxes on other pages.

- You can enter much more than one or two words. Suppose you are looking for an Elgin pocket watch—but not any pocket watch. You want a railroad-grade watch in the big 18S size. You don't want one with a case. You could enter a simple group of terms such as "Elgin pocket watch 18S RR," but this would exclude any listings that spell out the word *railroad* rather than using the RR abbreviation. You would get more accurate results by creating a complex search, such as:

```
Elgin watch and pocket (18S,size18) -(case), (RR,railroad)
```

 *You'll learn more about creating complex searches in Chapter 5. You'll also learn how to save those searches so you can use them over and over again.*

## Basic Search

Think how you shop at a crowded flea market or estate sale. First, you do a quick scan: You look around and try to spot the tables that have the goodies you want. You quickly look over the table and grab as many things as you can that seem promising. Later, when you have a quiet moment or are waiting to check out, you do a more detailed evaluation. You inspect each item for cracks or other flaws, and take only the things you really want.

Similarly, eBay gives you two options for conducting searches: Basic Search and Advanced Search. The Basic Search page, which you access either by clicking Search in the navigation bar or by going directly to http://pages.ebay.com/search/items/basicsearch.html, may be basic, but it isn't really all that simple. Along with a search box, you get various check boxes and pull-down menus that enable you to refine what you're looking for. These features are described in more detail in Chapter 5.

## Advanced Search

You get to Advanced Search by going to the Basic Search page and then clicking the Advanced tab, or by going directly to http://pages.ebay.com/search/items/search_adv.html. The most popular reason for conducting an advanced search is the ability to research eBay's database of completed auctions. You do this by following these steps:

1. Check Completed Items Only.

2. Enter your search terms in the Search Keywords or Item Number field.

3. Click Search.

4. Enter your user ID and password if prompted.

You'll see results not from sales that are still being offered on eBay but from sales that have already ended. Scanning the results gives you invaluable information about what sells successfully, what items fail to attract bids, when sales tend to end successfully, and what others have paid for the items you are seeking.

**WATCH OUT!**    *If you want to track a specific auction that ended a week or two ago, do your Completed Items Only search quickly. eBay has been steadily limiting the number of results you obtain from such searches. At this writing, a typical search returns only the previous two or three weeks' worth of sales. Auction services such as Andale (http://www.andale.com) give you access to a far wider range of completed auction results—for a monthly subscription fee.*

# Researching Collectibles

Most collectors probably think of eBay simply as a place to buy and sell. But you can also learn a lot of fascinating details about the items you love by surfing and reading the descriptions of items currently for sale. Often, experienced eBay sellers know a lot about what they sell, and they realize that, by sharing their knowledge of a particular item, they are likely to generate more interest in it.

## Beware of Fakes

There's another reason to read descriptions closely, inspect photos in detail, and ask for more information if you need it. The fact is that everything you see up for sale on eBay is not necessarily genuine. When it comes to collectors' items, one-of-a-kind collectibles, and antiques, you need to be aware of fakes. The strategies for detecting forgeries on eBay is the same as in the "real" world. Much of it has to do with the seller. If someone has dozens or even hundreds of positive feedback comments, seems knowledgeable about the subject, and is prompt in answering your questions, you can feel good about making a purchase from that individual.

On the other hand, if the seller has a low feedback rating, boasts about "discovering" the item in a barn or overseas, does not say much about it, or posts descriptions that seem copied from a book or someone else's listing, you need to exercise a healthy skepticism. Sellers located in certain southern Pacific nations (such as Indonesia) are reputed to be likely sellers of forged or faked valuables on eBay. Before you place a bid, research both the seller and the item itself. Search the Web for tips on qualities you need to look for in an item. If you are in doubt, ask other collectors, either on eBay's own discussion forums or on newsgroups.

## Evaluating a Collectible's Condition

eBay is so popular that it has developed its own subculture. Like any subculture, it has a language all its own. Abbreviations and terms used to describe the condition of collectibles and other merchandise frequently turn up in auction listings. Sometimes sellers are in the process of listing a dozen or more objects, or a hired assistant is preparing the description based on the seller's information; whatever the reason, descriptions should be read carefully and any terms need to be deciphered.

Sometimes, the language used is universal and can apply to any type of collectible. Here are some examples of the more popular abbreviations you are likely to see:

■ **NIB (new in box)**   The item comes with its original box and is brand-new; in other words, it has never been used. You might also see the similar listing NRFB (never removed from box). In either case, you should ask about the condition of the box.

■ **MIB (mint in box)**   The item being sold is in its original box. This *does not* necessarily mean it was never taken out of the box, just that the item is in mint condition and comes with the original box. MIB doesn't say anything about the condition of the box; it may be in something less than mint condition.

■ **NM (near mint)**   Almost mint condition. This is a deceptively vague term. It can mean virtually the same thing as "almost new"—the condition is nearly flawless, but there has been some sort of wear. It's best to ask the seller exactly what signs of wear there are.

■ **COA (certificate of authenticity)**   Many collectible items come with a certificate of some sort—some are numbered, some not. Check to make sure the number on the collectible actually matches the number on your COA. It may not matter if you decide to keep the object forever, but it could cause problems if and when you decide to sell it.

■ **Vintage**   This is one of those terms that can mean almost anything, and as a result, has almost no meaning. Vintage, technically, means "old," but does that mean it's 10, 50, or 100 years old? The description needs to provide more information than this.

Other terms are specific to a specific type of merchandise, and you probably won't see them used in connection with any other kind of collectible item. If you see some of these that you don't understand, you should either ask someone in eBay's Answer Center for an explanation, or you should visit a site that's specially set aside for collectors of the item in question and that explains the qualities that go into evaluating its overall condition. Table 2-1 presents just a few examples of the many item-specific terms you might encounter.

## Asking for More Information

The preceding suggestions apply to terms that are included in descriptions. As a savvy collector, you should always be conscious of terms that are *not* mentioned in descriptions. Some qualities don't show up in photos, no matter how well-lit and sharp the images. For example:

- **Odors**   Dolls and other items that include cloth, or that are made of cloth, can smell musty, mildewed, or like cigarettes. Such problems can detract from an item's value, especially if they can't be washed out.

- **Completeness**   You may see a number of components in the auction photos. But that doesn't mean all the accessories are available. If you do

| Type of Collectible | Term | What It Means |
| --- | --- | --- |
| Dolls | Deboxed | The doll is not in its original box; box is not available. |
| Dolls | ©Mattel *[date]* | Copyright notice that appears on Barbie dolls. |
| Dolls | Original outfit (O/O) | The doll's original outfit, in which it was originally clothed. |
| Dolls | Customized | A doll with a face that has been repainted or hair that has been altered. |
| Dolls | Straight leg | A doll with legs that do not bend. |
| Dolls | Paling | A lightening of the vinyl on the head or face of the doll compared to its body. |
| Pens | Brassing | The gold plating on the pen is worn so the brass underneath shows. |
| Pens | Re-saced | The fountain pen has had its rubber ink sac replaced. |
| Royal Doulton figurines | Acid-etched | Figurine has been decorated by glazing, then washed in acid to remove parts that are not to have the decoration. |
| Record albums | Ringwear | The album cover is marked with the impression of the record inside it. |

**TABLE 2-1**    Special Terms to Describe a Collectible Item's Condition

your research, looking up similar items on the Web or on eBay itself, you may well discover that some pieces are missing. It may not mean that the seller is intentionally trying to mislead you; he or she may not be aware of the other pieces, either.

■ **Repairs**   Some items up for sale on eBay have undergone repairs. But sellers don't necessarily have to disclose this in their descriptions. If you have any doubts, or if you are experienced enough with the items you collect that you know some models are prone to cracks or other damage, ask about repairs.

If you have a question about a specific sale that is currently active on eBay, feel free to post a message in one of eBay's community forums asking knowledgeable collectors to evaluate the item. If someone has the time and is willing to help, you might just get the answer you need.

## Browsing for Treasures

Browsing through cases, boxes, tables, or rooms full of bric-a-brac brings you a sense of anticipation that can't be matched any other way. Every time your eye falls on a new object, there's a chance that it'll be just the item you have been looking for. Browsing through the approximately 26,000 categories on eBay brings the same sense of anticipation. While searching brings you focused results quickly, browsing is more likely to turn up a surprise: an item you didn't know existed, a listing that has been misspelled and is not likely to get attention from crowds of collectors, or something that has been listed in the wrong place.

Browsing on eBay, like many other buying and selling functions, can be performed in a variety of different ways. From the home page, you can click one of the main categories listed in a narrow column on the left-hand side under the heading Categories. You'll find a similar list of categories in the site map. When you click one of the category links, you go to a category opening page (such pages are described in the following section). Another option is to click the Browse button on the left-hand side of the eBay navigation bar. You go to the Browse page (see Figure 2-4), which contains a listing of all eBay's main categories of merchandise for sale.

Click a category name to go to a category opening page, where you can click subcategories until you find the specific types of things you collect. For instance, if you collect pins with firefighting logos on them, you could click the main category Collectibles, the subcategory Historical Memorabilia, then Firefighting, then Pins, Buttons. Of course, the question naturally arises: How do you know in the first

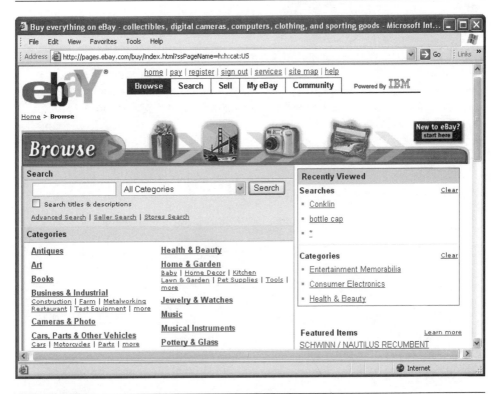

**FIGURE 2-4**    If you're in the mood to browse through categories, this page is a good place to start.

place that the subcategory Pins, Buttons contains firefighting memorabilia? How do you find the right subcategory in the first place, when there are so many to choose from? You could do a search for the terms "Firefighter Pins" or "Firefighter Buttons" and then make note of the category in which the items you want are located. You could also search through eBay's categories. This feature is fairly well hidden within the eBay web site, but it's described in the section that follows.

**TIP**    *Here's another way to find categories worth browsing through on eBay: Do a search for the items you collect using Basic Search or Advanced Search. Click a few of the search results and make note of the category "tree" that describes where the items are listed. Click the subcategory at the end of the tree, and then browse through the listings to find similar (if not identical) items.*

## Collecting Step-by-Step

To search through eBay category titles rather than the titles of items currently up for sale, you have two options. The first option is available to all eBay members; the second is accessible only if you have registered to sell on eBay, because it's part of the Sell Your Item form (see Chapter 3 for more.) The first option is easy; just follow these steps:

1. Go to the eBay home page (http://www.ebay.com) and click the link See All eBay Categories, at the bottom of the category list. Or click All Categories in the site map.

2. On the All Categories page, click Edit, Find (on This Page).

3. Enter the name of the category you want to find, or a keyword that applies to the category you want, and click Find. If the keyword is included on the All Categories page, it will be highlighted.

There is a flaw with this approach, however. It only enables you to search eBay's top-level categories and the first level of subcategories within each one, because these are the only ones that are included on the page. In order to search through all of eBay's categories, you need to follow this second approach:

1. In the eBay navigation bar, click Sell.

2. When the Sign In page appears, enter your eBay user ID and password, and click Sign In.

COLLECTOR'S NOTE  *You need to be registered as a seller (a process described in Chapter 3) before you can follow these steps.*

3. When the next page appears, leave Sell Item at Online Auction selected, and then click Continue.

4. When the Select Category page appears, enter your category keyword in the box labeled "Enter item keywords to find a category."

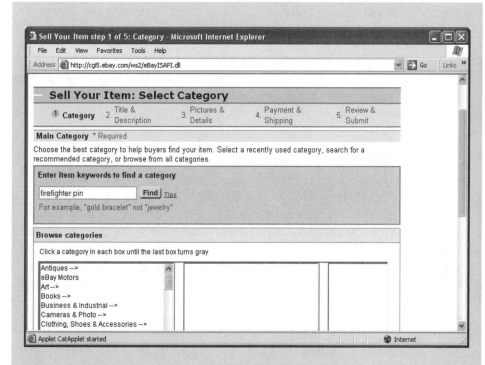

5. **Click Find.**

A new browser window appears with a list of categories and subcategories relating to your search. Each subcategory is presented with a list of the category tree it is contained in and with a percentage ranking that indicates how likely it is you'll find what you're looking for. For instance, if you search for the term "firefighter pins," you come up with the following results:

```
Collectibles : Historical Memorabilia : Firefighting : Pins, Buttons (36%)
Collectibles : Historical Memorabilia : Firefighting : Other Items (15%)
Collectibles : Disneyana : Contemporary (1968-now) : Pins, Buttons : Other (9%)
```

You'll find out more about the Find a Main Category page in Chapter 5.

You'll also find a sampling of eBay Stores on the Browse page. The stores listed on the Browse page have paid an extra fee to be advertised there. Click the

See All Stores link to go to the eBay Stores home page, where you can browse through all available user-created sales outlets.

 *eBay Stores can't be searched through Basic Search or Advanced Search. If you find an eBay seller who has items of the sort you collect, search that person's store individually using the search box on the eBay Stores home page (http://www.ebaystores.com).*

## Category Opening Pages

eBay maintains one of the most extensive sites on the Web. The site has plenty of virtual "nooks and crannies"—web pages that are easy to overlook and that sometimes contain special promotions. If you collect well-known brands such as Disney or Barbie, you might find new models at reduced price. On the Entertainment Memorabilia page, you're likely to find links to sales of props from recently released movies. In many categories, such as Coins and Stamps, you are likely to find links to upcoming collectors' shows. As any collector knows, the trick is finding places that like-minded enthusiasts tend to overlook.

Category opening pages are easily overlooked—it's quicker to do a search for merchandise than to browse through categories. But some category opening pages contain useful information for collectors. A category opening page is a sort of welcome page for a type of merchandise on eBay. The page includes links to subcategories within the main categories. But some category opening pages also list special sales promotions. Some also include links to collectors' clubs and other organizations of interest. All the pages list the most popular items within the category, based on the number of searches done within the category. You can get to a category opening page by clicking its link either in the site map or on the eBay home page. For instance, if you click the Stamps link to go to the Stamps category opening page (http://stamps.ebay.com) shown in Figure 2-5, you gain access to a variety of useful data, including links to the following:

- A page on the American Philatelic Society's (APS's) web site, where you can find a local APS club in your area

- The APS's "code of conduct" for selling stamps on eBay

- Professional Stamp Experts' stamp authentication and grading site

- An About Me page created by an eBay member who presents information on the American Stamp Dealers Association

- Linns.com, the web site of a weekly stamp newsletter

■ Discussion groups on eBay designed especially to bring buyers and sellers of stamps together

FIGURE 2-5 **FIGURE 2-5** Category opening pages often contain links of interest to collectors.

# Buying and Winning Collectibles on eBay

In order to play any game well, you need to know its ground rules. On eBay, the rules and procedures for buying merchandise differ depending on the type of sale. Sales on eBay fall into two general types:

■ **Auctions**    A seller puts one or more items up for auction, and interested parties place bids. When the sale ends, the merchandise goes to the highest bidder.

■ **Fixed-price sales**    A seller puts something up for sale at a fixed price. The fixed price option may appear in conjunction with an auction: buyers can either place bids and compete with other bidders or pay the seller's fixed price and purchase it immediately. Or the item may be put up for sale with a fixed price only and no bidding. The exact options are set by the seller.

eBay is best known for its auctions, and the different types of auction sales are described in the following sections. These descriptions are followed by instructions on how to place bids or make fixed-price purchases yourself.

## Standard Auctions

A standard auction is the simplest kind of auction sale on eBay. The seller publishes a description of an item on eBay (a process described in Chapter 3). A standard auction description contains the features shown in Figure 2-6.

The basic process is like any other auction: bidders place bids and counterbids, and at the end of the sale, the item goes to the highest bidder. But there are some important differences between eBay auctions and those held in a traditional, brick-and-mortar auction house. The primary differences are described in Table 2-2.

## Reserve Auctions

eBay sellers don't have any way of knowing just how much a collectible they put up for sale will actually fetch. But chances are they don't want to lose money on what they sell: if a seller originally paid $10 for that Barry Bonds baseball card, he or she doesn't want to end up letting it go for $8.

There is a way of guaranteeing that sellers won't have to sell something for less than a desired amount; it's called a *reserve price*. A reserve price is the minimum a seller is willing to accept in order to sell something. In the Barry Bonds example,

Category tree      Current high bid                    Item number

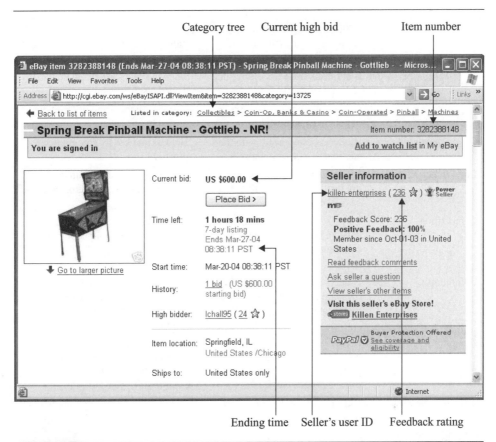

Ending time    Seller's user ID    Feedback rating

**FIGURE 2-6**    An item description enables you to research it, the seller, and other bidders.

a seller could do one of two things to provide a guaranteed minimum sale price. First, the seller could set a starting bid at the desired amount of $10. That way, no one can even place a bid unless the amount the seller wants to get is matched.

Alternatively, the seller can specify a reserve price of $10 when creating an auction description. In this case, the desired price—the reserve price—is kept secret. Collectors like you only know that there is a reserve by the words "Reserve Not Met," which appear next to the starting bid, as shown in Figure 2-7.

When someone's bid meets the reserve, the message next to the starting bid changes to "Reserve Met." When this message appears, bidders know for sure that auction will end with a completed sale.

| Aspect | Traditional Auction | eBay Auction |
|---|---|---|
| Who runs the sale | A professional auctioneer | Individual sellers |
| Length of sale | When bidding stops–the exact end is at the auctioneer's discretion | At an exact time determined by when the sale started and how many days the seller wants it to last |
| Inspection | Collectibles need to be inspected in person or in a catalog | You view photos and descriptions posted by the seller |
| Communication | Bidders communicate with the auctioneer, not with the seller | Bidders and sellers communicate directly |
| Level of participation | Bidders and sellers have no interest in the auction house or marketplace itself | All participants contribute to making the eBay marketplace work |
| Competition | Large-scale, veteran collectors have an advantage because they can spend more and put more up for sale | Casual collectors and veterans compete on an even playing field |
| Community | Bidders and sellers are on their own and generally don't share their thoughts | Bidders and sellers can share tips and ideas, and voice concerns, in the community forums and chat rooms |
| Geography | If you can't visit the auction house in person, you have to participate on the phone and order a printed catalog | You can view eBay's catalog instantly, for free, and shop from sellers who come from around the world |
| Timing | Bids are placed during a narrow period of time | Bids can be placed any time before the sale ends |

**TABLE 2-2**    Traditional Sales Versus eBay

# eBay Enriches a Collector's Life

Paula Amato knows a lot about both traditional auctions and the high-tech auctions on eBay. When she was a girl her parents, both avid collectors, took her to a variety of high-end auctions at Sotheby's in New York. "You had to wear a dress and gloves on a Saturday," she recalls. "I was at the auction of the Shah of Iran, the Kennedy auction. We even went to the invitation-only sales. Today, when I'm on eBay, my uniform is whatever I have on. Sometimes I answer the door and I think, 'Whoops, I'm not even dressed!'"

Amato, who now lives in Fort Lauderdale, Florida, calls herself an "eclectic collector." "I collect everything I can get my hands on," she says. "I surround myself with Oriental things. That's why I like doing eBay. I can get an item, and if I don't like it or get tired of it, I can turn around and sell it."

Amato got started on eBay after coming to Florida to care for her father, who had been injured in an auto accident. "After a while I was bored to tears," she says. "I got my first computer in September 2000, and the first thing I did was look up eBay, and I started buying, and I said, 'This is way too easy.' Then, after six months, started selling myself. Now I'm almost obsessed with finding things to sell. I go to estate sales, thrift shops, some consignment, any place."

When it comes to buying, Amato suggests searching for descriptions with misspellings in the titles. They are likely to be overlooked by other collectors, and the sellers don't always realize their true value. "One time, I saw a listing for a lot of 12 or 13 items. I was having heart failure; I couldn't believe what I was looking at. I knew some of the things being sold were from a famous shipwreck. I had a $300 proxy bid on it, but I got it for $20. I kept a couple of the more important pieces and sold the rest."

The most amazing thing Amato has sold on eBay is a cane created by a tramp: she found it in a consignment shop for $20, and sold it for $1000 on eBay. "I just sold something to someone in Slovenia," she exclaims. "I never even heard of the country."

eBay has changed Amato's life in both material and interpersonal ways. "I am able to decorate my house with items I could never afford otherwise. eBay has also opened a lot of doors: I have met a lot of unbelievable people. I've met many people I have been speaking to for years. When people I have met on eBay come to Florida for a vacation, we get together; I had dinner with one girl from Canada the other day. I also belong to a local eBay user's group; we meet every six weeks for dinner. We share ideas, and we are not selfish about what we know. If you don't enjoy what you're doing, or if you are just doing it for the money, it's just not a good idea."

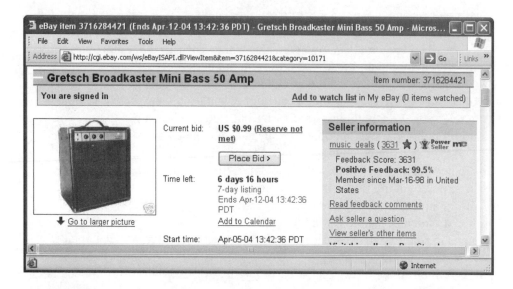

**FIGURE 2-7** The words indicate that the seller has a reserve and that bidding has not yet matched it.

Reserve auctions have their pros and cons. Like many aspects of eBay, members disagree strongly on them. Some sellers believe reserves are a necessary protection. Others think they discourage bids; they prefer to set a starting price. Many believe the starting price option attracts more bids. The key is research and knowledge. If you do your homework and know what something is worth, you'll be able to decide whether to continue bidding until the reserve is met or give up when your own maximum is reached.

## Multiple-Item Auctions

Sometimes collectors can't help buying more than one of something. In the quest to find the perfect Indian head penny, they buy a bag full of 19th-century coins. In order to get one Angelina Jolie refrigerator magnet, they have to buy a set of six. Other times, it's to their advantage to purchase a set. For instance, collectibles on eBay are often made available as groups, and a discount is offered, such as, "If you buy three of these cards, you get a fourth one free." If you take advantage of such an offer, you may be able to sell one of the items you received and thus make back some of your expenses.

Multiple-item sales are the format eBay provides for sellers who want to sell off multiple instances of the same item at one time. Multiple items can be offered either at a fixed price or at an auction. When multiple items are offered at auction, the sale is sometimes called a Dutch auction.

In a Dutch auction, the seller specifies how many items are available and sets a starting bid. Potential bidders can bid at, or above, the minimum for one or more of the objects being offered. At the close of the auction, all winning bidders pay the lowest successful price (that is, the lowest bid that is still above the minimum price). Dutch auctions and the concept of "successful price" can be hard to understand. An example may help clarify this type of sale:

Suppose you uncover a box full of 10 Chuckles-the-Cat Bean Bag Babies at a garage sale. You put all 10 up for sale at the same time in a single Dutch auction. You specify a minimum bid of $20 for each cat. Eighteen separate bidders place bids: one bids $30, two bid $25, three bid $24, two bid $22, two bid $21, and the rest bid $20. The 10 highest bidders win: the individuals who bid $30, $25, $22, and $21, respectively. However—and this is the confusing part—in a Dutch auction, they all purchase at the *lowest* successful price, which is $21. Those who bid $20 lose out because there are only 10 cats available.

> **TIP**
>
> *One area on eBay is set aside for people who want to sell multiple items as a group, often for bargain prices. It's called Wholesale Lots (http://pages.ebay.com/catindex/catwholesale.html). It's mostly for business and industrial purchasers, but occasionally you find some collectibles in this category as well.*

# Making an Offer

Whether you are approaching someone behind a card table at a garage sale or behind a counter in a store, a critical moment for many collectors comes when you say the magic words "How much is this?" or "Would you take ___ for this?" You hope your offer isn't too low or too high; you realize you may be starting up the time-honored process of haggling. On eBay, you don't actually haggle over merchandise. You either place a bid or purchase something at a fixed Buy It Now price, as described in the sections that follow.

## Placing Bids

When you're thinking of buying something, don't be in a hurry. It pays to take some time to research what comes up for sale on eBay, who bids on the type of item you collect, and how much is typically bid. I have been looking for a particular type of pen for a long time. I see one come up, and I start to recognize the same names. I can actually look back at past auctions (if I have saved the information) and see how much that person bid the last time the same type of pen appeared. Also, if you are seriously interested in something you see, it's a good idea to ask the seller a question if you have one: you'll find out more about the item and about what kind of customer service the seller provides.

The actual process of placing a bid is easy: click the Place Bid button in the auction description, enter the amount you want to bid, click Continue, review your bid to make sure it is accurate, and then click Submit. If someone outbids you while the sale is still active, you'll receive an e-mail message so that you can place another bid if you want to. If you win, you'll receive an e-mail message from eBay after the auction ends, informing you of the good news.

## Buying It Now

The more I collect—or try to collect—on eBay, the more enamored I am of Buy It Now (or BIN, as it is commonly abbreviated). Buy It Now is an option that enables a seller to buy something at a fixed price. When a BIN price is available, you only have to click the button conspicuously labeled "Buy It Now" in order to make the purchase.

## Trade Talk

Don't overlook the process of "sniping" when it comes to winning eBay auctions. Sniping is the act of placing a bid at the very last minute or even within a few seconds before the auction is scheduled to end. If the last-second offer is higher than anyone else's bid, the snipe bid turns out to be the winner, because other bidders don't have the opportunity to place a counterbid. You can either place a bid manually by being present at the end of the auction and waiting until the last second to place a bid or by using a sniping service.

Generally, sniping services work like this: you identify the eBay item number, specify your maximum bid, and determine how close to the auction end you want your bid executed. One popular web site, AuctionStealer (http://www.auctionstealer.com), allows your bid to be entered three seconds prior to the close of bidding. This makes it almost impossible for another bid to be recorded prior to auction end. Some eBay members feel this is an unfair way of winning an item, but many others see nothing wrong with "playing your card" so late that no one else can respond.

A BIN price can be offered as a fixed-price option along with an item that's up for auction. It can also be offered as the only sales option. BIN prices might seem to run counter to eBay's reputation as a place where bidders can compete against one another and the winners end up with bargains. But the fact is that, as eBay becomes ever more popular, bidding becomes more competitive and it grows harder to find any collectibles that can accurately be described as bargains.

I do a lot of searching for bass guitars, for instance. There's a particular kind I wish I could buy, a Rickenbacker, that regularly sells for $900 to $1100. As I write this, the following such instruments are being offered on eBay:

- A "fireglow" bass that has attracted 16 bids, with the current high bid at $916

- A white one with 13 bids, currently listed at $1025

- A black model with a single bid of $600 (reserve not yet met) and a Buy It Now price of $900

The Buy It Now price of $900 looks pretty good in the light of what other models sell for. But other, higher Buy It Now prices in the $1500 range might be reasonable too. BIN prices give the first person to spot the item a chance to get it right away at a reasonable price without having to wait a week for the sale to end and worry about trying to beat out other bidders. It's the difference between getting something you really want and paying extra for it or bidding in the hope

## Trade Talk

When BIN prices are offered as part of standard and reserve auctions, special rules apply that determine how long the BIN price is available. In a reserve auction, the BIN price remains while bidding goes on until someone places a bid that meets the reserve. When the reserve is met, the BIN price is removed and bidding continues until the auction ends. In a standard auction with a BIN option, the BIN price is only available until the first bid is placed. If you see a BIN price on an auction with no reserve, you may need to move fast; someone could buy the item from you or someone could place a bid, thus eliminating the BIN price. In fact, some bidders intentionally place bids that act as "BIN killers," thus preventing anyone from buying something and ending the competitive bidding process.

of saving money and possibly not getting it. For things that are in demand—things that collectors tend to compete over—Buy It Now can be an attractive option.

# Sealing the Deal

It's easy to purchase the special objects you collect when you find them in the real, rather than the virtual, world. In the real world, you hand a real person some tangible form of payment, whether it's a check, a credit card, or cash. The person gives you your change and asks for your signature. It seems so safe and secure. Can you get the same level of security in the virtual world, and specifically, on eBay itself?

In reality, every form of commerce has its pitfalls. Even if you pay in person, you need to trust the merchant not to charge more than the agreed-upon price. You hope someone won't steal your credit card number or checking account information. The same things that can happen to real-world payments can happen to you online. Your credit card information can be stolen by hackers who manage to break into a business's web site that is supposed to store them securely. Or you can be tricked into giving out the information from someone attempting to "verify" your identity for security purposes. But if you observe some wise, secure practices, you should be able to avoid such trouble and pay for what you buy on eBay. Your options are described in the sections that follow.

## Paper Money: Cashier's Checks and Money Orders

When it comes to sending payment, you can't get much simpler than old-fashioned paper checks or money orders. First of all, virtually all sellers accept them—even those who don't accept credit cards or some form of electronic payment. Cashier's checks and money orders are especially popular with sellers because they won't bounce—you have already paid to obtain them. They're also popular with buyers because they produce a quicker shipment than personal checks. Many sellers do accept personal checks, but only with the requirement that they wait a week or 10 days for the check to clear before they will ship what you have purchased.

Cashier's checks can be obtained from your bank or credit union. Depending on the bank's policies, you may have to pay a fee of $3 to $5 to obtain one. The U.S. Postal Service (your local post office) will issue you a money order for a reasonable fee. The most popular options are Western Union Auction Payments, which charges $2.95 for money orders of $10.01 to $30, and the U.S. Postal Service, which charges only ninety cents for money orders of the same amount.

If you aren't in a hurry to receive what you have purchased, personal checks can be a practical option. You just have to wait for the check to clear—a process that varies greatly depending on the speed with which your check gets to the seller, the speed with which the seller deposits the check, and the speed with which the banks transfer the money. The process might only take a few days, but because of the unpredictability, most sellers say they will wait up to 10 days before they ship.

**WATCH OUT!**  *Paying with cash might work fine when you're buying something in person. But in case you ever consider mailing in a cash payment, repeat after me: Never send cash! If you are ever asked by an eBay buyer or seller to pay with cash, politely say no and suggest an alternative, such as a money order or check.*

# PayPal

PayPal is eBay's own electronic payment service. An electronic payment service functions as an intermediary between someone who provides goods or services and someone who pays for them. Many financial institutions provide electronic payment services for customers who want to pay their bills online: you sign up for the service, pay the bills with your credit card, and the financial institution sees that it is transferred to the appropriate company.

## PayPal and Credit Card Payments

PayPal presents both buyers and sellers with a number of advantages. One of the biggest is convenience. As a buyer, you don't have to pay anything to use the service to make payments. You sign up for an account at PayPal's web site (http:// www.paypal.com). (The seller also has to have an account with PayPal to make the transaction work.) Another advantage is the ability to pay for eBay merchandise with a credit card. When you sign up for a PayPal account, you submit your credit card information to PayPal. You then depend on PayPal to keep your information secure. When you pay for an auction item using PayPal, you send the purchase amount to PayPal, along with the seller's e-mail address. PayPal then debits your credit card account and transfers the money to the seller's PayPal account.

Yet another advantage of using PayPal to pay for auction items with your credit card is PayPal's Buyer Protection program. The program provides you with purchase insurance that you can obtain in addition to eBay's own $250 worth of fraud protection. The buyer protection applies to items that were purchased on eBay and that were either not received after you paid for them or that turned out to be significantly different than described in the auction listing. The important thing to remember is that not all sellers who use PayPal offer buyer protection. Sellers must live in the United States or Canada, have an eBay feedback rating (the total of positive and negative feedbacks; see "Putting Feedback to Work for You" later in this chapter) of at least 50, at least 98 percent positive feedback, and meet other requirements. If buyer protection is available to you, you'll see the icon shown in Figure 2-8 at the bottom of the Seller Information box.

## PayPal and eChecks

You don't necessarily have to have funds charged to your credit card when you use PayPal to make payments. Instead, you can pay with an "eCheck" or electronic check, deducting the purchase amount from your checking account. The process should be familiar to anyone who uses debit cards.

You should be aware, though, that eChecks require some extra time to process. If you've used a debit card to make a purchase, you may have discovered that you can use the card even if your account does not have sufficient funds. eChecks can

**FIGURE 2-8**    Some, but not all, sellers who accept PayPal also offer buyer protection.

## Trade Talk

Many eBay members use PayPal for years without encountering problems. But it should be noted that some eBay members are deeply dissatisfied with the service. They object to the way PayPal investigates (or allegedly, fails to investigate) cases of fraud. In such cases, a buyer pays for something with PayPal and the seller never delivers it. Or a seller accepts payment from someone who turns out to have paid with a fraudulent credit card number. One of the complaints about PayPal concerns credit card transactions. As part of PayPal's user agreement, if you pay for something with a credit card and the seller fails to deliver, you can either have PayPal investigate the problem or receive a refund from your credit card company through its fraud protection—not both. PayPal's convenience and widespread use mean that, at the very least, you should sign up for an account as a buyer. But you should still investigate sellers through their feedback before you make a purchase, rather than depending on PayPal to solve problems should you run into them.

"bounce," just like regular checks. For that reason, sellers typically include a note like this in their auction description:

Listing 2-2
```
An eCheck is also acceptable but must first clear prior to shipment
of goods. This will delay the shipment.
```

PayPal requests an eCheck from the buyer's bank immediately upon request, but it can take four to five days before the bank actually releases the funds. The threat of eChecks' bouncing should not discourage you from paying with them. Just use your common sense, and be prepared to wait a week to receive what you've bought.

## Western Union Auction Payments

Many eBay members who are unhappy with PayPal turn to Western Union as an alternative. Like PayPal, Western Union Auction Payments (http://www.auctionpayments.com/) also functions as an intermediary for electronic payments. But transactions are not totally electronic. In order for the transaction to work, only the buyer has to sign up for an account with Western Union, and it's free to set up accounts so you can send payments. You pay with your credit or debit card; Western Union debits your credit card account and charges you a transaction fee as well. It then issues a paper money order and mails it to the seller. The fee is:

- $1.95 for money orders of $10 and under

- $2.95 for money orders of $10.01 to $30

- $3.95 for money orders of $30.01 to $50

- $4.95 for money orders of $50.01 to $100

- $4.95 plus 2.25 percent of the face value of the money order for money orders of $100.01 to $700.

Once the seller receives a confirmation e-mail from Western Union saying that the money order has been mailed, he or she has the option to either ship the merchandise immediately or wait until the money order actually arrives.

*Western Union Auction Payments limits its transactions to $700 or less, including shipping fees.*

# Putting Feedback to Work for You

You're probably familiar with word of mouth and the role it plays in your collecting. If someone tells you that a particular individual has a lot of items for sale that you are interested in, you are more likely to buy from that person. If someone else tells you that the collectibles in a particular store are overpriced, you may well decide to shop somewhere else.

eBay has taken the time-honored tradition of word of mouth and turned it into an organized feedback system. The innovative thing about feedback on eBay is that it not only gives you informed opinions about whether or not someone has behaved honorably in the course of completing a transaction, but it also acts as an incentive to reward good behavior and deter bad behavior, as described in the sections that follow.

## Feedback Types

What exactly is feedback? The term refers to the comments that buyers and sellers register about one another on eBay. After a transaction has been completed, members type evaluations into an online form, and eBay posts them on a part of its site called the Feedback Forum. The comments from the latest buyer or seller with whom an individual has done business are added to comments received in connection with previous transactions. Feedback can take one of three forms:

- **Positive**  Positive comments praise a seller's prompt delivery or a buyer's prompt and reliable payment. Each positive comment adds one point (+1) to the member's total feedback rating.

- **Negative**  Negative comments are registered when a seller fails to ship, a buyer fails to pay, or something else happens that ruins a transaction. Negative comments result in a single point (–1) being subtracted from the member's feedback rating.

- **Neutral**  Neutral comments are registered when a transaction is completed successfully, but something happens that isn't quite right and that isn't necessarily the fault of a buyer or seller; the shipper loses the item or is slow in delivering it, for instance. Neutral comments have no effect (0) on a member's feedback rating.

The accumulated feedback comments are added up to create the individual's feedback rating, a numeric total that appears in parentheses next to every eBay member's User ID. When you are first starting out on eBay, your feedback rating is 0; after you have bought or sold lots of items, it can climb into the hundreds, thousands, or even (for a few particularly successful users) the hundreds of thousands. One of the highest feedback ratings ever recorded on eBay was earned by a husband-and-wife team, Jay and Marie Senese, who are well known for selling "1 cent CDs" and "1 cent DVDs" on eBay. Their astounding feedback number is shown in Figure 2-9.

The star icon that appears next to a member's feedback rating indicates how much positive feedback they have received. The Seneses are known as "shooting stars" because of their special feedback icon. But any collector on eBay should try to gain high feedback numbers. Feedback tells a prospective buyer or seller that you can be trusted and that you are experienced with doing business on eBay.

## Research Feedback

Whenever you want to research someone's feedback, you only need to click his or her feedback number. If you have written down the user ID or someone has sent it to you in an e-mail message, you can look up feedback in one of two ways. Here's the first way: go to the Find Members page (click Search, then click Find Members in the navigation bar) and enter the person's user ID in the Feedback Profile box at the top of the page.

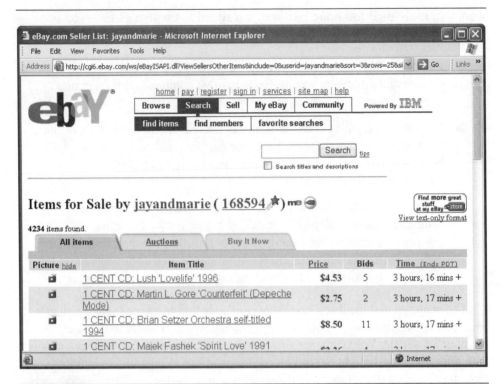

**FIGURE 2-9**   A few busy sellers have managed to earn "shooting star" icons for high feedback ratings.

The full-featured way to research feedback is through the Feedback Forum page (http://pages.ebay.com/services/forum/feedback.html). A research box at the top of the page lets you enter the user ID of an eBay member whose feedback you want to review. A series of links enabling you to perform common functions is presented near the top of the page. Click the link that corresponds to the kind of research you want to conduct. The following options are available:

■ Review and respond to feedback comments left for you

■ Review and follow up on feedback you have left about others

■ Hide your feedback. This enables your feedback to be private, so it can be seen only by you. You should avoid doing this unless you have some negative comments you don't want others to see. Hiding your feedback will likely cause other eBay members to avoid doing business with you.

When you enter a user ID in the search box at the top of the page and click Find Member, you view the member's feedback summary as well as individual feedback comments left for that individual. If the person's feedback rating is high, you may gain access to pages and pages of feedback comments. You can view not only comments left for the member but comments the person has left for other eBay members. Viewing feedback left for others gives you a better picture of the individual's dealings with other buyers and sellers.

When you click one of the other links, you'll generally be asked to sign in with your user ID and password. You'll then go to a form where you can view feedback, leave feedback, or perform other functions. As you can see, you get not only the opportunity to leave feedback for someone but to add your own comments in response to feedback that has been left for you. On occasion, members who lose their temper do leave angry and sometimes vulgar comments. You might want to add your own "rebuttal" or further explanation to clarify what's been said.

## Leaving Feedback

When you are ready to leave feedback, go to the Feedback Forum page and click Leave Feedback. You'll go a page that displays any transactions for which you have not yet left feedback. Click the link for the transaction you want, and enter your comments in the feedback form provided for you.

Feedback comments are an important way to be a contributing member of the eBay community. Yet most members toss off feedback comments quickly, without giving them much thought. The comments you leave for other people are easily accessed as part of your member profile, along with the comments others leave for you. In order to build a good reputation and develop trust, try to make your feedback comments courteous yet specific. Often, members simply reuse standard feedback phrases, such as "smooth transaction" or "fast response." They use lots of quotation marks and make comments like the following:

- "AAAA+++++!!!!! Great seller!"

- "Fast shipping, good packing. Cheers!"

- "Speedy delivery, good customer service. Highly recommended!"

There's nothing wrong with such phrases. But consider describing, simply and briefly, the exact experience you had with someone during a transaction. To me, the most valuable feedback comments are those that get more precise about how long it took to receive something, or how an item was shipped. For example:

- "Shipped in less than 5 days; video was top quality."

- "Received CD-ROM within three days of payment."

- "E-mail responses came in less than six hours; shipment received 3 days after payment."

- "I appreciated double-boxing and Priority Mail option."

Also be aware of the option to leave neutral feedback. A negative comment should be left if you feel someone didn't behave in a satisfactory way—if an item arrived damaged and you weren't offered a refund or a discount; if the high bidder didn't pay up; if the seller didn't ship. Neutral feedback is appropriate if something went wrong with the transaction but it wasn't necessarily the buyer or seller's fault: Payment was slow because the buyer was out of town, or the package got lost by the shipping company, for instance.

COLLECTOR'S NOTE    *Be careful when deciding between positive or neutral feedback. Neutral feedback is perceived by most eBay members as having a negative connotation, so only leave it if you were really unhappy with how a transaction turned out.*

Be sure not to leave feedback until an item is shipped and actually arrives at its destination. "I leave feedback when I get confirmation that the item has arrived safely—safely in someone's hands, when the whole thing is over with," says Paula Amato.

COLLECTOR'S NOTE    *eBay itself won't erase feedback comments acting on its own. The process is involved, but those buyers or sellers who dispute comments left by someone else or who want to "clean up" their feedback comments in order to improve their overall rating can pay a fee to have them reviewed by a third-party company called SquareTrade (http://www.squaretrade .com). SquareTrade is in the business of giving a seal of approval to companies that want to do business online. It has entered into a partnership with eBay to provide arbitration services in case of a feedback dispute.*

## Links for Collectors

| Web Site/Page | Address | What's There |
|---|---|---|
| Browse | http://pages.ebay.com/buy/index.html | Links to all eBay's main categories of merchandise, as well as featured eBay Stores, selected Themes, and selected Regions |
| All Categories | http://listings.ebay.com | A list of all eBay's main categories and the first level of subcategories within each one |
| Basic Search | http://pages.ebay.com/search/items/basicsearch.html | A search form that lets you search titles and descriptions, specific categories, or specific eBay locations around the world |
| Advanced Search | http://pages.ebay.com/search/items/search_adv.html | A search form that lets you search for completed auctions, Buy It Now auctions, and other options |
| Feedback Forum | http://pages.ebay.com/services/forum/feedback.html | A page full of links that let you view feedback, leave feedback, and respond to comments that have been left about you |
| PayPal | http://www.paypal.com | eBay's own electronic payment service |
| Western Union Auction Payments | http://www.auctionpayments.com/ | Service that allows buyers to pay by debit or credit card, then issues paper money order to sellers |

# Chapter 3

# eBay for Sellers: A One-Hour Primer

## In This Chapter You'll Learn...

■ How to identify the right collectibles to sell on eBay

■ How to write sales descriptions that encourage bids

■ How to take high-quality digital images of your merchandise

■ How to fill out eBay's Sell Your Item form

■ How to make sure your merchandise reaches its destination

When you move from buying to selling, collecting takes on a whole new dimension. All of a sudden, you're thinking not only of yourself and your interests when you go collecting. You have to look for things that you can resell. You try to anticipate how much profit you might make on a particular object and whether it will attract bids. You have to answer questions from potential customers, and you have to make sure the buyer is satisfied.

eBay started out primarily as a place to buy and sell collectibles. In recent years, it's become more and more populated by businesses and consumer goods. But collectibles haven't gone away. If anything, you are more likely to find some desirable objects now on eBay than you were five or six years ago. The number of potential buyers is still on the upswing, and that means there is still a chance for collectors like you to start selling successfully. This chapter provides you with an overview of what it takes to start selling on eBay and how to complete transactions safely.

# Deciding What to Sell

Sometimes, the best buys on eBay are the things that people put up for sale without having any idea what they are. They go up with no reserve, they are misspelled, or they are put in the wrong category. The seller's lack of knowledge can easily be turned into a bidder's good fortune. The key is to take the time to know what you have and how much it is worth. When you do your research, you will be able to describe things more accurately, place them in the right category, and know whether they are worth enhancements such as bold listings, highlighting, or placement in featured categories.

If you sell collectibles in an area in which you are already knowledgeable, you won't mind doing research and taking care with your descriptions. Start by selling what you already know and love. You're likely to have some duplicate items in this area or objects that are no longer the primary focus of your collection and that you won't mind selling online. Once you become familiar with selling on eBay in your own specialty, you can go on to master your sales methods and move into additional areas for buying and selling.

# Know What You Have

As I was starting to work on this chapter, I came across an album in the local resale shop by the famous country singer Kitty Wells. When I turned the album cover over to look at the back, there was a signature: Kitty Wells. Naturally, I paid 50 cents for the album and took it home, wondering all the time if this was really signed by the singer herself and, if so, was this album worth anything?

I was faced with the first questions that need to be answered by anyone who wants to sell collectibles on eBay:

- Is it authentic?

- What is it worth? Are people going to bid on this?

It's true, you could simply put up what you have for sale, show good photos of it, and let the market decide. Bidders could inspect your item and determine its authenticity based on copyright marks, makers' marks, trademarks, or other characteristics. Their bids could determine what it's worth. Chances are there's a collector out there who knows as much, or more, about your item than you do and who can evaluate the authenticity by asking you questions and relying on long experience. Lots of sellers, in fact, focus on volume: they take photos and get descriptions online as quickly as they can, so they can have time for other tasks. But I'm convinced—and sellers have told me—that when you take time and prepare an authoritative, compelling description, you get more bids.

Researching your merchandise tells people that you care about what you sell, that you are knowledgeable, and that you can be trusted. Developing a good reputation and providing good customer service are almost as important to successfully selling on eBay as having some good things to sell. Some suggestions on how to research your merchandise follow.

## Is It Authentic?

Authenticity, as you probably know already, is an essential quality that goes into making something a collectible. How do you determine something is authentic, such as a Kitty Wells signature? Even if I could find Kitty Wells herself (and since she is still alive and has a web site, I could), she wouldn't remember signing the back of an album years ago. I could take the album to one of the appraisers on *Antiques Roadshow,* but they have already been to Chicago and probably won't be back for a while.

Luckily, I have a resource at my fingertips that appraisers and collectors didn't have until recently: the Internet. It turns out there is no shortage of real Kitty Wells signatures online. When I typed the words "Kitty Wells autograph" into Google's search engine, I immediately found a signed photograph of the singer that had already been sold for $55. Plenty of signed programs, cards, and photos turned up, I was able to compare the signatures on these photos with the one on my album, and I found several similarities in the way the letters are formed that tell me this signature must be the real thing. Compare the photo shown on the right in Figure 3-1 and my album signature and see what you think.

Google is, of course, only one place to research the authenticity of an item. There are lots of other resources. One of the obvious is Kitty Wells's own web site, which includes yet another autographed photo (http://www.kittywells.com/facts.html). There are a variety of celebrity autograph sites, such as History for Sale (http://www.historyforsale.com), which include signatures of Kitty Wells and other celebrities. Unless you have a certificate of authenticity or a letter certifying that the object is authentic, you can't know with 100 percent certainty that an item is "for real." But you can do research that lets you and your prospective bidders know that, with reasonable certainty, it is.

COLLECTOR'S NOTE    *Brian J. Graham, an experienced collector of Belleek pottery, provides detailed information on Belleek sales on eBay as well as tips on how to date pieces using variations in the Belleek marks (http://www3.bc.sympatico.ca/bjgcelt/conventionpresentation.html). It's a good example of the importance of carefully examining items, watching out for fakes, and studying a field closely when you seek to sell on eBay.*

## How Much Is It Worth?

This question, too, can be answered up to a point by researching on the Web. You can search through completed sales and determine how many similar items (if any) have been sold on eBay recently. (See Chapter 2 for instructions on how to conduct such a search using eBay's Advanced Search tab.) When I did a search for "Kitty Wells autograph" I came up with a few not-very-encouraging results:

- Kitty Wells Autograph on Arts Cover: Starting bid $5.95, 0 bids received

- Kitty Wells Autograph First Day Cover: Starting bid $9.99, 0 bids received

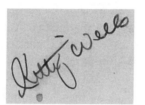

**FIGURE 3-1**   Use the Internet and take the time to research what you plan to sell on eBay.

Such a search only tells me how many items have sold in recent weeks. To get a better idea of how much Kitty Wells items can fetch on eBay, I went to the auction service Andale (http://www.andale.com). Andale sells a wide variety of software tools that auction buyers and sellers can use. One of the most popular features is not a software program but information culled from eBay's database of past auctions. You have to pay a monthly fee to access eBay data on a regular basis, but you can try out the service for free. I found that, in the preceding six weeks, 14 Kitty Wells autograph items have been up for sale on eBay. Of those, six auctions ended with bids and a completed sale; the other eight auctions had no bids. Two of the six successful auctions were record albums: one sold for $9.99, the other for only $2. The other four were photos, and these sold for $3, $9.99, $5.50, and $17.28, respectively. I get the definite impression that photos are more desirable than albums and that I can't expect to make more than $10 on this album. It's not encouraging news, but I feel better for knowing what to expect.

Andale's database report also includes a variety of suggestions for making a successful sale and even some charts that illustrate what makes such sales work. The suggestions include:

- ■ Set the starting bid between $1.99 and $3.98, but don't set a reserve bid.

- ■ List the auction to start on a Sunday and run for seven days, so that it ends on a Sunday, when many people are home from work and likely to be shopping online. List the item between 4 and 10 P.M.

- ■ Don't spend money on features designed to bring more attention to the item, such as highlighting the title in bold or in a color; at least, these did not work in the six successful auctions reported.

- ■ List the item in the category Collectibles : Autographs : Other Autographs. If you decide to list in a second category as well, choose Entertainment Memorabilia : Autographs : Music : Country : Original.

Some of the impressive-looking charts used to back up these recommendations are shown in Figure 3-2.

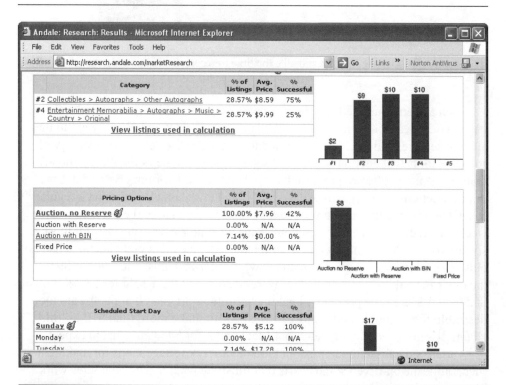

**FIGURE 3-2** Andale provides useful data and makes suggestions based on sales of similar items.

**3**

I've learned quite a bit about Kitty Wells autographs so far. Probably, they aren't terribly valuable because she has been around for a while, is still alive, and has apparently signed lots of different types of items in her career. Is there anything else I can research to try to gain more money by playing it up in the auction description? It would be helpful if the album itself was especially rare. I am encouraged by spotting the listing on a site called MusicStack, which functions as a marketplace for rare albums and CDs. I notice that some sellers are selling the same album for $6.99, $10, and $12, respectively. I can look this up in a record price guide, but that only tells me what someone thinks the album is worth. The ultimate answer only comes when you put the item up for sale on eBay, and bidders indicate how much the item is really worth in the marketplace.

## How Do You Find the Right Bidder?

This book's technical editor, who sells on eBay, advocates a strategy for finding the right bidder for an object. It's an idea that some eBay members might find controversial, because it borders on invasion of privacy (in my opinion, at least). However, I couldn't find anything in eBay's Rules for Sellers that prohibits it, and I thought it was worth mentioning. It involves finding bidders who typically buy what you are selling and approaching them to make them aware of your sale.

The process works something like this: Do an advanced search on eBay for completed items that are similar to what you have to sell. Make note of the high bidders as well as some of the underbidders (the bidders who didn't win—you find them by clicking on the number of bids in the auction listing). Try to find people who place high bids for the items that are like yours. Notify these bidders by sending a message through eBay's message service that you are offering an item that might be of interest to them.

COLLECTOR'S NOTE    *eBay isn't the only place to put rare or especially valuable items up for sale. The music marketplace I found (http://www.musicstack.com) might be more likely to attract collectors of rare records. In my own area of interest, I know that fountain pens are frequently bought and sold on a site called PenBid (http://www.penbid.com). You might try selling one or two items on such specialty sites and see if you get better results than on eBay. At the very least, you should know whether these kinds of marketplaces exist for the things you collect and visit them occasionally to check out prices.*

## Avoid Common Sellers' Mistakes

Sometimes, the key to success is simply avoiding obvious mistakes. It's hard to make a really serious mistake when you are putting something up for sale; even if you get a date or model number wrong, you are allowed to edit a description until the first bid is placed. And after bids have come in you can still add to your description and correct any mistakes. In most cases, you can add to a description up to 12 hours before a sale ends. The kinds of mistakes listed here can hurt your sales, but they are easy to avoid:

- **You misspell the item.** When it comes to collectibles, accuracy counts. Typos as simple as typing the number 5 instead of 4 can cause big trouble. Any coin collector can tell you that an 1804 silver dollar is worth a great deal more than an 1805. In my field, pen collecting, a Waterman pen is far more desirable than a Waterson, which was just an imitation. The real trouble comes when you misspell a critical word in the auction title. Changes to the title can't be made if the item has received any bids or if less than 12 hours remain before the end of the sale. If the sale goes out with a brand name or model name spelled wrong, it can seriously hurt sales. Yet misspellings do occur with long words: instead of a Rickenbacker guitar, you see models spelled as Rickenbaker, for example. Misspellings are easy to fix: read the description twice, and use the spell-check feature built into the Sell Your Item form. (Having someone else proofread your typing is an effective way to catch mistakes.)

- **You put in a reserve when you don't need to.** There's nothing wrong with reserve prices. They are intended to help you minimize losses. As a seller of a valuable collectible, one of the first things you ask yourself is, "How can I guarantee that I'll get what I want for this?" But keep in mind that many sellers believe reserve prices discourage bids. If you don't get any bids, this could be one reason. When there is no reserve, bidders know for sure that someone will win the item, and this encourages more bids.

- **You put in a high starting bid that discourages bidding.** Don't feel hesitant to set a starting bid that represents the minimum you want to accept for something. But keep in mind that eBay charges you an

**3**

insertion fee (the fee for listing an item) based on the starting bid; a starting bid of $300 on something worth $275 is likely to discourage bids, and it will cost you $3.60 if the item sells. Set the starting bid as low as you can to encourage bargain hunters to bid.

■ **You don't include photos.** You don't have to include a photo with a sales description. But as you already know from your own shopping on eBay, almost all sales have one. The Web is inherently a visual medium. If shoppers don't see a photo in one of your sales, they are likely to move on to a sales description that does.

■ **You post bad photos.** By now, just about anyone can take a good digital photo. Even if you don't have a digital camera, you can develop your photos at the local pharmacy and have them printed on CD-ROM or online (see Chapter 8 for suggestions).

■ **You don't post enough photos.** Depending on your choice of hosting service, it can be very inexpensive to post photos of your merchandise online. To keep up with the increasing level of competition on eBay, you should include as many photos as you can afford. Include only one image and your item won't get as much attention as those of your competitors.

■ **You are too negative about the item.** Every item has its good and bad points. Your job is to talk about both honestly. While talking up the object you should also mention any flaws, but don't emphasize them too much in an attempt to be overly honest. Remember that you are selling something, not trying to apologize for it. Always end the description with the good points, and try to suggest how people can use or enjoy what you are selling.

■ **You end the sale at a bad time.** When in doubt, it's a good idea to end your auction on a weekend. That's when the largest number of buyers will be available to compete when the sale ends. End your sale during the week, and you will probably get fewer bids. End it during the conventional 9:00 to 5:00 working hours, you'll get even less. Of course, all of these are just generalizations that won't apply if an item is truly rare or valuable. Besides that, bidding services on the Web are available that place bids automatically for you at a time you specify. But for more common merchandise, you should try to end the sale on a weekend.

■ **You don't say enough about the item.** A one-sentence description might give the basic facts and figures about an object. But consider what such a description says about you: that you are in a hurry; that you don't pay attention to detail. Think about the sorts of descriptions that make you excited about something: chances are they are the ones that tell a story, that provide some juicy details and engage a viewer's imagination.

■ **You don't really know what you have.** Sellers are surprised all the time by what they have. People who sold the $31,857 fishing lure or the $19,000 beer can that I wrote about in my first book on eBay (*How to Do Everything With Your eBay Business,* McGraw-Hill Osborne; 2003) had no idea they were so valuable. But that's not the type of "ignorance" I'm talking about. I'm talking about when you misrepresent something or put it in the wrong category. Incorrect descriptions can lead to disgruntled customers and e-mails from knowledgeable collectors. Do a little homework beforehand, and you'll build up your reputation rather than tear it down.

## Think About Year-Round Sales

One of the eBay members I interviewed for this book collects and sells silver and porcelain household items. Those types of things are likely to sell at most times of the year. But when the end-of-the-year holidays roll around, sales drop off. That's because eBay shoppers tend to look for toys and gift items then. In order to cover sales over the holidays (and at other times of the year) she sells miniature figurines of dogs and other pets.

You should take a lesson from this seller and try to diversify; that way, you can be sure of being able to make sales all year round. Rather than collecting and trying to resell only Christmas ornaments or one type of collectible, for instance, consider supplementing your inventory by finding some wholesale items: items that you can purchase cheaply from a wholesale distributor and resell on eBay.

In recent years, I have talked to successful eBay sellers who distribute items like these:

| Seller's eBay User ID | Feedback as of April 2004 | Items Sold |
| --- | --- | --- |
| roniheart | 1562 | Folk art, Dreamsicles ornaments |
| bargain-hunters-dream | 3113 | Porcelain, handpainted figurines, kitchen tools, household items |
| smart_blonde330 | 1089 | Wholesale cosmetics, overstock items |
| venusrisinglimited | 1055 | High-quality bedding, luggage, bath items |

Finding a source for these items isn't difficult; finding good, desirable items that will attract customers and that you can resell at a profit is the hard part. Most of the longtime sellers who do it told me they had to look a while for a supplier. There are plenty of businesses that advertise themselves as "drop shippers" or sellers of "truckload inventory," but take care that what you get from them is really going to be desirable to eBay bidders. Often, they are selling overstock or discontinued items from retail stores—items that buyers have already rejected. Search for "wholesalers" or "liquidators" on Google, or do a search on eBay's own Wholesale Lots area.

> **TIP**
>
> *Try to pick something to sell that you are already interested in. If you are a cat lover, look for things having to do with cats, for instance. You'll have more fun writing descriptions and working with the items yourself. Also make sure what you want to sell isn't already widely sold on eBay (such as clothing, which is already plentiful).*

## Consider Categories

Another way to boost sales, even if you don't decide to sell wholesale items in bulk, is to choose collectibles that can be listed in many different sales categories on eBay. The more exposure you have across eBay's range of categories, the more potential buyers you will find. Consider the collectors who buy and sell porcelain-related items. Their merchandise can be spread around the following parts of eBay:

- Pottery & Glass : Pottery & China

- Home & Garden : Home Décor : Sculptures, Figure : Ceramic, Porcelain

- Dolls & Bears : Dolls : By Material : Porcelain

- Collectibles : Decorative Collectibles

It's also important to consider how easy your collectibles are going to be to ship when they are sold. You have an advantage if you sell something small and flat, like postcards and photos, rather than bird cages or electronic components.

## For This Collector, the Postcard's the Thing

Nancee Belshaw (eBay user ID revolving-door) sells thousands of collectibles on eBay each year. How does she do it? For one thing, she was wise enough to pick something to collect that's relatively inexpensive, easy to ship and store, and has lots of variations: postcards. The Los Angeles resident has only been collecting for five years but has accumulated 2000 postcards in her personal collection. She's also a dog lover, and she specializes in selling postcards with dogs and other animals depicted on them—as well as risqué postcards of women from the 1920s. Animal postcards are particularly popular around the world, she has discovered.

"I have one person who buys from me regularly and who collects Arabian horse postcards—and she has 6500. Postcards come in lots of subcategories. You can buy them for as little as $2. Thirty dollars is the most I spend as a seller; my top seller is the 1920s singing star Josephine Baker. I sold a postcard of her for $200. For me, that's a big deal because most of my stuff sells for $10, so I have to do a lot of volume to make a profit."

Selling on eBay isn't quite a full-time activity for Nancee. She still works part-time as a psychotherapist. She got started on eBay, in fact, when insurance restrictions caused her therapy business to dwindle dramatically. "I am trying to make eBay a replacement for that income, so I am working 97 hours a week. At any time, I have 500 postcards for sale on eBay. I hired an assistant to help me put them online. Someone else helps me with shipping. You have to learn that you don't have to do everything: You can delegate. I also sell through my web site, http://www.eyedealpostcards.com. If anyone is going to make a success at this business, you have to work 12 hours a day, every day of the week."

**3**

Having assistants to provide her with help enables Nancee to focus on what she loves: collecting. She frequently travels to Europe to attend conventions that attract postcard collectors. Often, she travels with overseas postcard enthusiasts she has befriended through her eBay sales. She's discovered that, when you buy and sell collectibles to people who love them, you've instantly got a basis for a friendship.

Nancee also sells figurines of dogs, cats, and other animals to ensure that she has buyers around the holiday season. "It's a good idea to have more than one thing you are selling. Collectors don't buy as much during the holidays, so this gift stuff has really helped me. They are easy to put up for sale on eBay; you put the same thing up over and over. One of the manufacturers I met at a gift show; the other two I found on the Internet. If you really look, you can find any wholesaler you want. Sometimes you have to spend a lot of time doing it, but you can."

When asked to provide advice for prospective eBay sellers, Nancee emphasizes the following: "Customer service is real important. A lot of people don't understand that. I think sometimes how you react to people affects the feedback you get and the number of sales you get. If you contact people really quickly, and mail out really quickly, it makes a difference. Unless you know how to talk to people, because people are going to get upset—sometimes for justifiable reasons, sometimes not—and you have to understand where they are coming from. Being a psychologist teaches me to be empathetic. As a result, I have only six negative feedback comments out of 13,000 total. My actual feedback number is lower than the number of total comments because I have lots of repeat customers: Each person buys at least three cards."

# Preparing Your Sales Description: The Preliminaries

It's easy to put something up for sale on eBay. When you're first starting out, you should use the form that eBay provides for creating sales listings. It's called the Sell Your Item form, and you access it by clicking the Sell button in the eBay navigation bar, then signing in with your user ID and password. After you've been selling for a while, when you have multiple listings you need to put online, you may choose to use special software programs that help you create sales listings and put them online in bulk (see Chapter 13 for descriptions of such programs).

But before you start filling out the form, you need to get your ducks in a row. By the time you start creating your listing, you need to have

- Done your research.

- Prepared your description, or at least a rough draft of it.

- Taken your photos and put them on a web server, unless you want eBay to host the photos. eBay lets you post one for free, and others cost 15 cents each.

- Determined how you are going to accept payments and set up an account with an electronic payment service such as PayPal if you decide to use one.

Once you handle the preliminaries it'll be that much easier to put your sale online. The following sections describe how to do it.

## Write Out Your Description

My eBay friend Jo Stavig told me the following story: A catalog copywriter named Wayne McKenzie—someone who obviously has a flair for writing—put a camera manual up for sale on eBay. In the description, McKenzie told a story. He had been hunting for clams on a beach in Nova Scotia when he lost his camera. He had no choice but to sell the manual itself. He went into elaborate detail on how wonderful the camera was and how much it meant to him. The woman who purchased the manual was so touched by the story that she eventually sent the manual back— along with the accompanying camera. She wanted the seller to get his long-lost camera back.

You don't have to write a description that gets that sort of reaction. But I think you'll get better results if you try to tell a story and make an effort to get buyers to fall in love with what you have to offer. Before you get to the Sell Your Item form, be sure to write out a preliminary description of your item that includes the research you have done to this point. Think like a buyer; provide all the information you would want if you were shopping for the item. In my own case, I type out the description in Microsoft Word so I can take advantage of Word's spell-checking capabilities. I then save the file so I can paste the contents into the Sell Your Item form when I get to that point. Saving the file enables me to include some "boilerplate" text—text that appears the same from sale to sale—so I can copy and paste it easily when it comes time to create a new listing. Here's the description I came up with for the Kitty Wells album:

3

I went to the local resale shop on a whim, and spotted this album immediately as I was coming down the stairs. I was interested because Kitty Wells is a classic country singer who has been called the "Queen of Country Music," and I love her simple, lovely songs along with the classic tinkling piano in the background. Imagine my surprise when I spotted the "Kitty Wells" signature on the back of the album. This is a pretty distinctive signature, and I have looked at many other examples of the way Wells signs her name. I'm certain this is an authentic Kitty Wells autograph, though I can't guarantee it. The album is rare and out of print. No manufacturer is listed, but the back of the album bears the serial number CLP-15588. I have seen it listed on rare record marketplaces for $10-$12. Both the record and the album cover are in very good condition: there is a little wear at the edge of the album, but the spine is virtually perfect, and I don't see any ringwear at all. There is no original paper sleeve inside the album cover, but I will provide one for shipping purposes.

This album contains many of Kitty's hits. Side 1: It Wasn't God Who Made Honky Tonk Angels; This White Circle; Mommy for a Day; Release Me; I Gave My Wedding Dress Away; Amigo's Guitar. Side 2: Heartbreak U.S.A.; I'll Repossess My Heart; Password; Searching (For Someone Like You); Making Believe. I will be traveling April 11-15 so responses to inquiries may be slow then.

Buyer pays shipping and handling fees, only Priority Mail with Delivery Confirmation (I will not ship UPS) is used (where allowed) and loss or breakage is only covered if insurance is taken. Your phone number is required for FedEx shipping. All insured claims are settled (paid for) by the Post Office and shipping fees are nonrefundable. No shipping to APO address without insurance. Checks are held for 10 business days and Illinois residents must pay sales tax. Seller has the right to refuse any PayPal payments without a confirmed address. Additional photos will be sent upon request. Please ask questions prior to bidding, as in traditional auctions items are sold as is and no returns. Items will be relisted in 10 days after the auction closes if I don't hear from the buyer and a negative Feedback will be left. Feedback will be left upon confirmation of the items arrival.

The first two paragraphs contain the information that is specific to this item; the third block of text is the boilerplate. Boilerplate is a huge time-saver. It helps organize your material in a logical order and enables you to place many sales online in a single day.

## Capture Digital Images

As a writer, I am biased toward the power of words. I tend to focus on the need to write a compelling description in order to attract bids. But even a wordsmith like me cannot deny the power of images in eBay sales listings. Having multiple clear close-ups of an item can hold a viewer's attention, generate inquiries, and induce bids.

You have to come up with a system for capturing good-quality images of your merchandise. You should take your photos and have them ready before you put a sale online. That's why this section provides you with a brief overview of the process of taking digital images before you actually post the item for sale on eBay. (For more details about digital images, see Chapter 8.)

### Taking Images

You've got plenty of options for taking pictures that you can add to your eBay auction listings. The most convenient and economical (in the long run) option is to use a digital camera. The qualifier "in the long run" is added because initially, you have to choose and purchase a digital camera. Once you have a good one, however, you should be able to use it for years to come, and it should save you money in photo developing and printing over time.

For this brief overview, I took some images with an Olympus Camedia camera, which has the ability to capture 5 million pixels (or 5 megapixels, as they are frequently known) of digital information within a single image.

## Did you know?    A Digital Pix Is Made of Pixels

A *pixel* is a tiny rectangle that contains one or more bits of digital information. Approximately 72 pixels are contained in an inch. The quality of a digital camera is frequently expressed in terms of megapixels. A 3-megapixel camera can take images up to 1500 × 2000 resolution.

3

For the Kitty Wells album described earlier in this chapter, I didn't have to take a lot of photos. The album cover only has two sides, so I wanted to capture both the front and the back. I took a close-up of the record label and of the signature. That's four photos in all. Two of them are shown in Figure 3-3.

The most important things to remember when taking digital photos are framing your object loosely (not cropping it too close), making sure you have adequate lighting, and getting as close as possible to the subject.

In order to photograph the signature on the album (see Figure 3-4), I used the camera's macro capability (a macro lens is one especially designed to take close-ups of small objects). I did not use the Camedia's built-in flash, but pointed two external lights at it, one from either side, in order to distribute the light more evenly without encountering light flares—bright flashes that reflect off shiny surfaces.

## Editing Images

After I took the images of the Kitty Wells album, I transferred them from the camera's memory card to my computer using a USB cable. I then opened them up in an image-editing program—software especially designed for adjusting computer images so they look better than they did originally. Even technically sophisticated digital cameras and scanners don't produce perfect images the first time. The album's

FIGURE 3-3    Be sure to photograph your object from as many angles as possible.

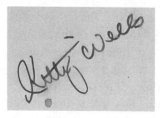

| FIGURE 3-4 | A camera with a special close-up lens or close-up capability is a must for eBay. |

back side, which was white, came out looking a dull gray in the digital photo. By editing the image in Adobe Photoshop Elements, I was able to make it look clean and white again. The gray version is on the left and the adjusted version is on the right in Figure 3-5.

Along with changing color, I crop the images. Cropping is the process of deleting the parts of the image you don't want. This reduces both the physical size of the image as well as its digital size—the amount of kilobytes or megabytes it consumes on disk. The smaller the image, the faster it travels over the Internet to

| FIGURE 3-5 | After capturing digital images, you need to edit them to optimize appearance. |

## Choose a Sales Format

When you're ready to create a sales listing, click Sell in the navigation bar, log in with your user ID and password, and click Sign In. Your browser goes to the first page of the Sell Your Item form, which is entitled Choose a Selling Format. You have three options:

- Sell Item at Online Auction
- Sell at a Fixed Price
- Advertise Your Real Estate

Since I want people to bid on my record, I leave the option Sell Item at Online Auction selected, and click Continue to move to the next page. You might choose Sell at a Fixed Price if you have opened an eBay Store (see Chapter 10). Real estate sales work differently than conventional standard or reserve auctions; the real estate can stay online for as long as 90 days, and purchases are not necessarily legally binding.

## Choose Categories

After you specify the type of sale you want to conduct and click Continue, you move to the page entitled "Sell Your Item step 1 of 5: Category." This is where you select one or more categories in which the item should be sold. If I wanted to do a search and have eBay suggest a category, I could enter the search keywords "Kitty Wells LP" in the Enter Item Keywords to find a category search box, click Find, and sell the album in the suggested category.

Here, I will fall back on the recommendations from Andale and sell the record in the following category:

```
Collectibles : Autographs : Other Autographs
```

To specify this category, I click Collectibles in the first Browse Categories box, Autographs in the second, and so on, as shown in Figure 3-6.

But this particular object crosses boundaries. It might not just appeal to collectors of autographs or of Kitty Wells memorabilia, but to country music record collectors as well. Therefore, I decide to spend an extra insertion fee and list in the second category:

```
Music : Records
```

shoppers' computers, where it can be displayed by their browsers. In this case, smaller is better.

### Hosting Photos

Everything you see on the Web has a home. Whether you are looking at text or photos, that home takes the form of a web server—a computer that is equipped to make content available (in other words, *serve* it) to anyone with a web browser. Such a computer typically has a very fast, direct connection to the Internet and is online all the time, so its contents are always accessible.

The textual part of your auction description automatically goes on one of eBay's web servers. But photos don't necessarily have to be hosted with eBay. It certainly is convenient to choose eBay as your host, and you might want to do this when you're starting out: eBay lets you post the first photo of an auction for free; after that, each subsequent image costs 15 cents. If you have lots of sales to put online and each one of those sales includes four or five photos, the cost can quickly add up. In that case, you can choose another host. Many third-party providers specialize in auction photo hosting, and these are described in Chapter 8. But before you sign up with one, consider hosting your photos on your own web server space.

All Internet service providers (ISPs) provide customers like you with space where you can post photos and web pages. If you use America Online, for instance, you are entitled to 5MB of server space for each of your screen names. The logical thing, if you have a limited number of photos to be hosted in conjunction with your eBay auctions, is to post one free photo with eBay and put the rest on your own web server space. That's what I did with the Kitty Wells auction. I put the photos on my web server using file transfer protocol (FTP) software (the method for transferring files from your computer to your web server varies from provider to provider). I made note of the URLs for each one:

```
http://www.literarychicago.com/ebay/kitty1.jpg
http://www.literarychicago.com/ebay/kitty2.jpg
http://www.literarychicago.com/ebay/kitty3.jpg
```

With the URLs written down, I can then paste them into the Sell Your Item form when the time comes to add them.

**WATCH OUT!** *Some ISPs frown on posting eBay photos on your web server space because they increase traffic to your site. Make sure you know exactly how much space you have and how much throughput (the amount of data transferred from a server to a browser when a file is viewed) you are allowed. You will be charged extra fees in addition to your regular Internet access fees if you put more files on your web server than you are allotted or if you get more page views than you are allowed. In that case, it makes sense to move to a hosting service that provides more space, such as the ones mentioned in Chapter 8.*

## Set Up a Payment Plan

It might seem illogical to suggest that you work out how your customers pay you before you even put anything up for sale. After all, although you hope you'll attract bidders, you don't know for sure that you will get any bids at all. But think positive; of course, you're going to get bids! When you get to the part of the Sell Your Item form that asks you to select your payment methods, you'll need to have that already figured out.

Since payments are the subject of an entire chapter (Chapter 11), I'm not going to go into great detail here—only to say that, if you're just starting out, you should accept four forms of payment:

- Cashier's checks

- Personal checks

- Money orders

- PayPal

The first three items don't really require you to do any setup beforehand. The fourth, though, does require you to decide what kind of account you want to set up with PayPal. PayPal offers two accounts: Personal and Premier. Both let you receive payments from eBay buyers or other PayPal users. However, the Personal account does not allow you to receive credit card payments—which is exactly why many buyers want to use PayPal. They want the convenience of paying with a credit card and the security of having PayPal transfer the money rather than having to send their credit card number and personal information over the Internet.

If you already have a Personal account, you should strongly consider an upgrade to a Premier account. The downside of such an account is that, for every payment

you receive, PayPal charges a fee of between 2.2 and 2.9 percent of the purchase amount, plus a 30 cent transaction fee. If you need to move from a Personal to a Premier account, follow these steps:

1. Go to the PayPal web site (http://www.paypal.com).

2. Log in with your PayPal username and password.

3. If you haven't yet "verified" your identity to PayPal by providing your checking account information, you'll be prompted to do so. If you don't want to verify your information, click Continue to My Account.

4. When the My Account page appears, click Upgrade Account.

5. When the Premier Account page appears, click Upgrade Now. You return to the My Account page, where your account has been changed automatically.

You don't have to have a PayPal account in order to accept credit card payments, of course. If you already accept credit card payments through a merchant account with a bank or other financial institution, you can use that instead of a PayPal account.

**TIP** *You can also bypass PayPal and set up an account with Western Union Auction Payments. That way, buyers can still pay you with a credit card, but you get a money order for the actual payment. Find out more in Chapter 11.*

## The Sell Your Item Form

Now that I've completed all the preliminaries, I can finally put my Kitty Wells album up for sale. I can do this any time I wish. In the course of filling out the form, you are given the option of scheduling the sale so that it begins at a particular time. The important thing about choosing the beginning time is that this determines the ending time, based on the number of days you want the sale to last. It's important to remember that you're in control of the sale process—that's the whole point of eBay; it puts individuals in control of buying and selling. Many collectors and other busy sellers try to schedule their sales so they don't interfere with day jobs, family life, or their hobby. (Before long, of course, eBay becomes *part of* their hobby.)

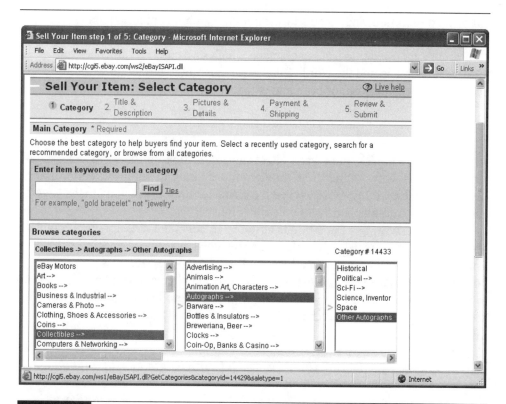

**FIGURE 3-6**    Take care when choosing the right category in which to list your item.

I have chosen to pay two 35 cent insertion fees, but I really want to maximize exposure and improve my chances of getting bids. I click the link for selling in a second category, choose Music, then Records in the second set of Browse Categories boxes, and then click Continue to move on to the next section.

# Create Your Description

The next page, entitled Describe Your Item, is the page where you put together your actual item description. The most important parts of the description are here.

## Create a Title with Keywords

First, you enter a title of 55 characters or less. Here, I can rely on advice given to me by Paula Amato, who was featured in Chapter 2: "In the description I would put 'Signed - Country Singer Kitty Wells Record Album'. This way many keywords are in the description, and when a buyer does a search it comes up in at least six searches."

Paula's suggested title is 48 characters, which gives me 7 more characters to spare. I decide to add the word "Rare" in an attempt to attract more interest, because the LP is long out of print and is listed on a rare record site. I enter:

```
Signed - Country Singer Kitty Wells Rare Record Album
```

Personally, I think people who collect signatures look for the word "autograph" rather than the word "signed," so they are more likely to enter this term in a keyword search on eBay. But I exceed the character limit if I include both "Rare" and the word "Autographed," so I go with "Signed."

The trick in writing a good title is not to be literary, and not to write a complete sentence, but to ensure that your sale will be included in as many keyword searches as possible. To do this, make an effort to insert as many keywords as you can into your title. Also make sure you use as many of the 55 characters that are available to you as you can: using all 55 characters will make your listing stand out from shorter titles in a page of search results. It also gives you more opportunities to insert keywords.

*You can also, for an extra 50 cents, put more information in a subtitle, which helps your title stand out from the crowd. That's one way to get around the 55-character limit, but you have to decide if it's worth the money.*

## Add More Specifics

After writing the title, the Sell Your Item form asks me to supply more specific information about the album based on the category Music : Records. The information requested (speed of album in RPM, size of the disc, and so on) corresponds to the search criteria shown in this category (see Figure 3-7).

## Format the Description

Since I have already typed my description in a Word document, I simply copy and paste it into the Description box. I take the time to do some formatting as provided by the controls at the top of the Description box: I create a heading, colored in red (see Figure 3-8), and make the typeface Arial. I press Enter twice to provide some separation between the actual description and the "boilerplate" information about

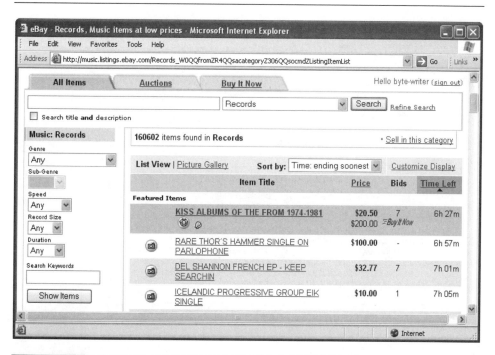

FIGURE 3-7     Add specifics in case shoppers do more detailed searches.

shipping and payment. I click Preview to get a look at my description, and then click Continue to move to the next page of the form.

## Specify Pricing and Duration

The starting price and reserve price, as well as the length of the sale, are three of the most important settings you can specify. Here, too, I am fortunate to have the advice of a longtime seller, Paula Amato:

> I don't use a reserve, nor do many sellers. A reserve will cost you an additional $1.00, and why would you spend the additional money on a low-priced item? You open for the lowest amount that you will take. I see that on the Web, similar albums sell for $9.95–$15.95, so I would open at $4.95. To save on listing fees you always go to the lowest amount that you are willing to take for an item and let it ride.

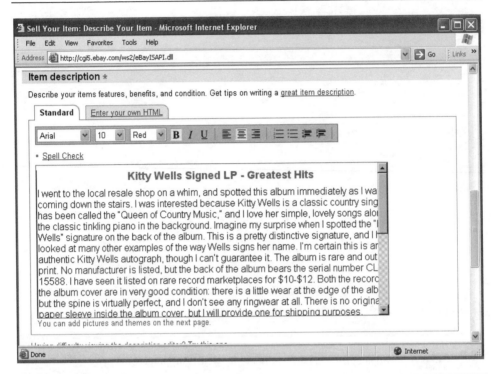

**FIGURE 3-8** The Sell Your Item form lets you format descriptions to make them more readable.

Accordingly, I go with no reserve and a starting bid of $4.95. I let the sale run for seven days. Even though I happen to be listing on a Sunday, I schedule the sale to end the following Sunday, in the evening, for an extra 10 cent scheduling fee.

> **TIP** *Always be aware of the break points for listing fees: the points at which fees go up. A listing that starts at $10 will cost the seller almost twice as much as a sale that starts at $9.99, for instance.*

## Add Photos

After specifying the starting price and sale duration, I add photos in the Add Pictures part of the Sell Your Item form. As stated earlier in this chapter, I can use my own web hosting space for the photos. However, in this case I decided to pay the extra 45 cents and have eBay host the images. This enabled me to see the images added to the form itself, as shown in Figure 3-9. If you add the photos using eBay Picture Services as your host, you can crop and rotate them as well.

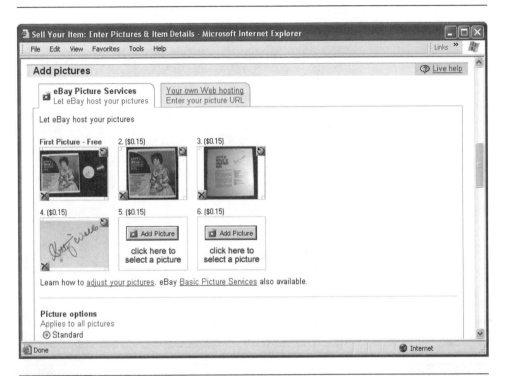

**FIGURE 3-9**    You can add, crop, and rotate images directly in the Sell Your Item form.

## Improve Appearance

The Sell Your Item form gives you an option to add some graphic interest to your sales description. For an extra 10 cent fee, you can use Listing Designer to select a set of colors and typefaces called a theme. You can even choose an arrangement for your photos. I decide not to do this, but instead to spend an extra 25 cents to add a Gallery photo. A Gallery photo is a small, thumbnail-size image that appears next to a sales listing's title in a page full of listings. Based on my experience as a buyer, I can tell you that images with such photos next to their titles do attract additional attention (see Figure 3-10). Therefore, I click the button next to Gallery.

After choosing a Gallery image, I have the option of specifying whether the sales description should be highlighted in bold, or in a band of color (an option called Highlighted). I skip these options (hoping that the item will in a sense "sell itself"), and click Continue, where I move on to the next-to-last part of the form.

**FIGURE 3-10** Gallery images help a listing stand out from the crowd.

## Payment Options

Since payment options were discussed earlier in this chapter and are the subject of Chapter 11, I won't go into much detail here, except to say that I check the PayPal option, as well as the Money Order or Cashier's Check option and the Personal Check option.

*The options that enable you to accept personal checks, money orders, or cashier's checks are not preselected when you reach the Enter Payment & Shipping page of Sell Your Item. Don't forget to select them if you want to include these options (and I suggest that you do).*

## Shipping Options

I specify that I will ship worldwide, and that I will charge a $4 fee for media mail in the United States. I decide to ship worldwide, in case overseas buyers are interested

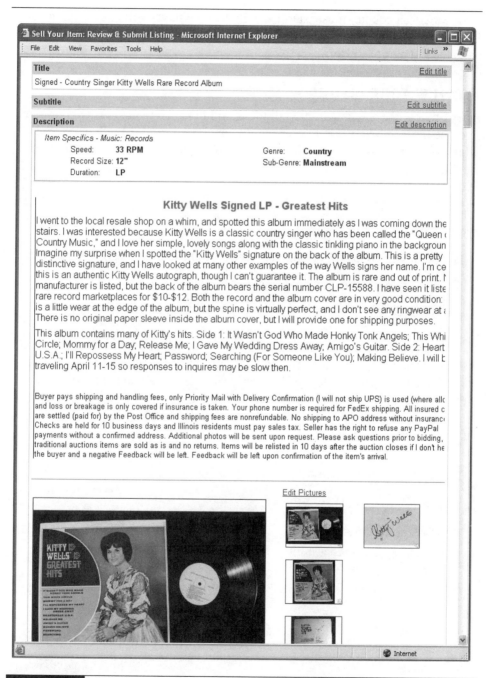

FIGURE 3-11 Be sure to preview and check your listing before it goes online.

in an American country music star. I specify that the buyer will pay shipping costs. I state that insurance is optional but highly recommended. When I'm done, I move on to the last part of the form.

## Preview Your Listing

After I fill out the shipping section of the form I move on to the next page, where I get the thrill of being able to preview my listing as it will actually appear on eBay (see Figure 3-11). I also learn that I have chosen options that add up to the following:

- Insertion fees: 70 cents

- Scheduling start time: 10 cents

- Additional photos (fee doubled because I chose two categories): 90 cents

- Gallery photo (fee doubled, again): 50 cents

- Total: $2.20

The upshot is that, if someone pays $4.95 for my album, I will have to pay eBay $2.20 and only make a profit of $2.75. This, of course, is what I hope won't happen: I hope someone will pay $10 or more for the album and really appreciate it the way I do. If no one ends up bidding at all, I don't have to pay eBay, and I have the option of relisting the item to try to sell it again. Finally, I click the Submit Listing button, and the sale is online.

## Links for Collectors

| Web Site | Address | What's There |
|---|---|---|
| Sell Your Item | Click Sell in the eBay navigation bar | A form you can fill out to put a sales listing online. |
| Andale | http://www.andale.com | An auction service that provides value-added tools for sellers on eBay and other online auctions. |
| PayPal | http://www.paypal.com | eBay's own electronic payment service. You can sign up with PayPal to receive payments from your auction winners. |

# Chapter 4

# The eBay Collectors' Community

## In This Chapter You'll Learn...

- Where to find collectors with interests that complement yours

- How to participate in eBay's discussion groups, chat rooms, and Answer Center

- How to join a user-created eBay Group—or start your own

- Where to look outside eBay for collectors' forums

- How to report trouble with sales or with other eBay members

You *can* collect all by yourself, either on or off the Internet. But when you hook up with other experienced collectors, you get more leads, you learn more about what you love, and all of your collecting activities become more enjoyable. eBay's community forums are among the most useful and satisfying parts of the site. People who visit eBay every day and spend several hours each day on the site aren't just bidding; they are having fun with friends and colleagues. Many users visit the forums each day; they chat with other members just like they were part of their extended family—and, in many cases, they are. They speak in a code composed of acronyms such as BBL and ROTFL.

For collectors, visiting eBay's community venues has both practical and intangible benefits. On the business side, you can get valuable tips and advice from people you approach online. On the personal, intangible side, the community forums make eBay into a communal activity. Just like friends that you see in the neighborhood from day to day, you now have people online with whom you can share complaints and celebrate successes. You also become a smarter collector: avoiding scams, winning more auctions, and selling more profitably. This chapter describes the ways you can enrich your collecting activities on eBay by making connections with other members.

# Finding Collectors Within a Category

When you are at an auction, you notice who the most active buyers are. You make note of the people who have "deep pockets," the ones who spend a lot of money on rare items. You also get to know buyers who either sell valuable and desirable collectibles or have a good eye for a bargain. On eBay, you can make note of their user IDs and track their bidding or selling patterns by doing a By Bidder or By Seller search. If you are *really* enterprising, you can send them an e-mail message and ask for advice. It's not a matter of being nosy or intrusive but of learning by example. You not only want to find out how to bid on objects and win them, you're looking for advice on what works and what to avoid. Even collectors who never attend an auction know who the authorities are in an area: they are the ones who publish newsletters, who run businesses related to the things they buy and sell, the ones with their own web sites.

On eBay, you find such people by following auctions and keeping track of the people who tend to sell in a category. You can identify these people by a number of signs:

- They have high feedback numbers.

- They run eBay stores.

- They have their own web sites.

- They have companies related to what they collect.

Here, as elsewhere, I can share my experiences with fountain pens. There are collectors who sell a lot and buy a lot. When they sell something, you can be sure it is of quality. Here are a few examples from the category of fountain pens:

- Berliner Pen Co. (user ID: penproaol). This seller takes pains to point out, in auction descriptions, that penproaol is the user ID for Berliner because it is such a well-known and highly regarded seller.

- David Nishimura (user ID: vintagepens). This seller offers pens both on eBay and through his web site (http://www.vintagepens.com). The web site includes a Frequently Asked Questions (FAQ) page for beginning collectors, as well as articles on selling pens, books of interest, and how to care for vintage pens.

- Regina Martini (user ID: Pencollectorscorner). This German collector has a web site (http://home.t-online.de/home/02195932018-001) in German.

Where, exactly, do you find these collectors? Over time, you find them by noticing their sales on eBay. Once you find their sales, you can visit their eBay store or web site. Once on their web site, you may find more useful information. For instance, if you visit the Berliner Pen web site (http://www.berlinerpen.com), you find the page shown in Figure 4-1, which provides links of interest to collectors. The links make it easy to enjoy newsletters, a mailing list, and a magazine, among other things.

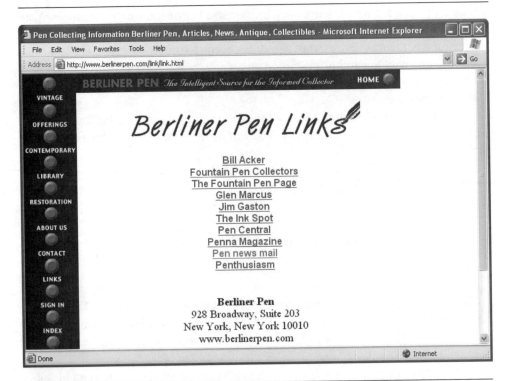

**FIGURE 4-1**   Prominent eBay sellers often provide information to collectors.

When I clicked the link for the mailing list, I found another link to an article that a pen collector wrote about a recent trip to London. He provided plenty of inside information on where to find great pens, how to get pens repaired in London, and lots of fascinating photos.

Why should you pay attention to what collectors do and what they sell on eBay? These are people you can seek out for advice. You get an idea of what is really valuable in a category. Then you can go to their web sites and ask them questions by e-mail. It's in the seller's interest to provide you with personal service, or at least with general information. By helping you, they build their reputation as an authority in the field. They also make it more likely that you'll actually buy something from them, either through their web site or on eBay.

# Finding Collectors in eBay's Community Forums

By now, you know that individual eBay members are easy to contact. Just click the Ask Seller a Question link that appears in someone's sales description, and you can send them a message using eBay's message system. If you want to reach someone and you don't know his or her user ID, you can use the Find Members form (http://cgi3.ebay.com/aw-cgi/eBayISAPI.dll?MemberSearchShow) to send them a message. But what if you have a question about a particular topic and don't need to reach an individual? You could ask eBay by filling out the Contact eBay form (http://pages.ebay.com/help/contact_inline/index.html), but don't expect to get an answer right away.

> **TIP** *You might get immediate access to someone at eBay by clicking the Live Chat icon on the home page and then typing a message to the staff person who responds. Live Chat doesn't operate at all times, however.*

You can get a quick answer by looking around eBay's community forums. By *forums*, I mean venues on eBay's web site where members can post messages to one another. All eBay's community forums function as electronic bulletin boards, rather than real-time conversations you might have in a chat room. You post messages on a forum's web page. Someone reads your message and hopefully posts a response. Others respond to the response, and a conversation develops.

## Trade Talk

eBay's message system isn't a direct e-mail contact method. You might be asking yourself why eBay doesn't publish users' e-mail addresses so that members can contact one another through their e-mail software. The answer is a four-letter word: S-P-A-M. In the early days of eBay, members could use their e-mail addresses as their user IDs. My own original user ID was my e-mail address, in fact. I had to cancel that account for several reasons; one of the biggest was the amount of unsolicited commercial e-mail (i.e., spam) I received by having the address openly visible on eBay. By requiring members to log in with their user ID and password and forwarding messages to other members without making their e-mail addresses public, eBay maintains privacy for its members and reduces spam.

Most questions that are specific to a collectible item, or a type of collectible, aren't the type you can pose to eBay's own support staff: they don't know what an authentic Tiffany trademark looks like, for instance. Such questions are best taken to the eBay community, where you're likely to find someone experienced who is willing to share his or her knowledge. Suppose I had a question about how to tell whether a wristwatch is solid gold, gold-plated, or rose gold. I would go straight to eBay's community forums by clicking Community in the navigation bar. Then I would do one or more of the following:

- Click eBay Workshops. I would look to see if eBay has already held an instructional workshop on watches or gold jewelry. If so, I can click the name of the workshop and read what was discussed, because such sessions have been archived (saved so others can review them later).

- Go to the Answer Center and ask my question, and then check back periodically to determine whether someone has posted a reply.

- Click Discussion Groups to see if someone has posted a similar question recently—or post my own question.

If I wanted to discuss watch collecting in general, I could "chat" informally with someone in the watches chat room, too. Many members would probably agree with me that it's in the chat rooms and discussion forums, as well as in the eBay Groups mentioned later in this chapter, where you find the "real" eBay—the place where people can relax, be funny and irreverent, kvetch when they have a complaint, or help each other out.

Each of these community forums has a slightly different purpose and style of communication (although there is some overlap). It's good to have an idea of how each is supposed to work so that veteran participants take you seriously and you don't appear naive. The differences are described in the sections that follow.

## Discussion Groups

Suppose you go to a collectors' convention. After an introductory talk, attendees break into smaller groups. The groups are assigned topics to talk about, and what they say is recorded so others can read about it later on. This is similar to the way eBay's discussion groups work—except that members can move in or out of each group at will and can bring up any topic that concerns them and that is more or less relevant to the group at hand.

Your first question related to discussion groups might well be: Why should I approach someone in a discussion group or read messages already posted there, rather than going to the Answer Center? The short answer is that nearly as many questions are posed on the discussion boards as in the Answer Center. To get started with discussion groups, click Community in the eBay navigation bar. Your browser goes to the Community Hub page shown in Figure 4-2.

FIGURE 4-2    The Community Hub page gives you access to all of eBay's community forums.

Once you are on the Community Hub page, click Discussion Boards to access the Discussion Boards page (http://pages.ebay.com/community/boards/index.html). This page lists a wide variety of discussion boards, which are broken into five categories:

- **Community Help Boards**   These boards are intended to help you with various aspects of eBay's site or with specific software and features offered on it.

- **Category-Specific Discussion Boards**   Each of these boards is focused on a particular type of item traded on eBay (antiques, comics, jewelry, and so on). Collectors should go here if they have questions or need help on specific models or on how to sell a particular object. If you want more specific advice about how to improve sales in an area, or if you have a question about how much something is worth, you are likely to find members who are experienced in a particular sales category and are willing to help.

- **General Discussion Boards**   These boards are intended for general chat and questions from newcomers. For instance, if you're just starting out and are bewildered or uncertain, go to the New to eBay board (http://forums .ebay.com/db1/forum.jsp?forum=120). Most of the other boards under the General Discussion Boards heading are social rather than instructional in nature. These include The Front Porch, The Homestead, The Park, The Town Square, and The Soap Box. You'll find jokes, games, and topics that go on and on, with thousands of contributions piling up over time.

- **Workshops**   These are online instructional sessions, held by eBay staff people and/or eBay members, on various topics of interest. All members have the opportunity to ask questions or make comments. If "hot" or controversial subjects are discussed, hundreds of comments may result. Workshops are an especially good resource for beginning collectors and are discussed in more detail in the "Workshops" section, later in this chapter.

- **Giving Board**   This board is intended for people to make inquiries pertaining to eBay Giving Works, which is the dedicated program for charity listings on eBay.

On each of these boards, you view discussions arranged by topic. You click the name of the topic to view individual comments (see Figure 4-3). This enables you to "shop around" conveniently for topics that match a question or interest you already have.

## Trade Talk

If you belong to a nonprofit institution that needs to raise funds, consider selling on eBay through Giving Works (http://givingworks.ebay.com). It's a place where socially minded shoppers can make purchases while also contributing to causes they care about. If you belong to a nonprofit group, you can announce your sale here and hopefully attract contributors.

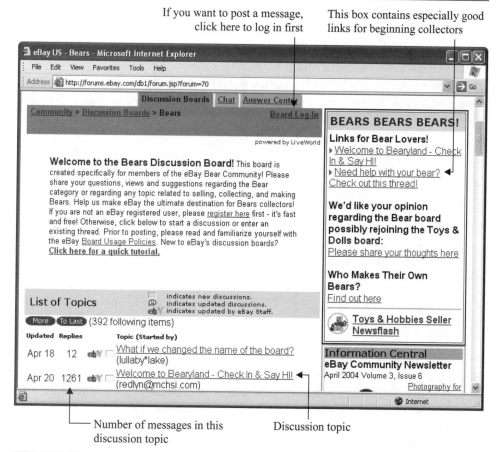

If you want to post a message, click here to log in first

This box contains especially good links for beginning collectors

Number of messages in this discussion topic

Discussion topic

**FIGURE 4-3**    Discussion boards are arranged by topics; each topic contains one or more sets of messages, which are called threads.

**COLLECTOR'S NOTE**    *As with anything, you have to take comments posted on message boards with a grain of salt. In other words, don't believe everything you read or take the accuracy of someone's word for granted. You never know if someone is giving you a truthful, unbiased opinion or if they have an axe to grind—or if they just don't know what they're talking about.*

When you click a discussion group topic, a new page opens that displays the messages within that topic. The Search button displayed at the bottom of the discussion group message window enables you to search for messages within the group that contain a keyword. The Post Message button lets you post your own message.

## Posting Your Own Messages

Reading the messages posted on the discussion boards (or in chat rooms or in the Answer Center) is informative and often entertaining. But it's even more fun to participate so that you can see your own comments online, as well as answers or comments other members have posted in response. Suppose you're reading a message and you want to post a response. You would follow these steps to let your voice be heard:

1.  To post a new message to the board and start a new discussion, click the Board Log-In link near the top of the message board.

2.  Enter your user ID and password, and click Sign In. You return to the message board window.

3.  Now that you have logged in, an Add Discussion button appears at the bottom of the list of messages. Click this button.

4.  Your browser displays a text-entry form into which you can type a message heading and a new message. Click Post Message to add your discussion to the message board.

When you want to post a reply to someone else's message, click either the Board Log-In link near the top of the message page or the Login button at the bottom of the page. After you enter your user ID and password and click Sign In, you return to the message page. At the bottom of the page, a text-entry box now appears (see Figure 4-4). Type your message in the box, and click Post Message to post your reply.

*It's always a good idea to spell-check your comments before you post them. Keep in mind that they will remain online for weeks at a time, if not longer. Misspellings and grammatical errors make you look unprofessional; take a few seconds before you click the Post Message button to make sure you have said what you really want and that you present yourself in the best possible light.*

## Adding Photos

Discussion boards and the Answer Center enable you to ask other collectors for help in identifying objects. But all the description in the world isn't as effective as

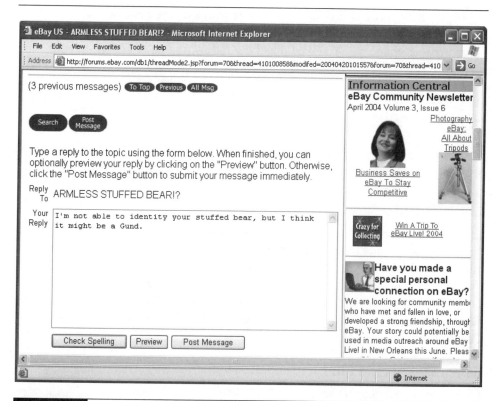

**FIGURE 4-4**    Log in and then type your message in this box to post a reply.

a single image that other participants can inspect and evaluate. In order to add an image, you need to do three things:

1. Obtain a clear, digital image that's small in both physical and file size.

2. Post the image on a web server.

3. Make a link to the image's location on the server with a line of HyperText Markup Language (HTML) that you add to your message posting.

If you have never created a web page or posted an image on the Web before, this is probably more difficult than it sounds. If you have already sold something on eBay and added images to an auction description, it's basically the same process described in the section "Capture Digital Images" in Chapter 3, and in more detail in Chapter 8. Suppose you've taken an image with a digital camera, edited it, and saved it on a web server with the following location: http://www.myserver.com/~myusername/image.jpg. You would add the following line of HTML to your message board posting:

```
<P>
<IMG SRC="http://www.myserver.com/~myusername/image.jpg">
```

The <P> command creates a paragraph in HTML and inserts a blank space between your message and the image you add.

# Chat Rooms

To continue the analogy of the collectors' convention, eBay's chat rooms are like the lunchrooms, hotel lounges, hallways, and other places where attendees meet informally. Whenever you just want to take a break from buying and selling (or from the kids, or from your job, or household chores, or anything else), click Community in the navigation bar, then click Chat. Your browser displays the Chat page, which is divided into two sections: General Chat Rooms and Category-Specific Chat Rooms.

## Category-Specific Chat

When you go to a party, to whom do you naturally gravitate? Someone who shares your interests or has the same background as you. The same is true on eBay. If you want to share stories and dreams with like-minded individuals, the category-specific chat rooms give you a place to go. Chat boards have been set up for people who love Elvis and memorabilia associated with him, Barbie dolls, Beanie Babies, and many more objects of interest.

Scrolling through messages in the Diecast chat room, the Glass chat room, or any number of other chat rooms can be a bewildering experience. You don't necessarily see lots of comments focusing on diecast collectibles, or glassware, or whatever the ostensible subject of the board happens to be. You see a lot of greetings, jokes, experiments with HTML formatting, and humorous icons, though. The things that tie people together in the chat rooms are their shared interest and the fact that they are eBay sellers. You can ask questions about manufacturers, models, or makers' marks in the chat rooms. But if you want an in-depth discussion, you might be better off visiting the category-specific discussion boards.

You may well ask (again) what the difference is between the category-specific discussion boards and the category-specific chat rooms? The names of the forums are virtually the same, but the difference is in how the discussions are presented. Discussion boards invite more in-depth exchanges compared to chat roomdiscussions, which tend to be short. You see the difference the moment you connect to one of the chat rooms; some messages from the Dolls category-specific chat room are shown in Figure 4-5.

4

Short questions and comments on virtually any topic are the hallmark of chat room discussions, as are photos and typefaces colored and formatted using HTML. If you don't have an issue to discuss and you just want to meet other collectors and gossip about what you've found, eBay's chat rooms are the place to go. But there isn't any formal dividing line separating what you can discuss here from other parts of the community. You'll find questions about identifying collectibles in the chat rooms and jokes and gossip in the discussion boards, too.

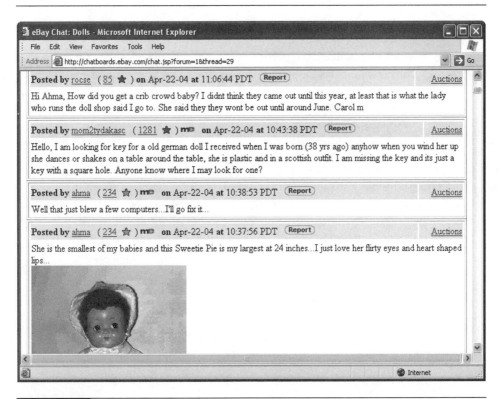

**FIGURE 4-5**    Chat room discussions are short and frequently use graphics and photos.

## General Chat

Most of eBay's general chat rooms are characterized by lighthearted humor. The eBay Q & A board and Images/HTML board, however, are for instructions and tips. If you're just starting out with eBay and need some questions answered, click Chat and visit the eBay Q & A board or the Images and HTML board. The best known part of the eBay community is the eBay Café. That's the original eBay community discussion board that still draws loyal members who visit regularly. The Holiday board, Giving board, Discuss Newest eBay Features board, and the international boards have a specific interest as their focus.

The Emergency Contact board deserves special mention. It is intended for people who aren't getting responses from buyers or sellers. Keep in mind that the problems you see listed here are the exception rather than the rule on eBay. It's good to be aware of what can happen by reading the messages posted to Emergency Contact, and to post your own message if someone proves to be nonresponsive.

## The Answer Center

eBay's Answer Center is like a suggestion box or question-and-answer session at a collectors' convention. eBay's Answer Center functions like a round-the-clock

## Trade Talk

If you're going to participate in the chat rooms, you had better learn to speak the language. In many cases, members save typing by using abbreviations. You'll find a good selection of common ones on the About Me page for the eBay member blue*eyes (http://members.ebay.com/aboutme/blue*eyes). You can come up with a whole conversation made up almost entirely of these abbreviations. Here's an example:

```
BTW GMTA I guess, and don't forget to CYE. I'm sure you'll be
ROTFL when you read it. Well I'm just about to POOF, so BBL.
```

As any experienced chat room member will tell you, this is translated as "*By the way, great minds think alike,* I guess, and don't forget to *check your e-mail.* I'm sure you'll be *rolling on the floor laughing* when you read it. Well, I'm just about to *leave,* so *be back later.*"

database of questions and answers that have been posted in the recent past, as well as a place to turn to describe your current situation and get answers from eBay members who are willing to help.

As stated in the preceding sections on discussion boards, the Answer Center is specially designed for members who want to ask a question—or, just as often, present a problem they're having with a feature on eBay that's not working right or that they don't know how to use. When you connect to an Answer Center, such as the Packaging & Shipping forum shown in Figure 4-6, you see a list of questions or topics that users have submitted. The number of replies to the question are given in parentheses. You can read the question or learn about the problem. If you click on the name of the question or problem, you can read the responses.

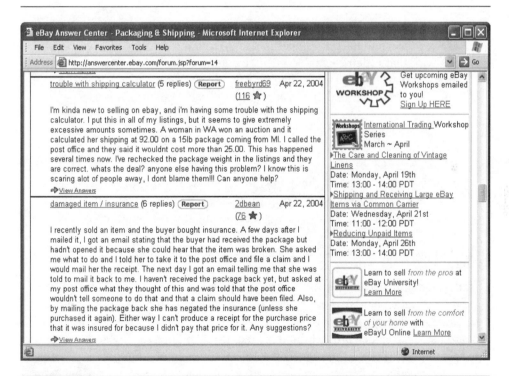

| FIGURE 4-6 | The Answer Center lets you read a full question or problem without having to click a topic name. |

# "Trolls," Feedback, and Posting Restrictions

In April 2004, as I was writing this chapter, controversy erupted on eBay. That's when eBay announced new restrictions on the number of postings that users with feedback ratings of 0 to 9 could make. Basically, members with feedback ratings in that range are now limited to 10 postings in the chat rooms or discussion groups in any 24-hour period. (The restriction does not apply to workshops or the Answer Center.) Before this, there were no restrictions at all; people with 0 feedback could, and frequently did, ask and answer questions and make comments on the boards and in the chat rooms.

Why the change? To quote the eBay staff person who moderated the workshop, which was called "Community Change: Posting Limits for Discussion & Chat Boards," held April 16, 2004:

> To preserve the health and vibrancy of eBay's online communities as we grow, we need to take new measures to discourage the type of negative behavior that is detrimental to positive community. We are discouraging problem behavior and those members that have "throw-away" IDs. If we think of eBay as a real-life community, you are not allowed to be anonymous or throw away your identity when you consciously decide to, and we are no longer allowing this type of activity to go unchecked on the boards.

eBay apparently created the policy to reduce the number of "trolls" on the message boards. *Troll* is eBay slang for someone who creates a user ID specifically for the purpose of causing trouble in a discussion group or chat room. Trolls bad-mouth other users or voice complaints. The decision caused a flood of protest in the workshop because many longtime users who try to be helpful members of the community post with special user IDs that have low feedback numbers (often, a 0 feedback rating, because the user ID is used only for the message boards). A member's feedback rating isn't always an indication of how long that person has been a member of eBay. Some longtime discussion board users have been around for years but use their "message board" user ID for posting, rather than the user ID they use for buying or selling.

Keep in mind, when you're just starting out, that you have this posting limitation. After 10 message postings, you will automatically be referred to the Answer Center, where you can ask more questions if you need to.

## Workshops

Many conventions include some how-to sessions for their members: instructional sessions that tell collectors how to identify and date models, make repairs, or perform other functions. eBay regularly holds its own online workshops. One of the many nice things about eBay's workshops is that some are conducted by members who are prominent and active collectors in their field. You get tips and opinions from people who know what they are talking about, and you can ask questions of these folks if you connect to the workshop while it is being held.

For instance, suppose I'm interested in collecting art glass and I want to know more about the subject. I could click Community in the navigation bar, then click Workshops to go to the Workshops discussion board (I could also go directly to http://forums.ebay.com/forum.jsp?forum=93). I could scan the list of workshops that have been held on eBay in the past several years. I'm in luck: I discover that a workshop was held September 26, 2002, on the subject of collecting art glass. The recorded comments are archived on eBay so anyone can review them. What's more, the workshop was held not by an eBay staff person but by a collector of art glass who has her own web site. She included many beautiful photos showing the different varieties that are sometimes bought or sold on eBay.

Not all hobbies have been covered in workshops, but at this writing, you can find instructions on collecting Disney pins, stamp collecting, miniatures, gemstones, and many other subjects. Besides scanning the list of past workshops, be sure to pay attention to the lists of upcoming workshops in the Information Central column on the right-hand side of the Workshops board opening page. You might find that a workshop is coming up in a subject you're interested in. If you attend "live," you can submit questions to the moderator and get answers in a matter of minutes.

 *If you attend a live workshop, you need to keep refreshing your browser window so you can see all the comments as they are made by the moderator, eBay staff people, and other participants. Be sure to review the Board Tutorial for instructions. There is a link to the tutorial near the beginning of all workshops.*

## Other Events and Gatherings

In the Woody Allen movie *The Purple Rose of Cairo,* the heroine gets to interact with "virtual" movie characters in the real world. You, too, have a chance to cross over from virtual interactions with buyers and sellers to meeting them in the flesh.

You not only get the opportunity to learn some new things about your favorite web site, but you just might make some friends, too.

## eBay University

Many of the people who are considered experts on eBay sign up to serve as instructors in what is sometimes affectionately referred to as eBay's "road show," a series of real-world classes held in various cities around the country. Go to the Event List, http://pages.ebay.com/community/events/eventsbydate.html, and see if a class will be held in your own area in the near future. In some cases (this depends on the subject), you have the option of either attending the course in person or taking it online.

## eBay Live

As I write this, eBay members are busily reserving hotel rooms and signing up for eBay's annual user convention, eBay Live, which is held once a year during the summer months. eBay Live is perhaps the best place to meet the "higher ups" in eBay, or at least to see them speak to those assembled. You may well see president and CEO Meg Whitman and founder Pierre Omidyar, for instance. The three-day event is full of opportunities to meet with other members from all over the world. Instruction sessions are held on buying and selling. To find out more, visit the eBay Live board under General Discussion Boards. You'll find photos from past meetings, registration information on classes to be held at the next eBay Live, and plenty of chances to meet other people.

## eBay Kaffeeklatsches

I'm probably betraying my age when I use the word *kaffeeklatsch;* it's a term you don't hear anymore. It used to refer to housewives' (another term you don't hear anymore) getting together over coffee to visit. A variation on the theme, the Tupperware party, enabled ordinary people to sell Tupperware to their own neighbors.

One of the most intriguing ways in which eBay members meet one another is by creating groups of users who live in the same city or geographic area. You find regional groups in eBay Groups (http://groups.ebay.com/index.jspa), the part of eBay's community that enables eBay members to create their own forums. As of this writing, you'll find groups in cities such as Charlotte, North Carolina; Jonesboro, Arkansas; and Kingman, Kansas—and others covering much wider regions such as northeast Kentucky, the state of South Dakota, central Massachusetts, and southeast Wisconsin.

# eBay Groups

Are you looking for a group where you can discuss collecting something really specialized, like dollhouse miniatures or coffee mugs? Or what if you want to meet eBay members with shared interests such as animal rescue, the writer Ayn Rand, or eBay-related vanity license plates? You can either join a group (if one exists—and, believe it or not, the license plate group does exist) or create your own eBay Group.

Other parts of the eBay community are more closely supervised than eBay Groups. Those other community groups are created by eBay itself, and eBay moderates discussions. eBay Groups are hosted by eBay, but members have considerably more freedom. Perhaps the biggest difference is the ability of members to organize their own group: to create it, invite members, and moderate discussions.

## Joining Groups

In keeping with the fact that they are created by eBay's own diverse user base, eBay Groups aren't all the same. Some are public and encourage everyone who is already a member of eBay to join up. Other private groups restrict membership or are by invitation only.

You may need to join more than one group in order to find one that's right for you. You can't actually read group discussions unless you are a member. To join a group, connect to the Groups home page (http://groups.ebay.com/index.jspa). Click through the available categories of groups, or enter a zip code or keyword in the search box to locate the one you want.

When you first click on a group's link on the eBay Groups home page, you access the group's Welcome page. Click the big Join Group button, then log in with your user ID and password. Click Sign In, and you view the group's home page. Unlike the Welcome page, the links on the left side of the page under Choose an Activity and Group Controls (see Figure 4-7) are now clickable links. They enable you to view photos that members have posted, learn about upcoming events, and join discussions.

**WATCH OUT!**   *Even though boards are created by users, that doesn't mean you can do anything you want on them. You can't post someone else's contact information, and you can't make profane comments. See the Restricted Group Activities list at http://pages.ebay.com/help/welcome/group-restricted-activities.html.*

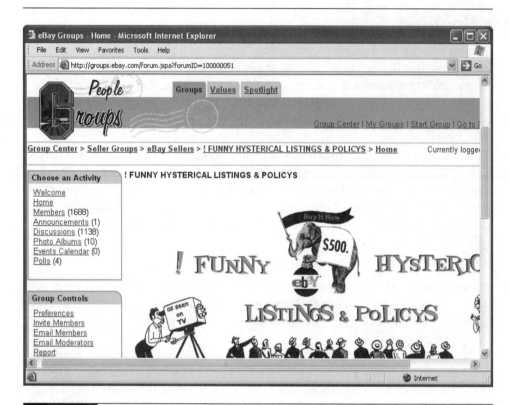

**FIGURE 4-7**     A group's home page contains the links you need to begin participating.

## Moderating a Group

Groups have less supervision than the other parts of the eBay community; on the other hand, they place more of a burden on members to run them closely and manage them so discussions are useful. Some of the tasks and requirements associated with running a group are:

- You must have a feedback rating of at least 50 in order to start a group and have been a registered member of eBay for at least 90 days.

- You need to develop a schedule of events, and you need to be available to moderate discussions.

■ You might be called upon to handle complaints and disputes between members, should they occur.

■ You might want to invite friends and other members with whom you've done business to join your groups.

■ You need to keep interest in your group: if there has been no activity for 90 days, eBay will delete it.

You don't have to do all the work yourself: a group can have a single administrator as well as one or more moderators. Once you know what's involved, it's easy to get the process started: just click the link Start Group near the top of the eBay Groups home page to get the process started. But before that, you should join a group called the eBay Groups Information Center. This group contains all the instructions you need on how to operate a group after you have formed it.

# Looking for Collectors Outside eBay

eBay isn't the only place where you can find groups of individuals who either share your interests or want to talk about eBay. By taking part in a forum that isn't hosted by eBay, you aren't subject to eBay's posting rules and restrictions. You can say what you like about eBay (as long as it doesn't violate the rules established by the forum's organizers).

## Usenet Newsgroups

Usenet (short for *users' network*) is the extensive, freewheeling, and unpredictable part of the Internet that is populated by thousands of newsgroups. A few of those groups are related to eBay:

■ **news.admin.net-abuse.sightings**   This newsgroup is full of information on e-mail scams and security problems that have plagued eBay users over the years. It's a good idea to scan the most recent posts to get an idea of what is currently causing problems for members.

■ **alt.marketing.online.ebay**   A forum primarily for people who want to sell more effectively on eBay, but it includes advice for buyers.

■ **alt.anti-ebay**   As you might expect, this group contains lots of posts complaining about fraud or eBay's treatment of members.

■ **alt.marketplace.online.ebay**   Almost all the posts to this group are advertisements for sales that are already posted on eBay.

From looking at these names, you notice one important fact about newsgroups: their names are broken into pieces that (like the URLs for web pages) are separated by dots. The first part of a newsgroup name is its top-level hierarchy. Some of the most common newsgroup categories are alt (for alternative or homegrown groups), biz (for business-related groups), comp (for computer-related topics), news (for news about Usenet itself), rec (for recreational topics), and soc (for social issues).

The parts of the name that come after this top-level hierarchy are subcategories. You find newsgroups in one of several different ways. Two of the most popular are to use Google as a web-based front end, or to use your web browser's own newsgroup software to access the newsgroups that are made available to you by your ISP. If you use Google, you can search through newsgroups and individual messages using the browser you're already familiar with. Go to the Google home page, http://www.google.com, and click Groups. Either enter part of the group's name in the search box, or click the top-level newsgroup name and "drill down" until you find the individual group you want.

*One nice thing about using Google as a newsgroup reader is that you can search for individual messages by keyword. If you enter the keyword "eBay," for example, you'll find a list of messages taken from different groups that concern the auction site. Another benefit of joining a group is the ability to increase your sales on eBay by sending links to your auctions to the group's members.*

## Collecting Step-by-Step

The two major browser packages, Microsoft Internet Explorer and Netscape, have newsgroup readers incorporated with e-mail software. In Netscape, you follow these steps:

1. Open the e-mail application by choosing Window | Mail & Newsgroups.

2. From the Inbox's menu bar, choose File | Subscribe.

**3.** When the Subscribe dialog box appears, choose your ISP's newsgroup account from the drop-down list. You may have to verify the name with your ISP; however, most news servers have an address such as news.[ISP name].com. A list of newsgroups appears in the main display area of the Subscribe dialog box.

**4.** Click the arrows next to the top-level newsgroup hierarchy that you want to explore (such as alt) and continue to click subcategories until you find the newsgroup you want. The group alt.marketplace.online.ebay is shown here.

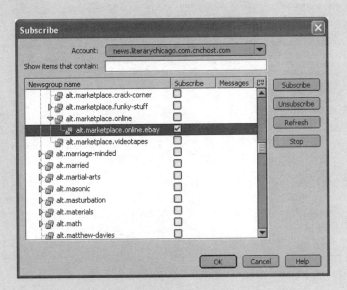

**5.** Check the Subscribe box next to the group you want to subscribe to, then click OK to close the dialog box.

Once you have subscribed to a group, you then scroll down the list of mail and news servers in the left-hand column of the Inbox window and select the name of the group. The messages in the group are downloaded to your computer, and you click on a message title to view it.

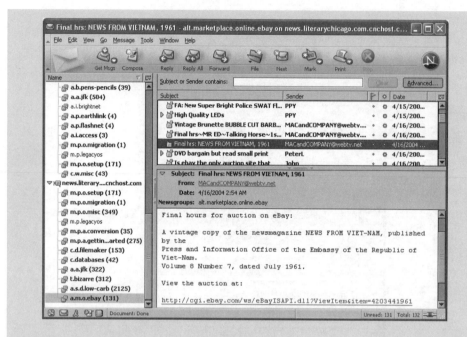

If you use Microsoft Outlook Express to read your e-mail, the process is similar:

**1.** Choose Tools | Newsgroups to open the Newsgroup Subscriptions dialog box.

**2.** Locate the newsgroup you want in the list of newsgroups shown in the main display area.

**3.** Select the group, then click Subscribe.

**4.** Click OK.

**5.** Click the name of the newsgroup in the list of mail and news servers on the left-hand side of the Outlook Express window, and then click a message title to read it.

TIP   *You can also use the Subscribe dialog box to find a newsgroup, if you know its name. Enter part of the newsgroup name in the Show Items That Contain box, and press Enter. A list of groups with contents that match your search terms appears in the main display area.*

Newsgroups give members a place to complain and spout off freely about eBay. That doesn't mean you can be profane, slanderous, or abusive. Unsolicited advertisements cannot be posted either. Some (by no means all) newsgroups are moderated by people who set ground rules and filter out postings that violate them.

**COLLECTOR'S NOTE** *Read the newsgroup's FAQ to find out exactly what those rules are. Scan the list of postings for one with "FAQ" in the title to find them.*

**4**

## Collecting Step-by-Step

America Online (AOL) has always been a popular haven for collectors. Its forums have been around for many years and are frequented by many experienced buyers and sellers. If you have an account with AOL, you can participate in its own set of collectors' groups by following these steps:

1. When the America Online window appears, click Favorites.

2. Click Meeting People and Staying in Touch; then click Groups@AOL.

3. When the Browse Groups window appears, click Collecting. The set of groups for collectors (shown in Figure 4-8) appears.

4. In the Search box at the top of the Browse Groups window, enter **eBay**, then click Search. A set of AOL groups devoted to eBay appears. When I conducted this search, I came up with no less than 68 eBay-related groups.

5. Click the name of the group you want to read messages in (see Figure 4-9). You can choose from groups with names such as eBay Addicts Anonymous, eBay Mommies, eBay PowerSellers, and the like.

AOL makes it easy for members to create their own groups. Just click on the link Create Group that appears in the upper right-hand corner of the first Browse Groups window. When you click a group's name to read its messages, you see a Join Now button. This button is somewhat misleading: you don't need to join the group to read messages, only to post them.

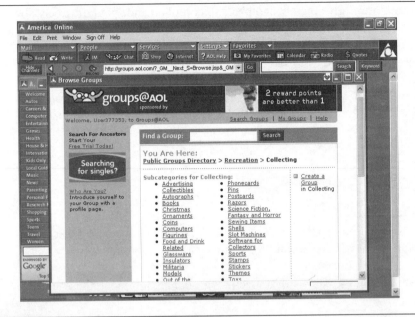

**FIGURE 4-8**   If you have an account with AOL, you can participate in its groups for collectors.

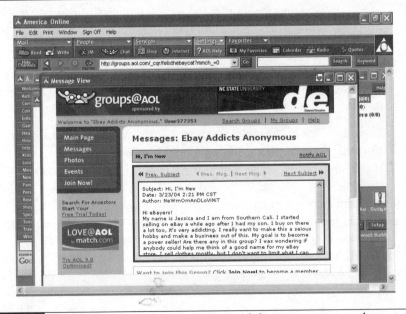

**FIGURE 4-9**   You don't have to join a group to read the messages currently posted.

4

## AuctionBytes

AuctionBytes, an independent web site (in other words, one that isn't directly affiliated with eBay or other auction sites), has established itself as a leading observer and commentator on online auctions in general. Because eBay is the "500 pound gorilla" in this field, it tends to get the most frequent coverage.

Go to the site's home page (http://www.auctionbytes.com) and click the Discussion Forums link under the heading Ongoing Features, near the bottom of the page. You'll come up with a list of forums related to eBay and other auction sites. Under the heading Collector's Forums, you'll discover a bunch of discussion areas related to hobbies such as book collecting, ephemera, fabric, glass, porcelain, records, and religious items.

## Trade Talk

If you collect something that's especially popular, you've probably attended a collectors' convention. Such events give you an excellent opportunity to meet people who share your interests and purchase objects that you might resell on eBay. For example, many large cities host conventions each year just for comic book collectors. Locally oriented events usually run for a single day, while national shows might last for three to five days.

# Reporting Trouble in the Community

Because any eBay member can post on the discussion boards and eBay can't monitor every single comment that appears, problems can occur. Insults and charges are exchanged; people bad-mouth one another; misleading information is posted. If you see such messages, it's your responsibility as a member of the community to report them. You can do this easily by logging in and then clicking the Report button, which appears just above the member's comments.

The discussion forums are also a good place to post messages about sales that seem fraudulent or bidding practices that seem improper and that other people should know about. Be sure, before you post such reports, that you are aware of what constitutes a violation of eBay's board usage policy. The policy is at http://pages.ebay.com/help/policies/everyone-boards.html. Along with the obvious things (don't threaten anyone, and don't use profane language), it states that users cannot

- Advertise merchandise, auctions, services, or commercial web sites, or make offers to trade

- Post "Wanted" messages

- Post someone else's contact information

**COLLECTOR'S NOTE** *Some of the most useful topics on the New to eBay Board discuss fraudulent e-mail messages that seem to be from eBay or from its payment service, PayPal. Typically, the messages have warning signs that point to them as being fraudulent: The English grammar is poor. The e-mail refers to the recipient as "Dear Customer" and not by name or user ID. The message claims that the recipient is being suspended, or needs to verify his or her identity. The recipient is asked to click a link in the e-mail message body or respond to the message and provide identification such as name, address, and financial information. Don't respond to such messages; rather, report them to eBay's address for fraudulent e-mail: spoof@eBay.com.*

# Links <sup>for</sup> Collectors

| Web Site | Address | What's There |
|---|---|---|
| Contact eBay form | http://pages.ebay.com/help/contact_inline/index.html | A form you fill out and send to eBay when you have a comment or need help with something. |
| Discussion Boards page | http://pages.ebay.com/community/boards/index.html | Links to all eBay's discussion boards, chat rooms, and other venues. |
| New to eBay Board page | http://forums.ebay.com/db1/forum.jsp?forum=120 | A discussion board where new users can ask basic questions about buying or selling. |
| Giving Works page | http://givingworks.ebay.com | A part of eBay's site that features auctions that benefit nonprofits and other charitable organizations. |
| Collection of discussion group acronyms | http://members.ebay.com/aboutme/blue*eyes | A selection of common acronyms used on eBay's discussion boards, as collected by an eBay member. |
| Event List page | http://pages.ebay.com/community/events/eventsbydate.html | A list of upcoming workshops, eBay University classes, and other events you can attend, either online or in the real world. |
| eBay Groups page | http://groups.ebay.com/index.jspa | An area devoted to user groups created and moderated by eBay users themselves. |

4

# Part II

# Shopping and Collecting

# Chapter 5

## Treasure Hunting on eBay

## In This Chapter You'll Learn...

■ New ways to search for and find what you collect on eBay

■ Advanced search options for saving searches and fine-tuning results

■ Smart strategies for protecting what you find and making sure you get what you want

■ How your My eBay page can help you organize your sales and buying activities

■ How your web browser can help you revisit your favorite eBay locations

The basic activity common to all collectors is searching for things and finding them—or not even searching for them but having them turn up out of the blue. If you ever watch *Antiques Roadshow* on PBS, you have probably been amused by the stories of how people find objects that turn out to be far more valuable than they ever dreamed. One recent show featured a woman who dug a rare vase out of the dirt, as well as a man who found a menu from the final dinner on the Titanic inside the frame of a mediocre painting.

On eBay, things don't just fall into your lap (unless you ask eBay to "watch" for auctions that meet your specified criteria, and e-mail you when they appear). You have to go out and find them. Then, when you find them, you have to research them and make sensible bids so you can add them to your collection without breaking your budget. This chapter gives you some advanced options for finding things and then purchasing them wisely.

## Becoming a Power Searcher

If you're a creature of habit, it's easy to get into the rut of clicking the same links and visiting the same pages each time you visit eBay. But it's important to break the mold of your usage patterns to access all that eBay's web site has to offer. The first step, of course, is to register with eBay and begin to shop and buy. Then you're ready to step back and take a look at all the resources that you can use. For starters, you can explore special sales, promotions, sellers, and merchandise you will never find unless you stray from the beaten path on eBay.

COLLECTOR'S NOTE   *When you scan a set of search results, don't overlook sellers with low feedback numbers who are obviously new to eBay. Newer sellers with a low feedback rating are often willing to start items well below market value, hoping to increase sales quickly in order to build up their feedback.*

## Making the World Your Oyster

It's easy to forget, especially if you live in the United States, that eBay can be found in different locations around the world. If you surf in this country, you connect by default to the U.S. eBay site. Because this is the primary web site for eBay, it contains far more items for sale than any of the other eBay sites around the world.

It's probably not a big surprise that the U.S site is considered eBay's "headquarters." But that doesn't mean that eBay users are limited to the red, white, and blue. In fact, there are a lot of separate sites operated by eBay that are designed for users in other parts of the world. Being fluent in different languages and familiar with different currencies will give you an advantage over other collectors who aren't brave enough to shop abroad. But even if it's all Greek to you, you should definitely expand your horizons by visiting some of these intriguing and eye-opening sites. For one thing, what you find on the global sites doesn't always appear on the U.S. site. There's a real thrill in finding local specialty foods and souvenirs of other cities and countries without getting on an airplane. You can also find great deals on hotels and cruises, for example.

In the United States, when you enter a term in eBay's search boxes, either on the home page or on a search results page, you search for items only in the U.S. In the United Kingdom, Canada, Brazil, or other eBay locations around the world, the default option is to search only your own country or region. However, in many areas outside the United States, the search box on the home page allows users to search either the home country or items worldwide. The Australian version of eBay, shown in Figure 5-1, shows the two options.

 *You can search international locations from the U.S. site from the Advanced Search page. In the section labeled Location/International, click "Items available to…" and then choose a country from the drop-down list.*

## Shopping at "Bad" Times

The resale shop near my home makes an effort to put out seasonal clothing at the right time: winter clothes come out in fall, summer clothes in the spring, and so on. If I make an effort to shop off-season, I can get some good deals for myself and my daughters. Off-season shopping applies to eBay, too. If you look at times when the millions of other eager collectors are less likely to be bidding, you stand a better chance of winning. Here are some suggestions of "bad" shopping times that can turn out to be "good" for you:

- ■ **During the week**   Many sales end in the afternoon or early evening on Saturdays and Sundays, when people who work Monday through Friday

5

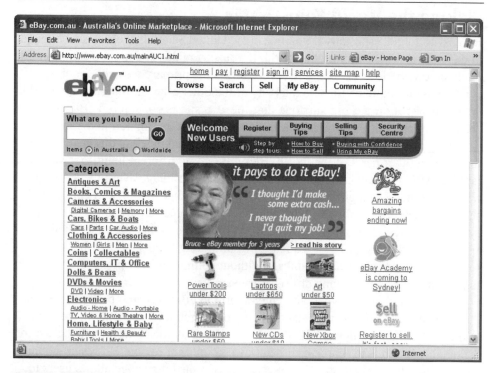

**FIGURE 5-1**   In locations outside the United States, the home page search box gives visitors two search options.

are likely to be home. But some sales end during the week as well. If you can find a sale that ends, say, on a Tuesday at 3 P.M., you stand a better chance of winning simply because fewer bidders are likely to be available.

■ **During the summer**   The summer months are known as the "dog days" among eBay sellers. Things slow down in July and August when people are busy traveling and not so likely to be at their computers. This is the time when you can really find bargains (provided you're not traveling yourself).

■ **After the holidays**   November and December are easily the busiest months on eBay, as buyers and sellers exchange potential holiday gifts and seasonal decorations. Just after the holidays, and especially after New Year's Day, the doldrums set in and you might be able to find some bargains then.

■ **The early morning hours**   Some sales that end in the early morning or the midmorning attract less attention because people are either heading to work or busy at work and can't bid.

This book's technical editor adds the following note about the benefits of early morning sales:

> Often, sellers don't consider the best ending time for their auctions. They are eager to get their listings done and don't use a program to schedule sales. As an example, a copy of the first issue of *Baseball Digest* magazine published in August of 1942 was recently sold by a major sports memorabilia auction house. The magazine is quite scarce, as it was published in the midst of World War II, when many potential readers were not able to obtain a copy. The auction house had furious bidding throughout the night, with the copy finally being hammered down at a whopping $1887. The very next day, an experienced eBay searcher found a copy in a very early morning auction with a Buy It Now price of $30.

COLLECTOR'S NOTE   *There are so many collectors on eBay, many of whom are already familiar with off-peak shopping, that you may still find competition, even for sales that end on a weekday or that take place at the end of summer. You still need to be present at the end of an auction and keep bidding as needed in order to win, in case you run into competition.*

# Exploring All of eBay's Search Options

eBay's database of current and completed auctions is one of its most valuable assets. Its powerful set of search utilities, which gives anyone the ability to sift through millions of sales in a matter of seconds, is another. Together, the two enable you to find virtually anything eBay has to offer (which, as time goes on, seems like virtually anything). But in order to take full advantage of these tools, you have to know how to use them. Chapter 2 gave you a brief introduction to searching eBay; the sections that follow examine your search options in greater detail.

## Basic Search Tips

When you are starting out, it's logical to search for keywords that are included in auction description titles. If you collect gold watches, your first step is to search for every auction that contains those particular words. But then you might want to expand your scope by searching for items manufactured by a certain company or in a certain location.

If you check the box next to Search Title and Description you'll turn up many more listings than you would if you only search titles. Don't forget that desirable auctions may have your keywords in the subtitles as well as in the descriptions. Think about terms that are important to what you collect (such as *nineteenth-century, gold, ruby, refurbished,* or *unopened*) and look for them in the auction descriptions. Explanations that are often found in the descriptions, but not the titles, include private auctions or auctions where bidders have to be preapproved.

When you click Search in the eBay navigation bar and then click Advanced (or when you go directly to http://pages.ebay.com/search/items/search_adv.html), your browser connects to the Advanced Search form. By using Advanced Search, you can search completed auctions by checking the Completed Items Only box. You can also specify what part of eBay you want to search—in your own region or around the world. Going global allows you to take advantage of favorable exchange rates or uncover more exotic merchandise. Aspects of buying and selling overseas on eBay are discussed in Chapter 6; other aspects of searching on eBay are examined in the next sections.

## Creating Complex Searches

The most common way to search eBay is to enter a single set of terms in the Search box. But power users can increase their success rates by being more creative with terms in a single search. This is done by including groups of terms in parentheses. A combined search—a search that uses a combination of multiple search terms— can be conducted from either the Basic Search or Advanced Search page.

For instance, the following search will find virtually all items on eBay that have to do with St. Louis:

```
("St. Louis", "arch","gateway","cardinals","Washington
University","blues")
```

Notice that each term is separated from the other by a single comma. Also note the use of quotation marks to find exact words. You can combine a search term with additional terms in parentheses to narrow it down. Instead of simply searching for the World's Columbian Exposition opening day program, for instance, you can search for memorabilia with the following:

```
Columbian exposition (opening day,program)
```

The preceding example will search for all the items that include the words *Columbian Exposition* and *opening day* or *program.*

In effect, the comma functions like the term *and/or* to include alternate terms in a search. Similarly, the minus sign (–) symbol functions like the NOT operator to exclude some search terms. The following example will exclude any sales in which eBay's payment service PayPal is not an option. In effect, it limits the search results to *only* those sales that include PayPal:

```
("paris","paris, france","city of lights","gay paree") -("no
paypal","do not accept paypal")
```

You can search for lots or pallets of items by combining two or more separate groups of search terms. Just put a single space between the parentheses:

```
(nails,screws,bolts,staples) ("lot of","case of","pallet of")
```

The most common combinations of search commands are shown in Table 5-1.

| Command | Search Performed | Example | Comments |
|---|---|---|---|
| "term1 term2" | Exactly the words contained in quotation marks | "San Francisco" | |
| (term1,term2) | Finds one term or the other or both | (michael jordan,m.j.) | Be sure not to insert blank spaces after commas in a series. |
| term1 term2 | Finds both terms only | basketball uniform | Insert one blank space between terms. |
| term1 –term2 | Finds the first term and excludes the term preceded by the minus sign | basketball –uniform | Keep one blank space between terms, but do not separate the minus sign from its accompanying term. |
| term1 –(term2, term3) | Excludes a series of words | baseball –(glove, hat) | There should be no space between minus sign and parenthesis. |
| term* | Finds any words that begin with a specified series of letters (The asterisk acts as a wildcard symbol.) | base* | There should be no space between asterisk and preceding character. |

**TABLE 5-1**   Complex Search Terms

5

When you are creating searches, consider looking for items sold in lots. In the case of magazines, you can search by year (for example, "magazines 1955" or "movie poster 1940"). Go through the decades year by year. As surprising as it may seem, you can frequently find magazines in lots of 10–20 copies or more selling for just a little more than a single copy.

**TIP** *You can also save your favorite searches, as described later in this chapter, which can come in very handy when you have spent a lot of time creating complex search criteria.*

## Sorting Search Results

When you get a set of search results, you don't have to accept them and start clicking immediately—especially if the search turned up 10, 20, or even dozens of pages of results. You can and should refine the results by using the options shown in the Search Options area in the left-hand column of the Search Results page (see Figure 5-2).

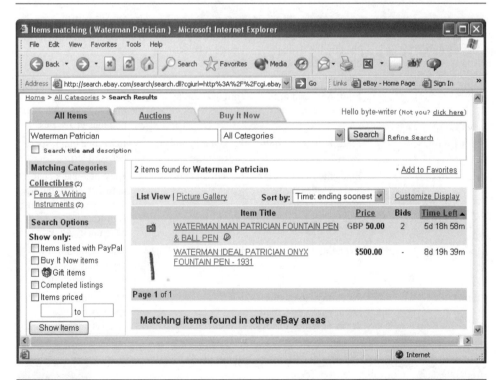

**FIGURE 5-2** You can refine search results to save time and improve accuracy.

As shown in Figure 5-2, the Search Options enable you to show items for which PayPal payments are accepted, Buy It Now items, Gift Items, items listed as lots, or completed auctions. You can also sort results by price. As this chapter was being written, eBay just started offering the additional filtering options under the Listings heading: Items Listed Today, Items Ending Today, or Items Ending in the Next 5 Hours. By clicking the Customize link just beneath the search options, you can choose different filter options from the list shown in Figure 5-3.

## Searching eBay Stores

5

eBay Stores are operated by eBay members, and eBay Stores sales items turn up in search results along with items offered at auction. But if you want to search eBay Stores only, you need to use a search box that's limited to eBay's fixed-price sales outlets. You access the Stores search utility in one of two ways:

- ■ Go to the eBay Stores home page (http://stores.ebay.com) and enter your search terms in the box on the left-hand side of the page (see Figure 5-4).

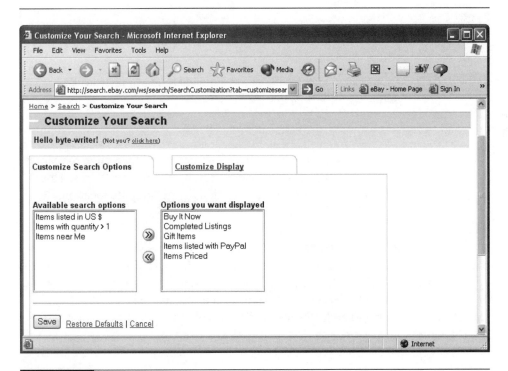

FIGURE 5-3    You can specify the kinds of filter options you plan to use most frequently.

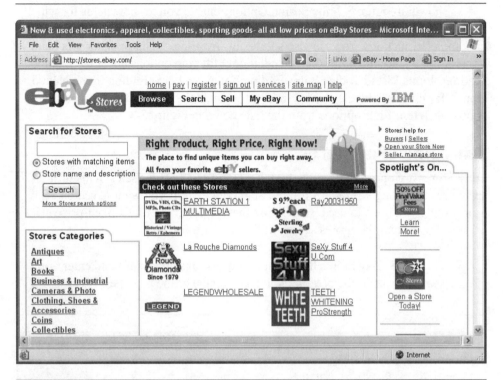

**FIGURE 5-4**    If you want to search only for items offered at a fixed price in eBay Stores, use the box on this page.

■ Click Search to connect to the Basic Search page, and then click the Stores tab. Your browser displays an advanced search page just for stores. This form lets you search by title and description, by geographic location, by price range, and by other criteria.

Many other items are offered at a fixed Buy It Now price not in eBay Stores, but on conventional category pages. You won't find these fixed-price items if you do a search through eBay Stores. To find them, do a conventional search using one of the search boxes on the eBay home page or on a category page. Then click the Buy It Now tab on the Search Results page (see Figure 5-5 to sort out the fixed-price items).

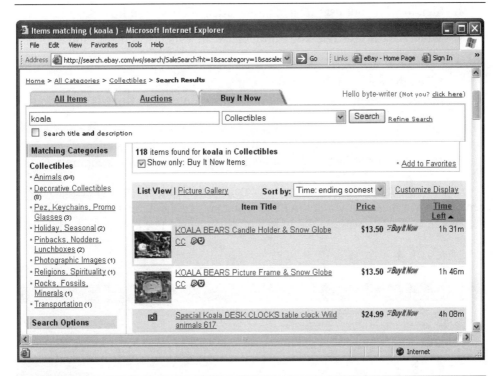

**FIGURE 5-5**  The Buy It Now tab turns up fixed-price merchandise in all of eBay, including eBay Stores.

## Searching Through Categories

You already know that eBay gives you plenty of ways to search for merchandise. But you can also search for categories. With thousands to choose from, you can easily spend many minutes browsing for the right one in which to sell something or find the collectibles you want to buy.

For instance, if you click Browse in the navigation bar and then click Collectibles, you go to the Collectibles page, which lists approximately 50 categories within this main category. At the end of this list, you see the link See All Collectibles Categories. Click this link, and you are confronted with a page that lists hundreds of categories and subcategories. When you consider that each one of the subcategories contains its own set of subcategories, you can quickly become overwhelmed.

Instead, if you're searching for a specific category, follow these steps:

**1.** Click Sell in the eBay navigation bar.

2. Sign in with your user ID and password, and click Sign In.

3. When the Choose a Selling Format page appears, leave the default option selected, then click Continue.

4. When the Sell Your Item: Select Category page appears, type a keyword that describes the category you want in the Enter Item Keywords to Find a Category box, near the top of the page.

5. Click Find. A list of suggested categories appears. For instance, if you enter the term "Hummel," you get the suggestions shown in Figure 5-6.

As you can see, the list of suggested categories is ranked by percentage. The percentage is a measurement telling you how many of the items sold on eBay that match your keywords are found in a given category. For instance, of all the

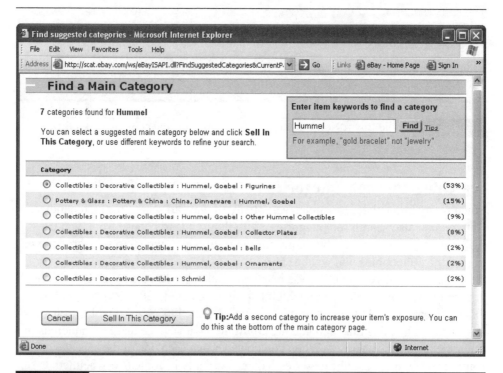

FIGURE 5-6    eBay ranks categories based on how often the specified items are found there.

Hummel-related items sold on eBay, 53 percent are found in the category listed at the top. This category is a particularly good one to buy or sell in, because you'll find more Hummel items there. You can also use the list to find items similar, though not identical, to the ones you collect. For instance, at the bottom of the list shown in Figure 5-6, you see a category for Schmid figurines, not Hummels.

*eBay only presents 10 suggestions in its list of category search results, even if your keywords might be found in more than 10 categories.*

# Being a Smart Collector

Finding treasure on eBay is only half the battle. The other half is making sure it gets to you and that it arrives in one piece—or at the very least, that you don't lose money if the item is damaged. Some tips for ensuring that transactions are successfully completed are presented below.

## Asking for Insurance

Many sellers won't automatically insure what they ship, especially if it isn't something that is fragile. Insurance does add a few dollars to the shipping charges, and that subtracts from the seller's profit. Besides, insurance is more for the seller's benefit than the buyer's. If something is damaged or lost in transit, the seller should (in order to be a good community member, and to prevent negative feedback) provide a full or partial refund to the buyer. The insurance can offset this cost to the seller.

Insurance is always an option for buyers, too, provided that you are willing to pay for it. If the collectible you purchase on eBay is one that you desire and value especially, by all means pay more for insurance. Then, if the item is damaged, you don't have to plead or negotiate with the seller for a refund. You work with the shipper to get the refund as part of their services. Typical insurance costs for the "Big Three" shippers for a 1-pound package being sent from New York City to Naperville, Illinois, are shown in Table 5-2.

Keep in mind that sellers who make a living on eBay or with a brick-and-mortar company might have parcel insurance as part of their business insurance package. In such a case, the seller pays a small flat fee to insure all parcels that are shipped. If this is the case, there is no charge to you, the bidder. Always ask if the seller has this type of coverage.

| Shipper | Amount of Insurance | Cost |
|---------|---------------------|------|
| USPS, Priority Mail | $100 | $2.20 |
| USPS, Priority Mail | $500 | $6.20 |
| UPS | $100 | N/A (All shipments are insured for up to $100.) |
| UPS | $200 | $0.35 (Excess value insurance costs 35 cents per $100 of value.) |
| FedEx 2Day | $100 | N/A (All shipments are insured for up to $100.) |
| FedEx 2Day | $200 | $2.56 |

**TABLE 5-2**    Examples of Insurance Costs

*FedEx Ground service, which includes FedEx Home Delivery, does not include any insurance. A service called Universal Parcel Insurance Coverage (U-PIC, http://www.u-pic.com) enables you to insure a single shipment at a substantial savings compared to USPS insurance rates.*

## Saving Photos of What You Purchase

After an auction ends and an item is purchased, busy sellers will remove the photos from the web servers on which they were hosted (or the services that host the photos will remove the photos automatically) in order to save server space. This is why, when you search through eBay's database of completed auctions, you often see descriptions that have only text and no images.

The savvy and security-conscious buyer on eBay will save photos of the items they purchase. The reason? When the item purchased actually arrives from the shipper, if there are any discrepancies the buyer can point to the original photos and even e-mail them back to the seller to prove that what was received was different from what was actually purchased.

*Be very careful before you complain that what you purchased is a different color than what you expected. You can't rely on web browsers to display colors accurately. Colors on the Web, except for a few dozen that are considered "browser safe," appear very differently depending on the monitor, browser, and computer operating system used.*

## Trade Talk

Sometimes, if you read eBay sales descriptions carefully, you uncover mistakes that aren't just typos but indicate more serious problems. Occasionally, collectors tell dealers that they are unwittingly (or perhaps knowingly) attempting to sell something that is a forgery. The web page called A Belleek Collector's Guide to eBay (http://www3.bc.sympatico.ca/bjgcelt/conventionpresentation.html) describes a Tridacna pattern saucer offered on eBay in 1999 as Belleek. (The forged pottery is shown at the very top of the web page; notice the misspelling of the word "Belleek" as "Beelleek.") It was described as "a VERY good forgery except for the forger's horrible spelling ability." Knowledgeable Belleek collectors spotted the mistake and informed the seller, who was apparently unaware the item wasn't genuine.

# Getting Organized with My eBay

How many times have you missed the annual collectors' convention or the rummage sale at the local church because you weren't on top of things and let the date slip by? Part of collecting is simply being at the right place at the right time. Not only that, but organization is one of the great joys of collecting. Sorting, classifying, and displaying what you have accumulated can give hours of pleasure. It also prevents hours of displeasure caused by misplacing and looking for things.

You've got to keep things straight, and My eBay is one of those organizational resources you might well overlook. It's a web page that eBay provides for each member, and it keeps track of that person's buying and selling activities. Not only that—it contains links to lots of utilities and forms you're bound to need sooner or later (and especially when you start selling).

I highly recommend that you spend a few minutes exploring your own My eBay page, if not to satisfy your need for organization then to see what's available to you. The sections that follow point you to a few features that are particularly useful aspects of My eBay.

## Configuring Your Summary

It's easy to find your page. It's automatically set up for you, so you don't have to create it yourself. Just click My eBay in the navigation bar, and then sign in with your user ID and password. eBay presents a page like the one shown in Figure 5-7.

When you first connect to My eBay, you are presented with a summary of your recent activities, which eBay has drawn from its database. If you haven't left

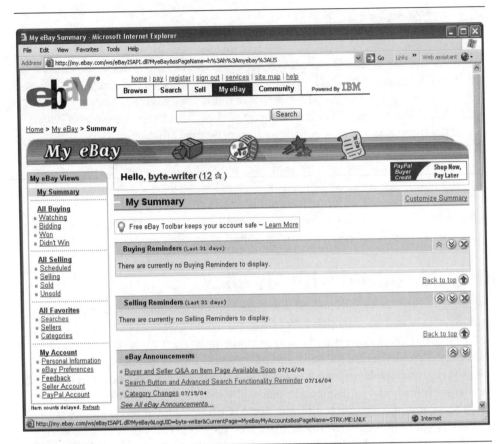

**FIGURE 5-7** My eBay gives you a way to track what you have bought and sold and find links to useful resources.

feedback, paid for a transaction, or received payment, eBay presents reminders on the summary page. But you can configure the summary page to view a wider range of useful activities. Just click the Customize Summary link near the top of the main My eBay page. You can then choose options from the Customize My Summary page (see Figure 5-8).

The Views to Display box shows the types of information currently displayed on your summary page. Scan the list of additional types of information in the Available Views box. When you see one you want to add, click it to highlight it. Then click the button that points to the Views to Display box. The selection is moved to that box. You can also reorder the items displayed in your summary by

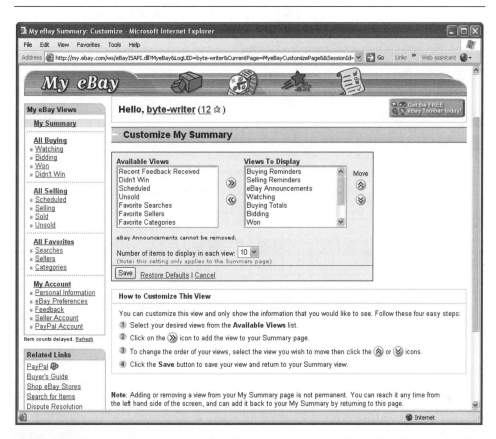

FIGURE 5-8    My eBay can instantly present your favorite searches and sellers as well as other options you want to view.

selecting the one you want to move and then clicking the up or down arrows next to Views to Display.

## Saving Searches

If you set up combined search terms, as described earlier in "Creating Complex Searches," and get a good set of results, there's no need to retype or paste the search terms into a search box every time you conduct subsequent searches. Instead you can save as many as 100 favorite searches in your My eBay page. Just follow these steps:

1. Click Search in the eBay navigation toolbar.

2. When the Basic Search page appears, fill in your search criteria—or click options on Advanced Search, By Bidder, By Seller, or Stores, and fill out the search terms you use frequently.

3. Click Search.

4. When the search results appear, click Add to Favorites.

5. When the Add to My Favorite Searches page appears (Figure 5-9), click one of the buttons to either create a new search or replace a previous search.

6. Check the box next to Email Preferences if you want eBay to e-mail you whenever an item appears that matches your search criteria. (Be aware that

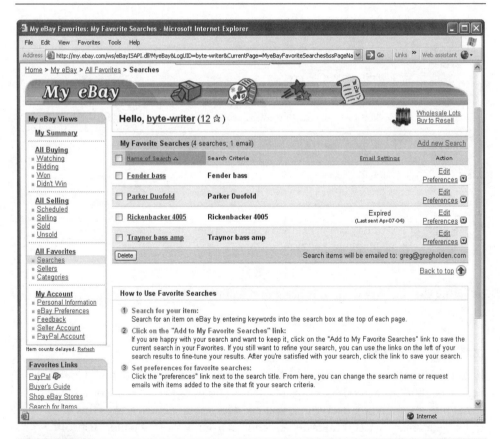

FIGURE 5-9    You can have eBay e-mail you when one of your search items is offered for sale.

you are likely to get lots of e-mail if you check this option, unless your search criteria are very specific.)

**7.** Click Submit.

When you want to conduct one of your saved searches, click My eBay in the navigation bar. When your My eBay page appears, you choose one of two options for viewing favorite searches:

■ If you have added favorite searches to your summary page, as described in the previous section, you simply scroll down to the list of favorite searches and click the one you want to conduct the search again.

■ If you haven't yet added favorite searches to your summary page, click Searches under All Favorites in the left-hand column of your My eBay page. When you want to do a search, click its name in the Name of Search column (see Figure 5-10). All the search criteria you stored will be used.

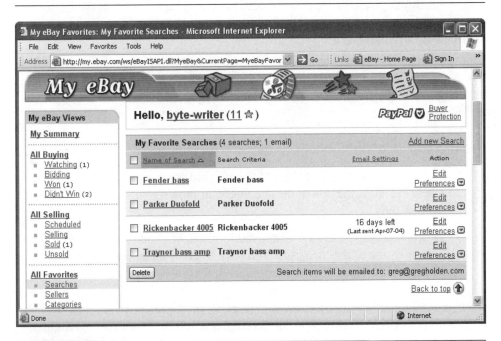

FIGURE 5-10    Whenever you want to conduct a saved search, click its name in this part of My eBay.

# Tracking Your Activity

One of My eBay's best features is that it gives you a convenient way to review your feedback comments and your account information, and to change your user preferences. It's eBay's way of personalizing the way you interact with the auction site. The various parts of the page (which are called Views) are presented in the My eBay Views column: My Summary, All Buying, All Selling, All Favorites, and My Account. The most important views are described in the sections that follow.

## All Buying: Tracking What You've Done

The first My eBay view is accessed by clicking All Buying. The All Buying view enables you to track sales from the standpoint of a buyer. You not only receive a record of any items on which you have placed bids, but you can also "watch" items you're interested in but haven't bid on as yet. Even if you're primarily interested in eBay from the standpoint of making bids, you'll probably want to purchase shipping supplies on the site. You may also shop around for items to add to your personal collection or bargains that you can turn around and resell at a profit. The subsections within All Buying are presented in the sections that follow.

### Items I'm Bidding On

This section presents items on which you have placed a bid recently. It provides you with a convenient way to keep track of your bids so you don't miss out on anything you really want. You can tell which auctions need attention by their color coding:

- Auctions in which your bid is currently the high bid are displayed in green.

- Auctions in which your bid is not the high bid are displayed in red. To place a new bid, click the title of the auction; your browser will jump to that sale immediately.

- Dutch auctions are always displayed in black, whether or not your bid is currently one of the high bids. You have to go to the auction page itself to find out if you have high bidder status in that sale.

In addition, the My Max Bid column displays the amount of your most recent bid, so you can decide whether or not to increase it, if you're not the high bidder. Also on the All Buying page, My eBay provides you with a total of the amount you have bid on all items, so you can make sure you don't overspend. Once one of the sales in the Items I'm Bidding On section ends, it moves to either Items I've Won or Items I Didn't Win.

 *By default, only the items you have bid on in the previous two days appear in this section. You can view up to 60 days' worth of activity, however. To change the default, choose a new value from the Period drop-down list, then click Go. This applies to both Items I've Won and Items I Didn't Win.*

## Items I've Won

This section allows you to track auctions you have won and items you have purchased through Buy It Now. If you have won a number of items in the past 30 days and you are waiting for them to arrive from various sellers, this is the perfect place to keep track of them. The information presented in this section is shown in Figure 5-11.

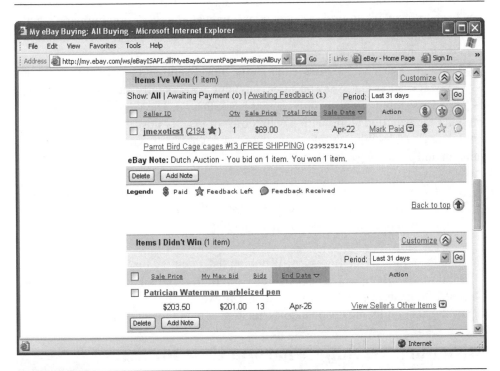

**FIGURE 5-11**   Items I've Won tells you whether feedback has been received, whether you have paid, and how much you paid.

### Items I Didn't Win

Items on which you placed bids that didn't turn out to be the winner are moved to this section after the sale in question ends. The items listed in this section give you a chance to do some more searching in an effort to change your luck: click the seller link to find items by the same seller that might be similar to the one you wanted. Click the category name to do some browsing for similar merchandise you might be able to win.

### Buying Reminders

If you have bought something on eBay but have not paid for it or have paid but have yet to leave feedback, eBay will provide you with a reminder in this section.

### Watching Sales

The Items I'm Watching section in All Buying gives you a formal way to mark sales you want to track so that you can bid on them when the auction nears its end or check on current prices while the sale is going on. If you don't "watch" a sale, you have to re-search to find the sale or simply keep the sale's auction page open on your computer screen for hours or days at a time, which consumes computer resources unnecessarily.

The Items I'm Watching list is one of the most useful and practical features on My eBay. It ensures that you won't miss anything you're really interested in (as long as you keep visiting My eBay on a regular basis, that is). The view (see Figure 5-12) presents each auction along with a countdown of exactly how much time is left until the sale ends. When a sale nears the final few minutes, you can hopefully jump in and place the winning bid.

> **TIP** *When you have found something of interest through a search or through browsing, be sure to check that seller's other auctions. You might find items similar to the one you are watching.*

To add an item to the Items I'm Watching list, click the link Watch This Item (Track It in My eBay), which appears in the top right corner of any sales description. Once the item has been added to the Items I'm Watching list, the message at the top of the auction listing changes to "This item is being tracked in My eBay."

## All Selling: Tracking What You Have for Sale

If you become a seller on eBay, this view gives you a convenient place to keep track of your auction listings. The page is divided into five sections: Items I'm Selling, Items I've Sold, Unsold Items, Scheduled Items, and Selling Reminders.

**FIGURE 5-12**    Any sales you are interested in are listed in this view under All Buying.

## Items I'm Selling

This section of the All Selling page enables you to see which of your sales are attracting bids, who the high bidder is, and so on. Color coding is used so you can quickly see which of your auctions have bids that have met or exceeded your reserve price, if you have one:

- Auction sales listed in green have bids that have met your reserve price; they will sell when the auction is over.

- Auction sales listed in red either have not attracted any bids as yet or the bids have not yet met your reserve.

- Any Dutch auctions you have listed are presented in black; you have to click on the auction title to check the bidding and see how many people have the high bids.

You have only to click the title of one of your auctions to verify that the photos and other contents appear the way you want. You can check how many visitors the sale has attracted by observing your counter, if you have installed one. The Payment Reminder column lets you know about sales for which the high bidder hasn't responded for three days. Click Payment Reminder, and eBay sends out a friendly reminder of its own telling the high bidder to get in touch with you.

## Items I've Sold

Any merchandise that has attracted winning bids is listed in this section (see Figure 5-13). Transactions that are listed in this category are ones that you need to resolve with the high bidder so you can arrange for shipping.

If you are selling a small number of items at a time, this area gives you a quick and simple way to view your auction activity. Any items that did not sell, either because they failed to attract any bids or because the bidders did not meet your reserve price, move to the Unsold Items section of the All Selling page after the auction ends. Each listing includes a convenient Relist link so that you can put the item up for sale again.

> **TIP** *Listing services like those provided by Marketworks (http://www .auctionworks.com) and the auction services listed in Appendix C enable you to schedule a sale days or even weeks in advance.*

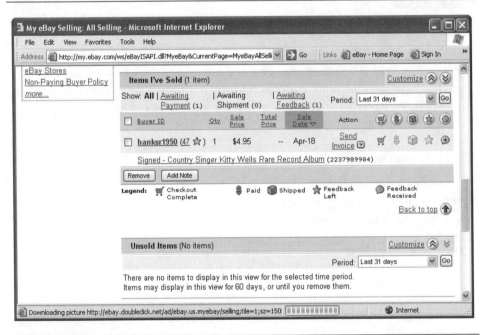

**FIGURE 5-13**   You can track what you've sold and whether feedback has been left in this section.

## Scheduled Items

You may be interested in relisting an item at a specified date in the future. In addition, you may have placed an item up for auction for the first time at a specified future date. Any items that are waiting to go on the virtual auction block are listed in this section. A Reschedule button appears along with each sale, enabling you to change the date at which you want the sale to start. Another button, Edit, enables you to change the listing before it goes online.

## Selling Reminders

Selling Reminders are messages from eBay that are designed to tell you what you need to do next in the process of selling something. You might need to send out an e-mail notification, send an invoice, or leave feedback, for instance. If you click on an item presented as a link under the Selling Reminders heading, you go to a web page where you can either complete the task or find out more about what it means or why you have to do it. The reminders are automatically updated as you proceed with a transaction.

# All Favorites: Accessing Data You Need Frequently

All Favorites provides you with a place to store information you access on a regular basis on eBay. If you save a set of search results or search terms, they are stored here so you can click on them and instantly access them. You can also add a seller to a Favorite Sellers section of the All Favorites page. In addition, any categories you designate as "Favorites" are stored in the My Favorite Categories page. To add a seller or a category, click the link at the far right-hand edge of the section: the link Add New Seller or Store lets you add a new source of merchandise you might want to buy or browse through. The link Add Category lets you designate a favorite category where you shop on a regular basis.

# My Account: Setting Your Preferences

The My Account section of My eBay collects information about how you pay for merchandise you have purchased, as well as the fees you pay to eBay. The page is divided into five sections:

- My PayPal Account information stores your PayPal account history.

- My Seller tells you whether you currently owe any Final Value Fees or listing fees to eBay.

- Automatic Payments enables you to designate a checking account or credit card from which eBay can automatically deduct your fees.

- Recent feedback provides you with a quick view of feedback comments your buyers or sellers have left for you.

- A convenient box at the bottom of the My Account page provides you with a listing of any seller fees you currently owe to eBay and links to payment options.

# Turning Your Browser into an Organizer

When you start shopping, collecting, or selling online, your primary navigational and transactional tool is your web browser. You use your browser as a combined road map, credit card, and sales receipt. It only makes sense, then, to use your browser to organize your collecting activities (or, for that matter, any other activity you conduct online). Your browser can keep track of web sites you visit frequently, and want to revisit, through its Bookmarks/Favorites feature. In addition, both Microsoft Internet Explorer (IE) and Netscape have a History feature that enables you to revisit web sites you've viewed in the recent past.

An even more convenient way to mark web pages you want to revisit on a regular basis—such as the parts of eBay you visit most frequently—is to customize your browser's toolbars. A toolbar is a set of navigational buttons and/or labels. All browsers have toolbars with buttons labeled Back, Forward, Reload or Refresh, Home, Print, Stop, and other common commands. You can add toolbars that help you perform more specific functions, or customize special toolbars that your browser provides to give you a set of links to your favorite locations on the Web.

## Installing eBay's Toolbar

If you need to stay on top of eBay auctions even while part of your browser window is doing other things, you can maintain your connection via the eBay toolbar. eBay's toolbar is free software that installs as an add-on to your web browser. It enables you to search eBay from wherever you are on the Web and receive alert messages in your browser window if you are outbid in an auction where you were the previous high bidder.

COLLECTOR'S NOTE  *You can find out more about the eBay toolbar at http://pages.ebay.com/ ebay_toolbar. The toolbar works with IE 5.01 or later or Netscape 4.51 through 4.79 (I was unable to install the toolbar on Netscape 7.0). It only works with Windows operating systems, however; Macintosh and Linux are not supported.*

## Collecting Step-by-Step

eBay makes its browser toolbar relatively easy to download and install. Follow these steps to get started:

1. Go to the eBay Toolbar page (http://pages.ebay.com/ebay_toolbar).

2. Read about the toolbar, make sure you have the required software to run the toolbar, and then click the Get eBay Toolbar Now button.

3. When the license agreement page appears, read the license terms, and then click Agree.

4. When a security warning page appears, click OK (if you use IE) or Grant (if you are using Netscape).

5. Your browser window refreshes, and the eBay toolbar is instantly added to the toolbars just above the main display area, as shown here.

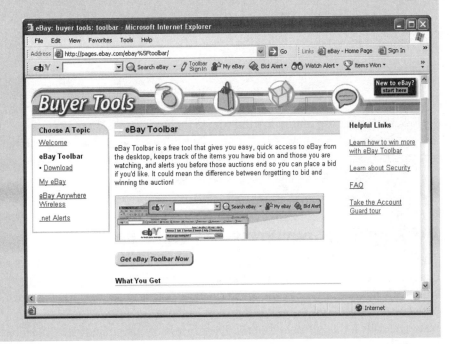

5

Once the toolbar is installed, you can use it to track auctions. First, you need to log in, either on the toolbar or on the site itself. Next, you can use the toolbar to search the site. If you click Search eBay, an extensive set of search options appears. The options at the top of the submenu let you choose how you want to search. The others provide you with categories and subcategories for searching. You choose an option and then enter a word or phrase in the toolbar's search box to actually conduct the search. You can also search within eBay Stores, by seller, and for Buy It Now items.

Alerts work with your Bid and Watch lists in My eBay. Whenever you bid on or watch a new item on eBay, the eBay toolbar will automatically refresh your Bid or Watch list. You can also manually refresh your toolbar lists by clicking the Refresh Bid/Watch List menu item in the appropriate Alert menu. The Watch Alert section changes color when an auction you are watching is about to end.

You can set Bid Alert to notify you 10, 15, 30, 60, or 75 minutes before an auction ends. When an item has reached the alert time you've selected, the Bid or Watch Alert button will be highlighted, an audio notification is sent, and a pop-up desktop alert listing your item will appear in the lower right corner of your browser window.

## Trade Talk

The eBay toolbar can be accessed at any time, and controlled, from an icon in your Windows system tray, the part of your desktop that also includes your clock. You have the option to close down the toolbar (this means you hide it from the browser window, not that you uninstall it for good). To close the toolbar, right-click the icon, and choose Exit from the shortcut menu. To recall it, click View, choose Toolbars, and choose eBay Toolbar.

## Working with Your Browser's Links Bar

The eBay toolbar doesn't work for Macintosh or Linux users, or even users of current versions of Netscape. And it takes up space in browser windows. In other words, it's not for everybody. As an alternative, you can use your web browser's own customizable Links toolbar. Internet Explorer calls it the Links toolbar; Netscape calls it the Personal toolbar. The process of customizing the Links bar to include eBay web sites is similar for both browsers:

1.  Display the Links bar. In Internet Explorer, choose View | Toolbars | Links. In Netscape Navigator, choose View | Show/Hide | Personal Toolbar. If you currently have either of these toolbars showing, choosing the aforementioned options hides them.

2.  Get rid of the buttons you don't want. Both toolbars come with a predetermined set of link buttons. Right-click each one you don't want, and choose Delete from the shortcut menu to delete it and make more room for the buttons you do want.

3.  Once you have cleared space on the toolbar, you can add buttons in one of two ways:

    ■ Go to a web page and drag the icon that appears next to the URL in the browser's Address bar into the Links bar.

    ■ Drag links you see on a web page into the Links bar. Click and hold down on a link, drag the link onto the Links bar, and release the mouse button.

The result is shown in Figure 5-14. Use your imagination when creating links: you can add buttons that point to your About Me page, your My eBay page, eBay's Basic Search page, or links to other pages you visit often.

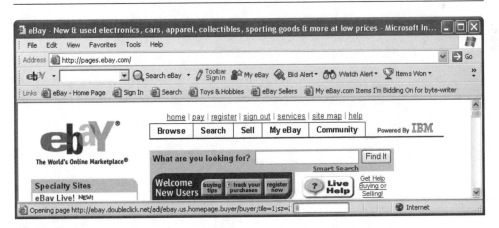

FIGURE 5-14    The Links/Personal toolbar can perform some of the functions of eBay's own toolbar.

## Links for Collectors

| Web Site | Address | What's There |
|---|---|---|
| Universal Parcel Insurance Coverage | http://www.u-pic.com | Low-cost alternative to insuring what you ship or receive on eBay |
| eBay toolbar | http://pages.ebay.com/ebay_toolbar | A browser toolbar that contains buttons and controls for tracking and searching eBay sales |
| My eBay page | Click My eBay in the navigation bar | A set of views that let you track what you have bought and sold and what you are interested in buying |

# Chapter 6

## Collecting Around the World

## In This Chapter You'll Learn...

■ How to explore eBay's multiple sites around the world

■ Ways to find travel bargains and regional items by shopping worldwide

■ About the additional costs usually incurred when paying for items purchased overseas

■ Special steps that may be needed to ensure safe shipping

■ Ways to chat with, consult, and learn from eBay international members on the message boards

The *Inter* in *Internet* doesn't stand for *international*, but it very well could. One of the things that makes the Internet so exciting is the ability to reach people around the globe in a matter of seconds. When you exchange your first e-mail or instant message with someone overseas, it's a great thrill. The same excitement applies to buying and selling on eBay with individuals in other countries.

It's amazingly easy to locate local and regional items virtually anywhere on eBay. The thing that tends to hold people back from making purchases is the process of finalizing transactions through payment, customs (if necessary), and shipping. It seems riskier and more complicated to pay someone across the ocean than a resident of your own country. But in both cases you're really using the same electronic methods when you send the payment. If you rely on the same principles that protect you when you buy domestically—researching sellers, reading feedback, making sure shipments are insured, and relying on the fraud protection provided by credit card companies and electronic payment services—buying overseas should not increase your risk. This chapter describes the many options eBay provides for shopping around the world, making friends in other countries, and completing international transactions successfully.

# Exploring eBay's International Sites

You naturally do most of your buying on eBay by visiting the version that's based in your own country. If you live in the United Kingdom, you visit eBay at http://ebay.co.uk, for instance. But if you scroll down to the bottom of the home page of your "home" version of eBay, you'll notice a box that lists many different international locations for eBay. These are all versions of eBay that are tailored for specific countries. At this writing, there are 22 such eBays, not counting the one in the United States. Some of them aren't actually called eBay: they go under names such as MercadoLibre, a marketplace that was purchased by eBay. That's the name used in countries such as Mexico and Argentina (see Figure 6-1).

If you collect something that's specific to a region of the world or that comes in varieties that are difficult to find outside the area where they are manufactured, these overseas eBay versions give you a great way to find them. Table 6-1 gives you a few examples of international eBay sites and what you can find if you do some shopping there.

## Searching eBay Overseas

The Web is a worldwide phenomenon. It gives sellers the ability to reach new customers around the world as well as around the corner from where they live. But on eBay, sellers can't actively reach out and find sellers in other countries.

6

**FIGURE 6-1**   eBay's international sites go by many different names.

| eBay Location | Home Page | Language | Collectors' Items |
|---|---|---|---|
| MercadoLibre Argentina | http://mercadolibre.com.ar | Spanish | 150 Argentinean postage stamps for $8 U.S. |
| Italy | http://ebay.it | Italian | Borsalino silk ties; autographed soccer jerseys |
| Netherlands | http://ebay.nl | Dutch | A Beatles miniature guitar and a brooch made in Holland in 1964 |
| Hong Kong | http://www.ebay.com.hk/home | Chinese | |
| New Zealand | http://ebay.com/nz | English | Maori weapons and other antiques |
| Spain | http://es.ebay.com | Spanish | An original drawing by Salvador Dali |
| Switzerland | http://ebay.ch | German | Swatch watches; ski sunglasses and goggles |

**TABLE 6-1**    Sites for International Collecting on eBay

When they sell, they can specify that what they have will be available either worldwide or to specified countries. It's up to you to go out and find those items, wherever they are available.

If you go a step beyond shopping in your own country and look in another one of eBay's web sites, you can find much more than you ever thought you would. There is an important way you can take advantage of the fact that most of the eBay sites around the world are separate from one another: very desirable items are available on overseas eBay sites to those who know the language and are not put off by the process of paying overseas sellers. It also pays, literally, to keep track of items that are listed in a currency with which your home currency has a favorable exchange rate. It's also very likely that there will be less competition on the foreign eBay sites than you face on the U.S. site. Some options for browsing other countries' sales items through the Advanced Search form are described in the sections that follow.

## Search Locations in Your Own Country

After you enter your search keywords and choose other options, you can optionally narrow the search to different geographic locations by making choices from the Location/International drop-down lists in Advanced Search. If you leave the option

Items from eBay.com (or eBay.co.uk, or your own country's home address) selected and then choose an option from the first drop-down list, you can choose a region within your own country (see Figure 6-2). In the U.S. location (eBay.com), you can choose one of the 50 states. In other eBay locations, you choose one of the major cities.

## Search for Items Available to Your Country

The second drop-down list in the Location/International section of Advanced Search, Items Available To..., specifies that you want to search for items that are available only to buyers from a particular country. Select the country from the Items Available To list. Some sellers exclude overseas bidders from their auctions; this option lets you find international sales that include your country as well as other parts of the world.

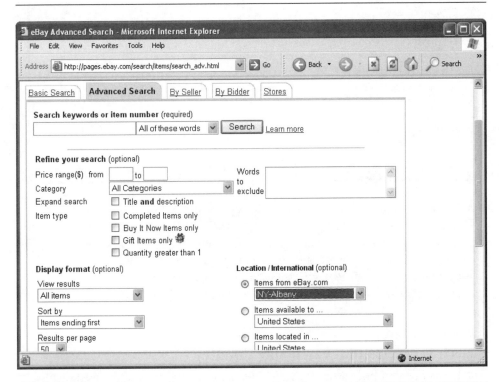

**FIGURE 6-2**    The Location/International options help you shop in other countries or in regions within your own country.

# Selling in Specific Countries

Sellers who want to make their items available to people in specific countries can do so through the Sell Your Item form. In the Ship-to Locations field of the Shipping & Payment Terms section of the form shown here, sellers can specify either that the item will ship worldwide, will ship only to the United States, or to the U.S. and selected countries or regions.

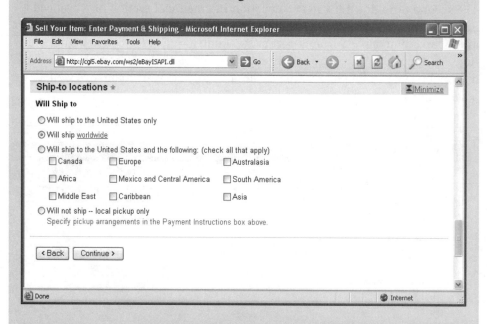

To ensure a smooth experience for buyers, helpful sellers should include the weight of the item as well as its physical dimensions. That way, you can calculate shipping costs, which can be considerable where international shipping is concerned. If the sales description does not include this information, be sure to ask the seller for it before you bid. That way, you won't be surprised by high international shipping costs if you win the auction.

## Search for Items in a Particular Country

The Items Located In... drop-down list yields more specific and focused results than the Items Available To... option. It enables you to choose a specific country to shop in. If you are looking for chocolate from Austria or rare paintings from

Italy, this is the list to use. Just make sure that the sellers are prepared to ship to your location. If you try to buy something from someone who has specified that they will not ship to your country, they are not obligated to sell to you.

> TIP    *Choose an option from the Currency drop-down list if you want to search for items being sold in a particular currency. Even if the item is not being sold in the currency you use at home, you can convert it using eBay's Universal Currency Converter. You can have your bank or Western Union convert it to the currency the seller desires.*

## Language Considerations

You have found someone in Holland selling a pair of old wooden shoes in just your size, and you are eager to bid on them as a gift for your Dutch relatives in the U.S. It's quite possible that the seller has some ability to speak English. But you can't depend on this. In this and other cases, you'll have the most satisfying experience if you have some fluency in the language of the country where you shop. If you don't, and you place a bid or click the Buy It Now button based on photos and a few words you can understand from a foreign-language description, you can quickly end up buying something you don't want. Be very careful to read descriptions closely.

If you see something you want (or you think you want) from an international seller and you can't completely understand the description, you can try one of two things to better understand what is being offered as well as the terms of the sale:

- Try an online translation service. The most popular service (which is also free) is called Babel Fish (http://babelfish.altavista.com).

- Ask for help. Some of the eBay members who frequent the International Trading discussion board have offered their own services as translators. See "Meeting eBay Members Around the World" later in this chapter.

> TIP    *If you sell as well as buy on eBay, the key to finding buyers overseas is not to depend on them to do their own translation but to keep your sentences short, simple, and easy to understand, and try to handle the translation yourself if you want it to be accurate. This can be very tricky. According to posts on the International Trading board, the word "hot" in English can be translated into either "spicy hot" or "hot in temperature" in Chinese, for instance.*

6

## Collecting Step-by-Step

Babel Fish, a service provided by the online search service AltaVista, is easy to use. Suppose you see a listing for a pen on the MercadoLibre site in Mexico like the one shown here.

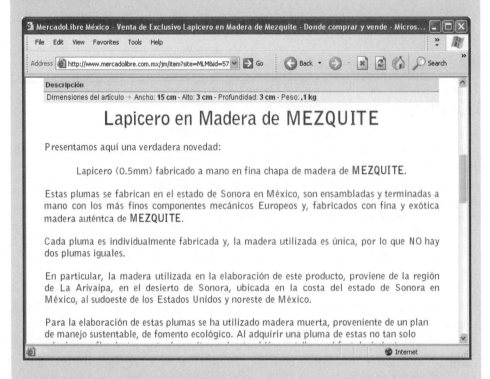

You can get a quick—though imperfect—translation from Babel Fish by following these steps:

1. Copy all or part of the auction description to your computer clipboard by scrolling across the text (keeping in mind that Babel Fish's text box can only translate a maximum of 150 words) and pressing CTRL-C.

2. Enter the address for the Babel Fish web site (http://babelfish .altavista.com) in your browser's address box, and press Enter to connect to the site.

3. Click inside the text box labeled Translate a Block of Text, and press CTRL-V to paste the text there.

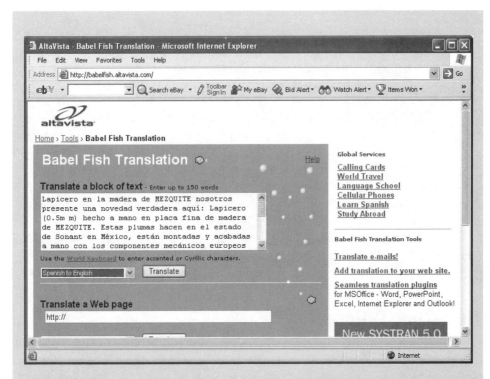

4. Choose the translation path (that is, *from* what language *to* what language) from the drop-down list beneath the text box. At this writing, Chinese, English, French, Japanese, Korean, Spanish, German, Italian, Portuguese, and Russian to English (but not English to Russian) are covered by the service. For this example, you would choose Spanish to English.

5. Click Translate.

The Babel Fish translation of the text shown in step 3 reads as follows:

```
Lapicero in Wood of MEZQUITE We presented/displayed a
true newness here: Lapicero (0.5mm) made by hand in
fine MEZQUITE wood plate. These pens make in the state
of Sonant in Mexico, are assembled and finished by hand
with the finest European mechanical components and,
made with fine and exotic wood auténtca of MEZQUITE.
Each pen individually is made and, the used wood is
```

```
unique, reason why there are not two equal pens. In
individual, the wood used in the elaboration of this
product, comes from the region of the Arivaipa, in the
desert of Sonant, located in the coast of the state of
Sonant in Mexico, to the southwest of the United States
and the northeast of Mexico.
```

This isn't going to win any awards for grammar, and I don't think all the terms are totally accurate. But it's enough to tell me why this pen is special and to give me the basic information I need to place a bid. (Remember that the shorter and simpler the text, the better your results.)

You also have the option of letting the service translate an entire web page: just enter the URL in the Translate a Web Page box.

## Time-Zone Differences

From a seller's standpoint, the time when an auction is scheduled to end is of great importance. Although it's true that reserve price auctions make it unnecessary for bidders to be present at the end, it's often the last hour or two of an auction that sees the most action. If the sale ends in the afternoon or evening on a weekend, more bids are likely to be received than if the sale ends in the wee hours of a weekday. But what if potential buyers are overseas and the time difference is six, eight, or even more hours?

## Trade Talk

A longtime topic on the International Trading board entitled "Languages—Translation" addresses many issues surrounding the subject of how best to make auction listings readable to people who don't actually read the seller's native language. Some members who participate on the board are so generous that they offer to translate short descriptions themselves. If you are lucky, you might find someone who speaks your language and is willing to help you out. Find out more by clicking Community and then International Trading, or go to http://forums.ebay.com/db2/forum.jsp?forum=31.

Sellers can try to schedule an auction so that it ends at a time when the largest number of potential bidders is available. Consider ending the sale Saturday around 2 P.M. Central time. That way, in Europe, it's Saturday evening and people can participate without having to stay up all night, while on the West Coast and in Hawaii it's still early in the day. You can determine the difference between eBay's official time and time zones around the world at the Time Zone Conversion page (http://pages.ebay.com/internationaltrading/timezones.html).

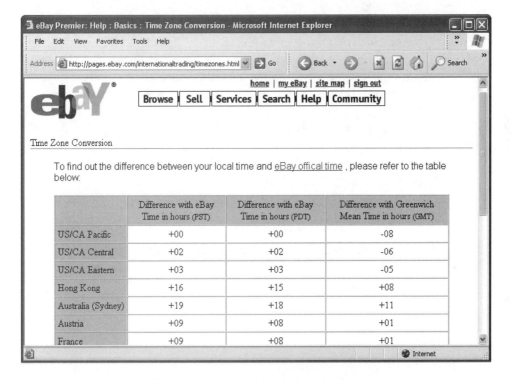

For buyers, time-zone differences are less critical because of proxy bidding. If the sale ends at a time when you just aren't around, you can place a proxy bid and eBay will continue bidding on your behalf until someone meets or exceeds your bid. Or, you can use a snipe bidding service such as eSnipe (http://www .esnipe.com) to place a bid at the last minute before a sale ends. But both of these options have potential flaws that can cause you to lose auctions. A proxy bid can be beat out at the last minute. A snipe bid won't be placed at all if the bidding has already met or exceeded the snipe bid amount you were planning to place. It's best to be present at the end of a sale of a collectible object you really want. Be aware of the ending time and calculate the ending time in your own time zone. A sale in

Australia that ends on May 8 at 17:16:04 Australian Eastern standard time (5:06:04 P.M.) ends nine hours later at eBay's home in California. That's 2:06:04 A.M. Pacific Daylight time on May 9. You'd better be prepared to either stay up late or place a high proxy bid before you go to bed.

## Collecting Step-by-Step

There's a trick you can try if you want to change the time zone and payment currency to your own from those of another country. This is useful if you see an item you want on a foreign language site, but are uncertain about your chances because the auction ending time is in the local time zone and the current bid is in a foreign currency. But be aware that it might not work in all countries and for all items.

Here's how it works: because all eBay auctions are contained in the same worldwide database, you can change the details of an auction into something more familiar by simply changing the URL. For example, assume that the URL of the auction listing looks like this:

```
http://cgi.ebay.it/ws/eBayISAPI.dll?ViewItem&Item=4860382911
```

The "eBay.it" part of the URL is being tailored for visitors to eBay Italia: the language is Italian, the default currency is the Euro, and so on. You can change the details as follows:

1. Make sure your browser's address bar shows the URL of the auction listing.

2. Change the domain to match your home domain. For example, changing the domain of the preceding URL to eBay.com, it would look like this:

   ```
   http://cgi.ebay.com/ws/eBayISAPI.dll?ViewItem&Item=4860382911
   ```

3. Now refresh the web page. eBay's database will tailor the same data to U.S. viewers.

By changing the URL to your local version of eBay, you'll not only have the start and end time of the auction translated to your own time zone, but you'll have the item (in this example, item number 4860382911) described in English, and the current high bid expressed in dollars.

# What Kinds of Things Can You Find Overseas?

Table 6-1 hinted at the range of items you can find if you are able to shop in other countries. But there are many more bargains you can uncover, whether you are looking for collectibles or not. Some examples are presented in the sections that follow.

## Vacation and Travel Bargains

As airline prices and fees go up and traditional travel agents disappear, the Internet is becoming the place to arrange travel. Train and air tickets are now routinely purchased online. People who are used to traveling through cyberspace are increasingly reluctant to turn their travel arrangements over to a travel agent. Click the Travel category (http://pages.ebay.com/travel) to start shopping. You'll immediately see a search box where you can get prices on airline tickets, hotel rooms, cars, and vacation packages. You will also see links for luggage, cruise deals, and many other travel-related categories (see Figure 6-3).

6

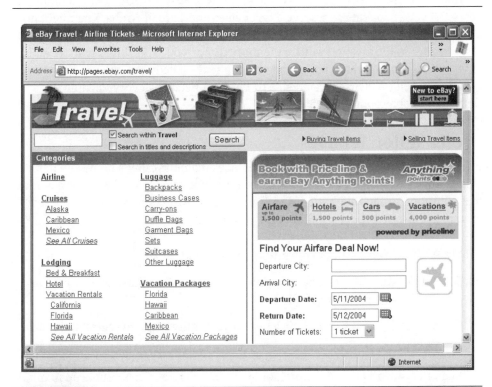

FIGURE 6-3    The Travel category opening page contains links to air, cruise, and hotel deals.

## Vacation Homes and Real Castles

Every day, thousands of real estate properties are up for sale on eBay, not only in your home country but abroad as well. Why turn to eBay rather than your local real estate company if you are looking for someplace to hang your hat? eBay is perfect if you are looking to relocate, because of its global reach. It's also great if you are looking to splurge on some luxury vacation property or if you just want to rent a beautiful condo or apartment for a week. And, if there is more than one of you making the decision on where to move or what property to buy, looking over the possibilities before having an actual on-site visit is the way to go.

Keep in mind that there's a big difference between sales in eBay's Real Estate section and other parts of eBay: many sales are "nonbinding." In other words, even if you turn out to be the high bidder, the owner is not always obliged to sell to you. As eBay obtains real estate licenses for each state, however, it is able to conduct binding real estate sales. Check the real estate section to see what's current in your own area.

If at all possible, arrange to view the property yourself before you bid on it. Of course, if you're looking to reserve a week in a timeshare in Aruba, you might not be able to take a trip right away (though it would be nice). In that case, you can hire a realtor in the area to evaluate the property for you. You'll find realtors and answers to questions about buying and selling real estate in the links and featured resources listed on the right-hand side of the Real Estate category opening page (http://pages.ebay.com/realestate).

## Exotic Motor Vehicles

eBay Motors can be found in many other places than just eBay's home site in the United States. You might be able to find an auto, motorcycle, or other vehicle abroad that is highly collectible but hard to find in your own country. Here are a few examples I discovered in searching eBay Motors in the U.K. for just a short time.

- A 1964 Morris Minor convertible (current bid, £1100).

- A 1977 Rolls Royce Shadow with 37,000 miles, available at a surprising Buy It Now price of £11,950.

- A 1951 Vincent Comet 500cc motorcycle, fully restored (current bid, £4,800).

Such items can't be found easily, or at all, in other countries. But keep in mind that, if you do end up the high bidder, you'll probably have to pay taxes, customs, and shipping costs that are far higher than if you are ordering a vehicle domestically, as described in the following section.

If you wish to purchase a vehicle that is to be imported into the United States, make sure that it meets DOT (Department of Transportation) requirements. Various things such as emissions controls, fuel consumption, and exhaust calibration could prevent a vehicle from being imported into the United States. In some instances, the cost to bring the vehicle into compliance could change the transaction from fantastic to prohibitive.

# Shipping Costs and Other Expenses

If you buy something from an overseas seller on eBay, it's generally assumed that you are willing to pay additional costs that may apply—things such as duties, taxes, and customs clearance fees. These fees can quickly turn what looks like a bargain into something other than a good buy, as described in the sections that follow.

## Shipping Considerations

You already know that you need to make sure a seller will actually ship to your location if you turn out to be the buyer or high bidder. Read the fine print carefully: In the description for the Vincent motorcycle mentioned in the preceding list, the seller does state that he or she will ship worldwide. But the Postage and Payment Details section states that "buyer pays for all postage costs," and no specific postage costs are given. For a heavy object like a motorcycle (not to mention a car), shipping can easily cost hundreds of dollars.

To get a rough idea of how much it might cost to ship a vehicle overseas, you can consult the web site for Dependable Auto Shippers (http://www.dasautoshippers .com), a vehicle shipping company that is affiliated with eBay (see Figure 6-4). The site includes shipping calculators that can help estimate domestic shipments and international shipments of cars, SUVs, and other motor vehicles; for other vehicles such as motorcycles, you'll have to e-mail the company for a quote.

When you do get a quote, keep in mind that international shipping rates may or may not include pickup and door-to-door delivery with customs clearance. If you live in an apartment building, the package might be delivered to the reception desk, but you might be required to pay extra to have it brought to your door. Some carriers will offer customs and brokerage services to help you learn more about what you need to tell your sellers about additional charges, duties, and taxes. An "extended area surcharge" may also apply depending on your location.

**FIGURE 6-4**    This shipping service can calculate costs for shipping vehicles both domestically and overseas.

## International Insurance

Insurance is as important for overseas shipments as for domestic ones. As usual, it's up to the buyer to obtain insurance if the seller doesn't offer to do this. At present, sellers can send goods insured from the United Kingdom to the United States via Parcel Force International Standard Mail, one of the U.K.'s Royal Mail services. Visit the Royal Mail web site (http://www.royalmail.com) to find out more about British shipments. For shipments from other countries, it's easiest to rely on the shipping service to provide you with insurance.

## Estimating Transit Time

How long will it take that doll or toy to get to you? Will it get to you in time for someone's birthday or for the holidays? You can fill out the form at http://www.servicecenter.ups.com/ebay/ebay.html#tnt to determine shipping times between different countries. You can also consult the European Transit Time

Maps on the UPS web site (http://ups.com) to get an idea. Enter the country and postal code where the shipment is originating, and you can estimate the transit time between various parts of Europe. This, of course, is only useful if your shipment is within Europe itself (see Figure 6-5).

TIP    *UPS also has a Global Advisor page full of links for those who trade internationally. The page (http://www.ups.com/content/us/en/resources/ advisor/index.html) includes information on documenting your shipment, obtaining insurance, and much more.*

## Customs and Other Fees

When it comes to international sales, a number of other costs may apply beyond the purchase price, shipping costs, and fees you pay to services like Western Union

6

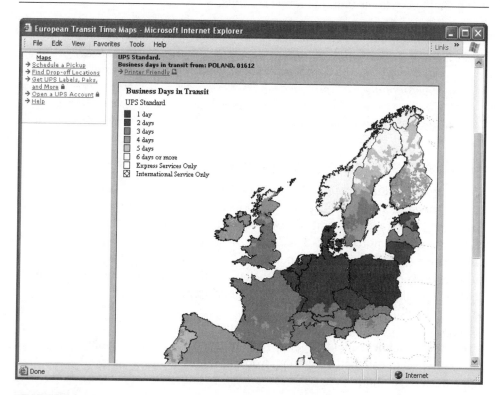

FIGURE 6-5    UPS maps help you estimate shipping times within Europe.

Auction Payments or PayPal. If your overseas seller doesn't accept one of the aforementioned payment methods or a personal check, you can obtain an international money order from your bank, but you'll have to pay a fee for this service.

There are also customs duties. U.S. Customs is an agency of the government that monitors what enters the country, either by shipment or carried by travelers. You might need to pay a customs fee (*duty*) for something you import from overseas. As you might expect, that cost has to be paid by you, the buyer. For the item to clear customs, your seller will certainly need to provide documentation about what it is, where it is coming from, and where it is going. Make sure the seller will include an invoice that provides such information. If you are buying something with a value of more than $2500, your shipper will need to file a Shipper's Export Declaration form with U.S. Customs. A Certificate of Original and Consular Invoice could also be needed. Your shipper needs to work these details out with the shipping company; if he or she does not, the item you purchase will be held in customs until the forms are filed.

**COLLECTOR'S NOTE** *You can find out more about customs fees on eBay's International Trading—Buyers page (http://pages.ebay.com/internationaltrading/ buyerhub.html). UPS can help you calculate customs duties as part of your shipping fees (provided your seller agrees to use UPS, of course). Find out more at http://www.ups.com/content/us/en/resources/select/ sending/customs/index.html.*

## North American Shipping Fees

Shipping to Canada from the United States might seem as if it should be straightforward, since it's just over the border. Not so. Although the North American Free Trade Agreement (NAFTA) made trade between the U.S., Canada, and Mexico flow more easily, that doesn't mean it's less expensive. In Canada, buyers are responsible for paying duties, a Goods and Services Tax, and applicable customs brokerage fees in addition to the cost of the merchandise you sell them. Buyers generally pay these fees upon receipt of shipment (although you can arrange to have UPS bill you beforehand).

If you live in Canada and import frequently from the United States, you may want to set up a nonresident importer (NRI) account with UPS (call 800-742-5877). The seller can then bill you up front for duties and taxes, as well as for shipping and handling.

*To find out more about Canadian customs charges, visit the Canada Customs and Revenue Agency at http://www.cbsa-asfc.gc.ca/menu-e.html.*

## Customs Restrictions

Sometimes the things you want to have shipped to you from overseas are prohibited by customs. You need to be aware of such restrictions beforehand. For instance, a seller on the eBay International Board asked if there are any restrictions on shipping ivory tusks to the United Kingdom. He was referred to the HM Customs and Excise site (http://www.hmce.gov.uk/contact/index.htm), which handles customs for the U.K. You can do a search there for restricted items; this leads to a phone number you can call to find out more.

UPS has a database of rules and regulations, organized by country, on its UPS Country Regulations page (http://www.ups.com/ga/CountryRegs?loc=en_US). Just enter the origin country and the destination country, and you get a page full of regulations you need to know about. You can also find out more about customs rules and regulations by visiting one of the customs offices listed in Table 6-2.

## Paying in Another Country's Currency

The prospect of paying someone who lives in another country for something you buy on one of eBay's sites can be intimidating, but it doesn't need to be. Many buyers and sellers use an electronic payment service such as Western Union Auction Payments (http://www.auctionpayments.com) or PayPal (http://www.paypal.com) and encounter no problems. Another electronic service, which specializes in dealing with European buyers and sellers, is also available. Through

| Country/Region | Customs Office URL |
| --- | --- |
| United States | http://www.customs.ustreas.gov |
| United Kingdom | http://www.hmce.gov.uk |
| Canada | http://www.cbsa-asfc.gc.ca/menu-e.html |
| Australia | http://www.customs.gov.au |
| France | http://www.douane.gouv.fr |
| Germany | http://www.zoll-d.de |
| Japan | http://www.mof.go.jp |
| Singapore | http://www.customs.gov.sg |

**TABLE 6-2**  Customs Offices in Selected Countries

Moneybookers (http://www.moneybookers.com) you pay a maximum of 0.50 Euros (62 cents when this book was published) to make an overseas payment and the service does the currency conversion for you. You do have to sign up for an account with Moneybookers to send a payment, however.

International money orders are favored by most sellers, rather than checks written in the buyer's currency. The reason is simple: it can cost the seller an extra fee to process foreign checks and deposit them. It can also take several weeks for such checks to clear. If you plan to make purchases often from a particular country (for instance, if you collect postal cards in France and frequently buy and sell with French collectors) you may want to consider opening a bank account in that country, which makes it considerably easier to transfer funds.

**WATCH OUT!**   *Wire transfers (in which funds are deducted from one person's account and moved to another account electronically) are a convenient and quick way to transfer payment from one country to another, and they often work smoothly. But fraudulent overseas sellers commonly demand wire transfers as a way to swindle buyers. Consider using an electronic payment service or sending an international money order rather than making a wire transfer.*

# Meeting eBay Members Around the World

Just as you can find unusual merchandise from around the globe on eBay, so too can you find people who can turn out to be just as valuable to you personally. Several of eBay's discussion boards and chat rooms have been set aside for members who want to discuss issues associated with trading globally. You can get help with translations or shipping questions, tips, and advice from experienced collectors who love the same things you do. Some suggestions for where to find overseas collectors are described in the following sections.

## Visiting the eBay International Trading Board

The International Trading discussion board (http://forums.ebay.com/db2/forum .jsp?forum=31) is the community area where eBay members from around the globe meet to discuss issues involved in trading internationally—or to simply meet one another and share stories about collecting in one another's respective countries.

The International Trading board is popular because it isn't available in every version of eBay around the world. Members in countries such as Australia or Switzerland are pointed to this board if they want to meet buyers and sellers from other lands. Some of the topics posted on this board are of passing interest ("I need advice on shipping to Australia"), while others are certain to be important to everyone, such as:

- Problems with wire transfers

- Whether a country uses only Euros or still uses lira/pounds/deutschemarks/ francs

- International shipping from the United States

- Languages and translation

When you participate on either this discussion board or one of those mentioned in the following section, keep in mind that you are not just representing yourself, but your country: try to avoid abusing or bad-mouthing other members or using profanity, for instance.

## Visiting Country-Specific Chat Rooms

Besides the International Trading board, which is intended for discussions about many different types of international trading, eBay also provides its users with country-specific chat rooms for the following countries:

- Australia Café: http://chatboards.ebay.com.au/chat.jsp?forum=1&thread=1

- Canada Board: http://chatboards.ebay.ca/chat.jsp?forum=1&thread=1

- eBay Deutschland Café: http://chatboards.ebay.de/ chat.jsp?forum=1&thread=3

- United Kingdom Board: http://chatboards.ebay.co.uk/ chat.jsp?forum=1&thread=1

Discussions in these chat rooms tend to be more casual, brief, and not nearly as serious as in the International Trading board. But they're a terrific place to have fun conversations and just gab with like-minded individuals living thousands of miles away.

TIP   *Many of the international eBay sites have their own discussion boards, where you are sure to meet buyers and sellers from that particular country or region. Go to the country's site, and click the Community link in the eBay toolbar of any international site.*

Anecdotal evidence gleaned from the eBay Global Trading message boards indicates that some countries (for instance, Indonesia) are more prone to fraudulent sales than others. Check out the boards before you say you'll accept shipments from everywhere in the world.

Do not take chances with international buyers who want to pay with a credit card. I recently heard about an eBay seller who received a winning bid for a laptop computer from a buyer in the Middle East. The buyer asked the seller to supply him with five additional computers to be resold in the buyer's retail computer store. A premium of $200 per unit was offered because that model was not available in the buyer's country. Payment was by credit card. The happy seller charged the buyer's card, went to CompUSA and bought the additional laptops, and shipped by FedEx. Everything was great until three weeks later, when the bank attempted to retrieve the funds that had been charged on a stolen card number. That particular seller is no longer offering items on eBay. Don't let a crook take you.

## Links for Collectors

| Web Site | Address | What's There |
| --- | --- | --- |
| The International Trading discussion board | http://forums.ebay.com/db1/forum.jsp?forum=31 | Discussion board devoted to tips and problems associated with selling or buying overseas |
| eBay's International Trading web page | http://pages.ebay.com/internationaltrading | A welcome page devoted to users who are interested in buying or selling overseas |
| United Parcel Service online rate calculator | http://www.servicecenter.ups.com/ebay/ebay.html#qcost | An online form for calculating rates for international shipments |
| Babel Fish | http://babelfish.altavista.com | Online translation form |
| eBay's Time Zone Conversion page | http://pages.ebay.com/internationaltrading/timezones.html | A table listing differences in hours, between Pacific time and other time zones around the world |

# Chapter 7

## Buying at Live Auctions

## In This Chapter You'll Learn...

■ How eBay's live auctions differ from conventional eBay auctions

■ How to register and bid, either on an absentee basis or in real time

■ How to research sellers and collectible items and be aware of extra charges you'll have to pay

■ Where to find other high-demand "premium" collectibles on eBay

If you feel the "need for speed" and are in love with the thrill of an auction's end, you need to explore a part of eBay that is easily overlooked—live auctions. eBay Live Auctions is the part of eBay's web site where sales at least loosely resemble those conducted in traditional auction houses like Sotheby's and Christie's.

eBay Live Auctions has its own system of conducting sales as well as a vocabulary that's much different than the rest of eBay. It's a terrific place to find precious objects you don't often (or ever) see on the rest of eBay, such as art and jewelry associated with a celebrity or other public figure, objects that illustrate the history of America, rare coins, or fine jewelry. This chapter will explain the system and help you get started with what can be a very rewarding place to shop for treasures.

# Collecting at Live Auctions

eBay's regular auctions are becoming more crowded all the time. But live auctions aren't as crowded, and therefore you stand a better chance of finding what you've been looking for. Best of all, they give you the feel of live bidding from the comfort of your own home.

There's a reason why live auctions on eBay aren't always marked by competition. They require more work than standard or reserve auctions, and there are extra charges you might not incur elsewhere. Live auctions are used by professional antiques dealers, auction houses, and other sellers. Often, sellers put the contents of an estate up all at once, because they can be sold in their entirety in a single day. Before you start shopping at a live auction, you have to do some browsing for what you collect, as described in the sections that follow.

## Trade Talk

If you want to sell rather than buy at Live Auctions, the added complexity means that you might want to consign some of your merchandise to a Live Auction dealer rather than going through the application process and learning to run such a sale yourself. If you do want to consign, make sure you get adequate background on the level of experience of your chosen seller. If possible, get references, and talk to them personally, either by e-mail or on the phone. Get all the seller's fees spelled out in advance. (You might encounter "hidden" or unexpected fees for photography, appraisal, insurance, and the like.) Make sure you get a written contract from the consignment seller spelling out all the fees that apply.

Be wary of a Live Auction seller whose representative entices you to allow them to auction your collection without a reserve or a high opening bid. Sometimes this strategy produces spectacular results, but there have been many instances where consignors were heavily disappointed when they received their checks from the auction company. See Chapter 10 for more on selling at Live Auctions.

**7**

## Lots of Catalogs, and Lots of Lots

eBay Live Auctions uses a different type of jargon than other parts of eBay. First of all, many different live auctions are held at predetermined times. Some live sales are conducted by auction houses and professional art dealers; others are run by individual antiques store owners. Each live auction event contains a group of items to be sold, which is called a *catalog*. Each listing in the catalog is designated by the old-style auction term *lot*. Items are sold one after another in rapid succession. Unless you place an absentee bid beforehand, you have only a matter of minutes or even seconds to bid on the collectible you want. But you know instantly whether or not you're the winner.

The differences between standard, or reserve, auctions on eBay and live auctions are shown in Table 7-1.

## Searching Through Lots

eBay's live auctions have many advantages for collectors. You can shop at leisure, bid without encountering sniping or the heated competition that is found in many

| Feature | eBay Auction | Live Auction |
|---|---|---|
| What is auctioned | Individual or multiple items | Lots, which may be a single items or a group of items |
| Seller | Any individual or business | Auction houses or dealers in art or collectibles |
| Buyer | Any eBay member | Any eBay member who has signed up for the live auction |
| Type of bids | Bids are accepted when placed | Bids are either made on an absentee basis or live |
| Cost to winner | Winning bid, shipping, insurance, sales tax | Same costs as for standard auction, plus buyer's premium |

**TABLE 7-1**   Differences Between Live and Traditional eBay Auctions

traditional eBay auctions, and you get instant results. However, searching for live auction merchandise is a separate process from using Basic Search or Advanced Search to look through traditional eBay sales listings. You have to go to the Live Auctions area and browse or search through the events that are going on currently or that are planned for the near future.

Let's say you have been looking for a long time for a Heywood-Wakefield dresser to go with your other Heywood-Wakefield furniture. It's easy to check out Live Auctions so you can see how the sales process works and see if there is anything you want. But you have to be careful with how you conduct your search, or you might miss some items of interest. Just follow these steps:

1. Go to the Live Auctions site by going directly to http://www.ebayliveauctions .com or by clicking Live Auctions from the eBay home page or the site map. The eBay Live Auctions home page appears (see Figure 7-1).

2. Browse or search. To look for something specific on eBay Live Auctions, you don't have to sign up. You can browse by doing one of three things:

   ■ Click one of the top-level categories listed on the left-hand side of the Live Auctions home page, and then click subcategory links until you find the item you want. However, this can force you to browse through dozens of pages, which is very time-consuming.

   ■ Enter a keyword or phrase in the Search Live Auctions box near the top of the page and click the Find It button. Then skim the live auction listings and see if one interests you. But note that the search box searches only titles, not descriptions, so if your spelling doesn't exactly match the auction lot's title, you'll miss it.

■ Click Search in the eBay Live Auctions toolbar and use the Advanced Search utility.

For some reason, searching on Live Auctions is trickier than on the rest of eBay. If you are really serious about finding something, I recommend trying all the alternatives or just skipping to the third option, Advanced Search, which usually yields the best results. The following sections discuss each of these alternatives in turn.

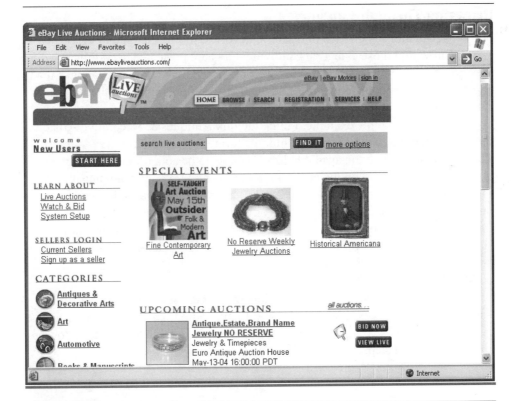

**FIGURE 7-1**    eBay Live Auctions can be a good place to uncover fine collectibles.

7

## Using the Search Box

For this example, I enter the words "Heywood-Wakefield" in the Search Live Auctions box (without the quotation marks, of course), and then click Find It. I get a search results page that says no items were found. This doesn't deter me, however. I know there are many possible ways to spell Heywood-Wakefield, and if my search terms don't match what's in the title, I won't turn up anything. I go on to the next option: browsing.

TIP    *You can combine search terms using commas or other operators, just as you can in the search boxes on the rest of eBay. But you can't save your searches and reuse them, as you can using My eBay. See Chapter 5 for more information on creating complex searches.*

## Browsing Through Categories

eBay Live Auctions is divided into sales categories, just as the regular eBay web site is. But within those categories, individual lots are presented according to when they go on sale. Since any given sale can contain hundreds of lots, it can take many pages' worth of listings before you find what you are looking for, if the first sales catalog presented does not have what you want.

To browse using this example, I click the link Antiques & Decorative Arts on the home page (there is no top-level link for furniture), then Furniture: American. Then I browse through the available lots. The lots to be sold on the first page are all scheduled to be sold by the auction house GoAntiques.com at an unusual time: 6 A.M. Pacific time on May 13, 2004. I mention this because it points up a problem with browsing through listings on Live Auctions. The contents of the first upcoming sale are listed first. Since GoAntiques.com does not have any Heywood-Wakefield furniture in its catalog for this particular sale, I have to go through three pages of listings until I find the next catalog, which is for a sale on May 15 (see Figure 7-2).

The problem is that I don't see any lots in the next several pages' worth of listings that say Heywood-Wakefield, and I have more than 10 pages to browse through (furniture is very popular on Live Auctions). I decide to abandon browsing and go to the next step: Advanced Search.

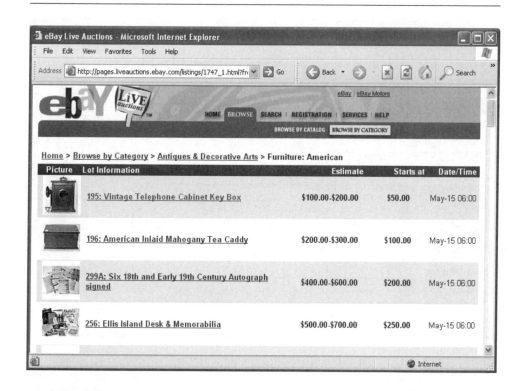

**FIGURE 7-2**   It can be time-consuming to browse through lengthy catalogs.

## Fine-Tuning Live Auction Searches

You get the most precise control over searches on Live Auctions when you use the Advanced Search function. To get to Advanced Search, I click the Search link in the toolbar (which includes the links Home, Browse, Search, Registration, Services, Help) near the top of nearly every eBay Live Auctions page. As you can see from Figure 7-3, the search page that appears enables you to search individual lots by title. A separate box enables you to restrict your search by catalog. There may be so many catalogs listed that you may want to narrow your search to only those sales focusing on jewelry or fine art, for instance.

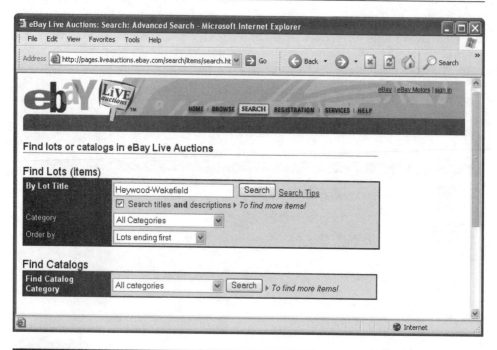

**FIGURE 7-3**    Advanced Search lets you search through individual lots or types of catalogs.

When I first enter the keywords "Heywood-Wakefield" in the By Lot Title box, I don't get any results, even when I check the Search Titles and Descriptions check box. But when I shorten the search terms to the single word "Wakefield," I come up with the results shown in Figure 7-4.

It took four tries, and I only came up with five search results, but it turned out that two of those five were indeed Heywood-Wakefield furnishings, and they were going on sale the following day. I didn't find them earlier because the sellers didn't put the hyphen between Heywood and Wakefield.

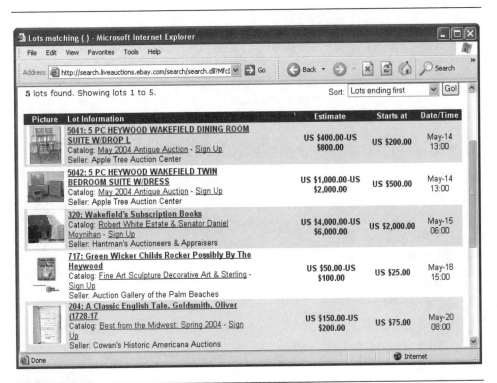

FIGURE 7-4    You may need to try different spellings to find a title match on eBay Live Auctions.

TIP

*Some of the larger companies that sell at Live Auctions produce paper catalogs to more fully describe the items being offered. Such catalogs often become collectors' items themselves. If you do get an auction catalog, don't dispose of it when the auction ends. It could be a desirable item in the not-too-distant future. It can also be a valuable reference tool in determining evaluations for items that you wish to sell on eBay.*

## Trade Talk

The eBay Live Auctions home page lists a half-dozen or so upcoming auctions. But these are by no means the only ones scheduled. If you click on the tiny link "All Auctions…" just above the list of featured auctions, you view a page that lists all the auctions scheduled; when I checked, there were more than 50. Any auctions that are currently being held live have a small paddle icon next to them. In the following illustration, the first sale listed is currently accepting bids on its lots.

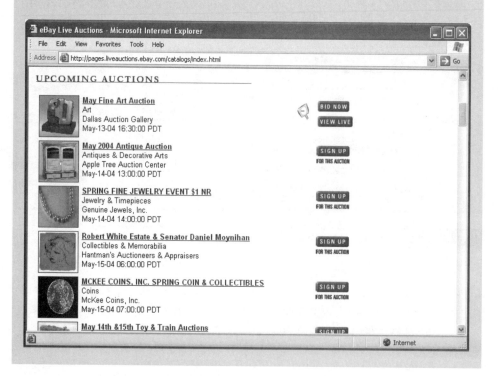

# Bidding in Real (or Almost-Real) Time

Once you find something on Live Auctions, you can place a bid. If the sale isn't "live" as yet, you can place an *absentee bid*. Otherwise, you can make a point of being present when the sale is held and wait for the item or items you are interested in. It's a good idea to watch a few sales before you start to participate in one, as described in the section that follows.

# Watching a Live Auction

It's fascinating, if a bit bewildering, to connect to the site and watch auction lots being put up for auction, one by one. Follow these steps to watch a sale as it occurs:

1.  When a sale is currently going on, click View Live. A page entitled "Auction in Process: View Live" appears (see Figure 7-5), listing viewing requirements for the sale.

2.  Read the requirements, and then click View Live Now. A separate browser window opens.

3.  Wait for the viewing page to appear. The Live Auctions site uses a Java applet to display items and refresh them when bids are received or when each sale ends. It might take a minute or more for the applet to execute and

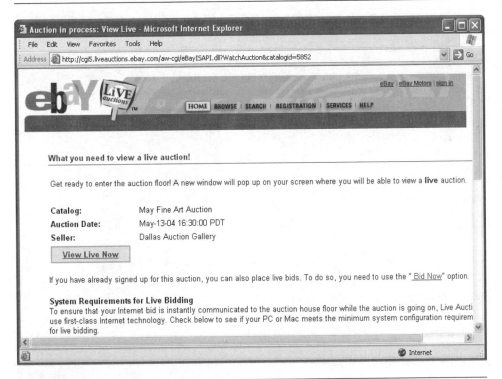

**FIGURE 7-5**    Read this page to make sure you meet the system requirements needed to take part in live sales.

begin displaying images. If it doesn't work, make sure your computer meets the minimum requirements for using live auctions.

4. Watch the sales go by. In a sales lot that contains hundreds of separate items, each item is sold with amazing speed.

Often, sales end without any bids. Occasionally, someone who placed an absentee bid in advance turns out to be the winner. On other occasions, bidders in a real-world auction house such as Sotheby's compete against cyberbidders like you for items. Even if you don't compete, it's exciting to watch the action, especially when bids climb high. Sometimes, you'll see a series of bids come in from the "auction house floor" (see Figure 7-6). This is the physical location where the sale is being held. You'll also see an "Internet bidder" place a bid

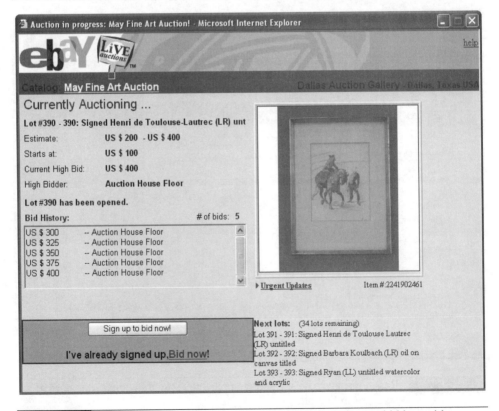

FIGURE 7-6    Bidders in the auction house compete against Internet bidders with lightning speed.

from time to time. Of course, it's even better when you see something you want and there are no bids or when the current bids are within your price range. The thing that takes some getting used to is the speed of the bidding: in less than a minute, the sale is over and the next lot is up for sale.

*The speed with which bids are posted in live auctions means that a broadband connection is a must have. A slow or intermittent dialup connection to the Internet can easily result in lost auctions.*

## Placing a Live Bid

A greater level of control is exerted by the sellers in eBay Live Auctions than in regular eBay. For one thing, you have to register yourself with the seller beforehand in order to place a bid. It's a good idea to do this well before the sale begins (at least a day, so you can be reasonably sure your registration is received) by clicking the Sign Up for This Auction button next to the sale's description. If a sale is currently going on live, you click the button Sign Up to Bid Now! that appears at the bottom of the Auction in Progress window. When you do so, the Welcome to Live Auctions page appears. It is virtually identical to the Sign In page used on the rest of eBay. Enter your eBay user ID and password, and click Sign In. The Live Auctions Registration page appears (see Figure 7-7).

It's tempting to skim through the terms and conditions of the sale quickly, especially if the sale is still going on live, but take some time to read them. At the very least, skip down to the section where the *premium* or *buyer's premium* is mentioned. This is an extra fee you will be charged if you are the high bidder, and it can be substantial. For the fine art sale shown in Figure 7-7, the premium was 12 percent for conventional bidders and 17 percent for those bidding on the Internet. That means that, if you are the high bidder at, say, $500, you will actually end up paying $585 for what you have purchased—and that does not include shipping charges or sales tax, if applicable.

When you have read the terms, check the box next to "I have read the terms and conditions of sale above and accept them." Then click Continue. Next, a Live Auctions user agreement appears. I suggest that you read this bit of legalese carefully, too. When you are done, check the box next to "I have read the User Agreement and accept all of its terms and conditions." Then click Submit.

Next, an eBay Bidder Approval page appears (see Figure 7-8). This is a page created by the auction house that is running the sale, in which the seller solicits your name and contact information as well as an assurance that you will follow through with payment if you actually win something—namely, your credit card

7

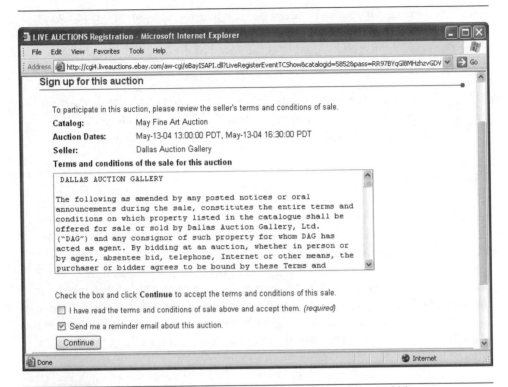

**FIGURE 7-7**      Read the terms of the sale carefully before deciding to bid.

information. Fill out this form and then Submit. Now you can finally begin to bid on items offered by this seller.

There is a good side to all the requirements and the registration process: it's likely to scare off many bidders. You are left with bidders who are truly serious and likely to be knowledgeable about what's being sold. Be sure to do your research beforehand so you know how much to bid and don't get carried away by competition and the hurried atmosphere in which bidding takes place.

TIP      *As you can tell by now, it's a good idea to register well before the sale actually begins. The registration process takes several minutes, and if you don't give yourself enough time, you'll miss the lots in which you are interested.*

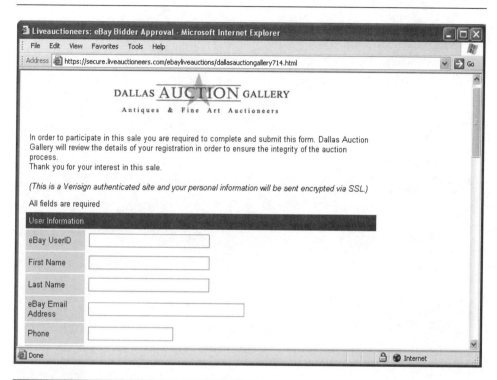

**FIGURE 7-8**    You need to submit contact and credit card information before you can bid.

## Placing an Absentee Bid

Live auctions on eBay are conducted so quickly that it might actually be impractical to bid while the sale is going on. For a "live" bid to work, you might have to wait an hour or more for the lot you are interested in to come up for sale. When it does, you have to act quickly, or you could well miss the sale. In case you can't be present at a computer during the actual sale, you can place an absentee bid.

Absentee bids can be submitted up to one hour before the live auction starts. When the auction starts, eBay calculates the absentee bids. If someone else has submitted an absentee bid that's higher than your initial bid, eBay places bids for you on a proxy basis until your maximum bid is reached. (Visit http://pages .liveauctions.ebay.com/help/before/laabsentee.html to find out more about how the

## Collecting Step-by-Step

Placing an absentee bid is easy: First, you find something you want. Then you register for the auction. Then you place the bid. Assuming you have located something, either by searching or by browsing and that you have signed up, you can follow these steps:

1. Click the title of the auction you are interested in. The auction page appears, as shown here.

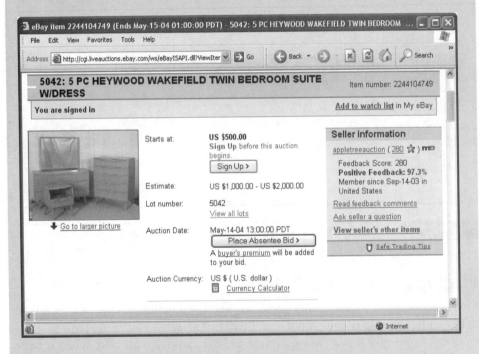

2. Scroll down to the bottom section of the auction description and read the terms of the sale. You find out who is selling the item, what the buyer's premium is, how much sales tax you have to pay, and how to handle shipping.

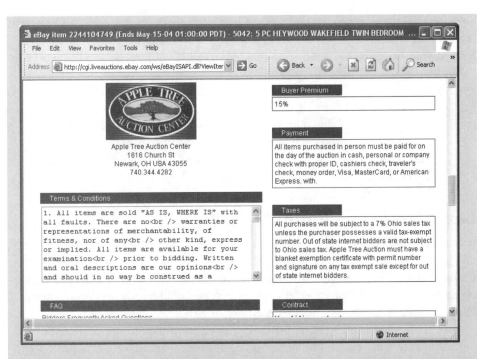

Screenshot content:

eBay item 2244104749 (Ends May-15-04 01:00:00 PDT) - 5042: 5 PC HEYWOOD WAKEFIELD TWIN BEDROOM ...

File   Edit   View   Favorites   Tools   Help

Address   http://cgi.liveauctions.ebay.com/ws/eBayISAPI.dll?ViewIter   Go    Back   Search

Apple Tree Auction Center
1616 Church St
Newark, OH USA 43055
740.344.4282

**Buyer Premium**
15%

**Payment**
All items purchased in person must be paid for on the day of the auction in cash, personal or company check with proper ID, cashiers check, traveler's check, money order, Visa, MasterCard, or American Express. with.

**Terms & Conditions**
1. All items are sold "AS IS, WHERE IS" with all faults. There are no<br /> warranties or representations of merchantability, of fitness, nor of any<br /> other kind, express or implied. All items are available for your examination<br /> prior to bidding. Written and oral descriptions are our opinions<br /> and should in no way be construed as a

**Taxes**
All purchases will be subject to a 7% Ohio sales tax unless the purchaser possesses a valid tax-exempt number. Out of state internet bidders are not subject to Ohio sales tax. Apple Tree Auction must have a blanket exemption certificate with permit number and signature on any tax exempt sale except for out of state internet bidders.

**FAQ**
Bidders Frequently Asked Questions

**Contract**

Internet

**3.** Calculate the total cost of the sale. Add in not only your bid but the premium and the sales tax. Make sure you understand exactly how much you're going to pay.

> **TIP** *It's also a good idea to calculate shipping costs. You can do so using one of the shipping calculators described in Chapter 11.*

**4.** Scroll down to the section of the page labeled Place Absentee Bid. Enter the amount of your bid, then click Place Absentee Bid. Your bid must be equal to or higher than the starting bid. You then view a page on which you review and confirm your bid. Click Continue to place the absentee bid.

absentee bid process works.) When the live auction starts, the high absentee bid is shown as an "Internet bid." Others participating in the live auction can then bid against your absentee bid—but if no one bids against your maximum bid, you win.

 *To participate in live auctions, you need a computer with a central processing unit running at 350 MHz or higher; at least 64MB of RAM; Windows 95 or later, and Internet Explorer 4.01 or Netscape 4.03 or later. You can use a 56 Kbps modem to connect to the Internet, but a cable modem or DSL connection is preferable. Macintosh and Linux users cannot place live bids; they must place absentee bids.*

## Being Aware of Additional Costs

As stated before, almost all sellers on eBay Live Auctions charge successful bidders a buyer's premium. For collectors who are used to shopping on regular eBay sales, the buyer's premium can come as a surprise. The premium is an additional percentage on each item sold. For example, if there is a 15 percent buyer's premium and the hammer price is $1000, the buyer's premium is $150.

Local sales tax is charged by virtually all sellers as well to out-of-state buyers, unless you are a tax-exempt organization or individual and have a certificate to prove it, or have a reseller's license. Sales tax is charged after the buyer's premium is added on. For example, if the local sales tax is 7 percent and your winning bid is $1000, you end up paying $1150 plus $80.50 sales tax, or a total of $1230.50.

 *Any bids you have placed are tracked in your My eBay page, just like sales on the rest of eBay. You can use My eBay to "watch" sales in eBay Live Auctions or keep a record of completed transactions.*

# Researching Items and Sellers

Sellers who offer objects of value on eBay Live Auctions can generally be trusted to behave in a reputable manner and to follow through with transactions because that is what they do for a living. In order to sell on eBay Live Auctions, an auction house or dealer has to go through an application process. They have to submit contact information for their company as well as the company's logo and a description of the types of items they usually sell.

The same feedback system used in the rest of eBay is in effect in eBay Live Auctions. To investigate a seller's previous transactions, click the feedback number next to his or her user ID in the Seller Information box. You go to the member's Feedback Profile page, where you can scan the comments left by previous buyers.

Because they are professional businesspeople, many Live Auctions sellers have their own About Me pages as well as their own web sites. Click the Me icon next to the user ID to view the About Me page. Often, the About Me page will provide you with a brief profile of the seller as well as a link to the company's web site. The seller shown in Figure 7-9 has such a link, along with the information at the top of the About Me page.

While it's true that you aren't likely to find out about buyer complaints or failed transactions on the seller's own web page, you can find out valuable information that can help you decide whether to invest your money in something the company is selling. You might discover that the company has been in business for a long time or that they have a knowledgeable staff of appraisers you can call or e-mail for more information. You also might find out about other sales they are conducting that may or may not involve eBay.

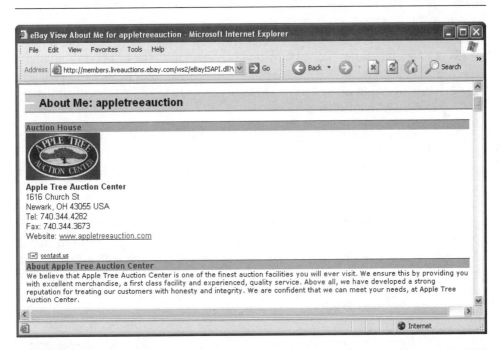

FIGURE 7-9   You can find out about most Live Auctions sellers on their own web pages.

# Other Options for High-End Collecting

eBay Live Auctions is one of the best places around to locate fine art, furniture, and other valuable collectibles. But you can also find high-end objects in the rest of eBay, too. You won't have to pay a buyer's premium, and you might not have to pay sales tax, either (depending on the seller's policy and whether or not you live in the same state as the seller). Some other options for locating valuable and rare items are described below.

## Big Ticket Items

For most collectors, the Big Ticket Items category isn't the place to do any sort of everyday shopping. You won't find any bargains here. Just to get listed, the starting bid or the current high bid must be $5000 or more. But that means this is the place to go if you collect exotic autos or expensive watches or other jewelry. Even if you don't, Big Ticket Items is a great place for daydreaming about all the luxury items you see there. You might even find some humorous items. I've seen the following for sale in this category:

- An auction for the phone number (212) 867-5309. The last seven digits of this phone number were made famous in a pop song. The sale attracted lots of attention in the media and spawned many copycat sales of similar numbers with different area codes.

- The entire country of Iraq. Vice President Dick Cheney was depicted as offering governing rights to Iraq (see Figure 7-10). The sale made it into this category because 29 eager bidders placed bids of up to $99,999,999 for the honor.

Once in a while, of course, you'll find a real collectible in Big Ticket Items. If you collect very expensive watches, this is a good place to go. On a random visit, I discovered a men's 18 karat gold Patek Philippe calendar watch with a starting bid of $21,900. If you collect exotic cars, you can practically always find one on this page, such as the Lamborghini Diablo VT Roadster with a starting bid of $155,000 that I spotted and sighed over.

 *Big Ticket Items isn't that easy to find. You can only get there by clicking Big Ticket in the site map, or by going directly to http://pages.ebay.com/ buy/bigticket/index.html.*

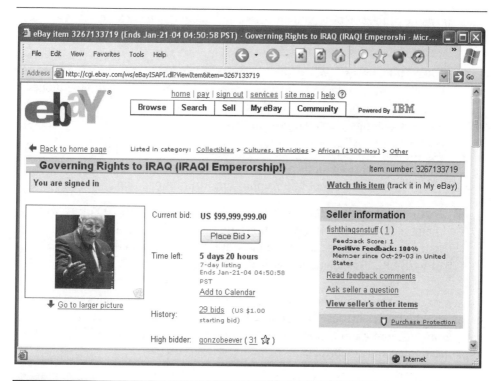

FIGURE 7-10   You might find collectors' items here, but mostly this section is for dreams and humorous auctions.

## Celebrity Auctions

Many television and movie stars and other public figures auction off collectible and valuable merchandise on eBay to benefit charitable causes. As I was working on this chapter, talk show host Ellen DeGeneres just announced that she was putting her $15,000-plus diamond wristwatch up for auction on eBay. The proceeds would go to benefit a charity of her choice. You won't find out about such sales on eBay auctions. In fact, celebrity auctions on eBay aren't as easy to find as they once were. Well-known entertainment figures used to have their auctions advertised on eBay's home page occasionally; I haven't seen such advertisements for a while.

One way to find celebrity auctions is to search for "celebrity auction eBay" on the search service Google (http://www.google.com). You can also use eBay's own Basic Search or Advanced Search and click the Search Titles and Descriptions box.

Enter the name of the celebrity you are interested in, and then click Search. Here are a few celebrities who often sell on eBay:

- **Ellen DeGeneres**   When she holds charity auctions that she advertises on her TV show, she doesn't always use the same user ID. The aforementioned watch was sold under the user ID kompolt-for-ellen, but it had 0 feedback and was obviously created just for this sale.

- **Jimmy Buffett**   The singer's Virtual Parrot Head Club (http://vphc.com) sometimes holds auctions on eBay. If an auction is currently being held, you'll find a link to it at http://vphc.com/forum/index.php.

- **Rosie O'Donnell**   Her For All Kids Foundation operates on eBay with the user ID 4allkids. If any auctions are being held, you'll find them listed on the group's About Me page at http://members.ebay.com/ws2/eBayISAPI.dll?ViewUserPage&userid=4allkids.

A search for the term "charity auction" will turn up plenty of sales that may or may not be by celebrities. The Entertainment Memorabilia category (http://entertainment-memorabilia.ebay.com) is a good place to find collectibles relating to public figures and celebrities.

## Links for Collectors

| Web Site | Address | What's There |
|---|---|---|
| eBay Live Auctions | http://www.ebayliveauctions.com | A part of eBay where professional dealers auction off merchandise live; auction house bidders compete with Internet bidders |
| Live Auctions Advanced Search | http://pages.liveauctions.ebay.com/search/items/search.html | A form that lets you search current lots for sale as well as entire catalogs |
| Big Ticket Items | http://pages.ebay.com/buy/bigticket/index.html | A group of sales items with a starting or current bid of $5,000 or more |

# Part III

# Selling Collectibles

# Chapter 8

# Images, Presentation, and Marketing

## In This Chapter You'll Learn…

■ How to provide the details and credibility that collectors crave in auction descriptions

■ How to write sales descriptions that engage a collector's imagination

■ Ways to use images to build interest and accurately describe an item's condition

■ How to create eye-catching designs that complement your merchandise

■ Ways of marketing yourself and your sales with a web site

You probably already know from your own buying and shopping on eBay what makes a good auction description. It can be summed up in a simple sentence: Include as many details as needed to induce bids and complete transactions. What does that mean, exactly? It means that you provide all the information you can about an object, and that you make sure there are plenty of clear photos including close-ups, if needed. Good descriptions and photos have a direct bearing on whether an item—a "collectible" or a run-of-the-mill household staple like a coffeemaker—gets bids and finds buyers.

Good auction descriptions are always important, no matter what you're selling. But some requirements are especially important when it comes to selling collectibles. In order to attract the attention of devoted and knowledgeable collectors, you need to provide all the information you can. You need to be conscious of the identifying markers and features that collectors are looking for, and you need to be up-front about condition. Marketing your auctions through keywords and advertising can also help your sale stand out from the crowd. This chapter examines how to create auction descriptions for the sales of your collectible items on eBay.

# Attracting Bids from Other Collectors

This book assumes you are a collector, just like the bidders or buyers you want to attract. Accordingly, chances are your primary goal as a seller is to make money from what you collect, so you can buy more collectibles. To do this, you need to attract bids from as many other collectors as possible. Your first task, then, is an easy one: build on what you already know—think like the collector you are. What do *you* like to see when you browse for the objects you want? What makes you click the Place Bid or Buy It Now button? Some suggestions are presented in the sections that follow.

## Details, Details

On television, images sell. On radio, catchy slogans sell. On the Internet—in a way that is perhaps unique to all media—information sells. The more you can say about a sales item, the more likely you'll generate interest in it. As a collector-seller, you have an advantage: you can draw upon your enthusiasm for what you collect and your past experience to create descriptions that attract bids.

The most knowledgeable sellers try to create descriptions that engage the viewer's imagination. They induce viewers to imagine what that pair of gloves might feel like, or how they might use that automatic juicer, or how that old Ford Thunderbird would look in their driveway. They tell stories about how they found the item or how they found the identifying trademark, because they know these are exactly the kinds of things collectors love to hear. Remember, there is no length limit for auction descriptions on eBay. You should try to keep your description from stretching more than, say, two computer screens in length, just so you don't overwhelm prospective customers. But don't be reluctant to tell a story, either.

In my book *How to Do Everything with eBay,* I described an auction entitled "Uncle Bob's Glass Eye." The seller told a long story about the glass eye he was selling, which his uncle was issued after losing an eye while serving in World War II. It seems Uncle Bob left the eye to his nephew in his will. The seller-raconteur was able to sell the glass eye on eBay.

## Prove Your Knowledge and Trustworthiness

Whether they are obsessive collectors or casual shoppers, people on eBay need the same sorts of things. They want to trust you. They want to feel that they can rely on you more than all of those other sellers that populate eBay's auction listings. They also want to feel sure they'll get what they have purchased, quickly and in good condition. Above all, they are looking for a bargain. To some extent, you can't control whether they get a bargain or not. You put an item up for no reserve, or you set a modest reserve, and the market takes care of the rest.

You can, however, control how much trust your bidders can place in you. In many professions, service providers go to school to add some significant letters to their names, such as Ph.D., M.D., J.D., or C.P.A. You can do the same in auction sales. You can become a licensed auctioneer through the National Auctioneers Association (http://www.auctioneers.org/becomeAuctioneer), like one eBay seller

I know. But you don't have to go that far yourself; you can demonstrate that you know something about what you're selling by

- ■ Operating a web site or online store devoted to your area of interest. Chris Byrne calls himself the Toy Guy, for instance (http://www.thetoyguy.com/About.html).

- ■ Moderating a discussion group (popularly called a newsgroup) devoted to what you buy or sell. It's relatively easy to set up a newsgroup in the Alt category (groups in other areas are more difficult to establish and maintain). Microsoft FrontPage software can help you set up a discussion group on your own web site.

- ■ Answering questions in Internet newsgroups about your area of interest.

- ■ Contributing articles or pricing information to the collectors' price guide that covers your area of interest.

- ■ Answering questions on eBay's message boards or other eBay venues. Jeff Francis is an eBay seller and also the curator of the Piccadilly Museum of Transportation Memorabilia and Advertising Art in Montana (http://www .piccadillymuseum.com; shown here). He boosted his reputation by writing an essay for eBay's Seller Newsflash newsletter; see http://pages.ebay.com/collectiblesnewsletter/Mar03_sub.html.

If you have written any essays or books about the type of merchandise you typically sell, so much the better. Even if you don't do any of the foregoing, you can still create an About Me web page that tells visitors something about you and what you do and your commitment to customer service. E. S. James's About Me page (see Figure 8-1 and http://members.ebay.com/ws2/eBayISAPI .dll?ViewUserPage&userid=aglimpseofthepast.net) promotes her qualifications as a dealer in antiques and depicts some of the items she has sold on eBay (as well as those that didn't sell, and one that she'll never sell). See "Creating an About Me Page," later in this chapter, for more.

## Prove You Are a Professional

You can boost your sales if you are able to show people that you are professional in your manners and your behavior. Being professional doesn't mean you need to sell on eBay full time or that you need to run your own online business. Rather, it

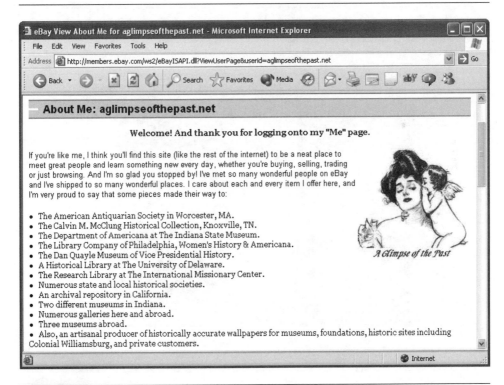

**FIGURE 8-1**   An About Me page can be used to build your credibility as an eBay businessperson.

has to do with how you communicate: how quickly and completely you respond to questions from bidders, how well you deal with problems, and how promptly and carefully you pack and ship what you sell.

## Maker's Marks and Other Identifiers

Signatures and maker's marks are among the most important things you should depict and describe in auction descriptions when you are selling collectibles. Make sure your digital camera or conventional camera is able to take sharp close-ups that can clearly show such marks. Most good-quality digital cameras have a close-up (or *macro*) function built in to the device. A few require you to purchase separate macro lenses or attachments. With such a lens, you can take photos like the ones shown in Figure 8-2. Make sure you photograph as many of the marks as you can find, and from several angles if necessary. Be sure to get a close-up as well, especially if you are selling a signed photograph.

FIGURE 8-2    Be sure to include clear close-ups of maker's marks, trademarks, and model or serial numbers with your sales listings.

If you don't recognize the mark that is on an item, ask about it on the discussion forums or in the Answer Center. In Figure 8-3, you see a question about a mark on a ceramic figure of a puppy that was immediately answered by another eBay member.

## Condition: Critical

Used car salesmen are notorious for concealing leaks, cracks, or other flaws in the vehicles they attempt to sell. In the real world, they might find some gullible customers they can take in, especially if those customers simply wander onto the car lot without doing any research. On eBay, buyers are drastically different. For instance, consider cars: Often, the people looking for used cars on eBay are collectors. Collectors will know everything about what they want to buy. They know what parts tend to rust out, what parts of the trim tend to break or fall off, and exactly how unscrupulous sellers attempt to conceal flaws.

8

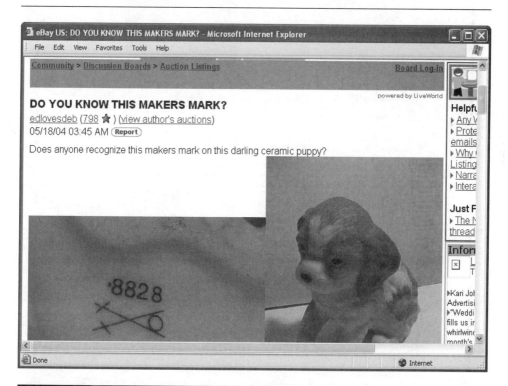

**FIGURE 8-3**   Be sure you correctly identify maker's marks; if you're wrong, you'll look untrustworthy to knowledgeable collectors.

Honesty is definitely the best policy when it comes to selling on eBay. At the very least, it lets buyers know about any defects or flaws your merchandise has before they even bid, so they won't be surprised when they actually receive what they've purchased. Accuracy shows your customers that you are making every effort to be honest and up-front with them. It also encourages repeat buyers, which will ensure that you have long-term business. Some sellers go into lengthy detail about defects in their sales items, especially for items that they know are desirable in and of themselves. The description shown in Figure 8-4 is honest about defects

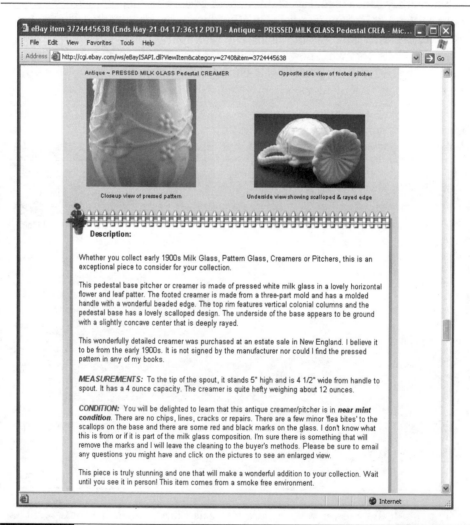

FIGURE 8-4    Be honest about defects, but don't forget to play up the good points, too.

such as "flea bites" in the pitcher shown, but the experienced seller also plays up the fact that the pitcher is in exceptionally good condition.

# Writing a Winning Description

The more information you include with your auction descriptions, the more likely you are to make a sale. That doesn't mean you have to spend acres of valuable computer-screen real estate getting to the point. You need to state, in the very first sentence, what you are selling and what qualities make this item stand out from the crowd. Be sure to mention if it is a one-of-a-kind piece, in perfect condition, or in a rare color. Try to get a one- or two-word mention of the item's most desirable quality in the auction title, if you can.

Auction bidders are in a hurry. They might stop in at your sale for only a short period of time before moving on to your competitors' wares. Suppose you're trying to sell something that might not seem desirable at first, like a pair of used sneakers. How, you ask, could you make sneakers seem attractive? Here are a few suggestions:

- **Write a good lead.** Hook your bidders' attention with some quick statements that show why your item is exceptional, such as, "Rare 1967 Chuck Taylor Converse All-Stars, Size 12." With 55 characters available in the title, you have an excellent opportunity to add in a few keywords that a collector might use when doing a search.

- **Provide some history.** Describe your item's provenance—which, in auction-speak, means the history or origin of an item. Tell where you got the object, how old it is, who used it, and so on: "This classic Gibson EB-0 bass, with the hard-to-find original pick guard, had only one owner—the seller's cousin. It has very little wear and even comes in the original hard case."

Not long ago, I found a platter made by the Stetson China Company in 1955. I wanted to see what it might be worth (not much), and I found a description of a similar platter by a seller who wrote a highly imaginative description. The seller created the title "Stetson Platter Is Cute But Such a Whiner. Please Adopt." The description began: "Older hand-painted platter says it's used to serving meals to large, happy gatherings, and wants that life again. Says its significant chips, stains, and wear marks had always been covered up by chicken grease or chocolate frosting before, so it really does not know how to cope with all its damn body-dysmorphia." (The word *dysmorphia,* according to an online medical dictionary, means "badness of form or shape.") The platter didn't sell for much—but it did sell.

8

## Accentuate the Positive

Just the other day, I was at a garage sale where one of my neighbors had some nice bicycles and a computer for sale. When I inquired about the items, he told me they were old, they needed repair, the bike tires needed replacing, and so on. All of this was obvious to me. It didn't affect my decision to buy or not (I bought the computer), but I wondered how many potential customers he turned off by being too negative.

Being honest doesn't mean you have to emphasize everything that is wrong with an object. Collectors, in particular, are knowledgeable enough that they can see from a glance, or can judge from their experience with similar items, just what sort of condition an item is in. But you'll still maximize your chances of getting bids if you make the following sales points:

- **Don't overlook the downside.** Once you've gotten everyone interested by gushing about the item's good points, be sure to avoid surprises or misunderstandings by describing any problems: "Although thoroughly dry cleaned, a subtle perfume odor remains. Some wear on right forearm; cuff buttons have been replaced."

- **Finish on a high note.** Don't end on a problem note; provide a closing sentence that reminds people why they should be buying this wonderful item. You might even provide a note about payment options or shipping costs, or restrictions (you don't take personal checks, or you won't ship overseas, for instance). Also try to end your descriptions with a reference to a price guide, such as: "Top price-guide value is $1000." Many collectors use the various price guides as a reference tool.

- **Don't make your terms too scary.** Often, the terms of sale tell you as much about a seller as the description. If the description is 1 or 2 sentences long and the terms of sale are 12 sentences long and filled with warnings and bad grammar, you might not want to buy from that person. What makes a terms of sale section scary are statements like the following:

  Serious Bidders Only!
  Have to contact seller within 48 hours!
  Only accept direct deposit and money order!
  I stress to leave your eBay item number for transfer description as items will not be dispatched if procedures are not followed.
  Let me do something to suit your needs. I will build your own combo if you wish!

Don't hesitate to ring me or send me an email!
Item picture could be changed without notice.

TIP    *You'll find more suggestions for writing good descriptions on the Auction Listings discussion board: http://forums.ebay.com/db1/ forum.jsp?forum=102.*

# Taking Good Images

Collectors who really know their stuff don't need long, detailed descriptions (though details can't hurt). They glance at the title and description. For them, a good series of photos is worth a thousand words.

For serious collectors, photos are perhaps the most important part of an auction listing—the part that produces inquiries, bids, and purchases. Photos can tell them just about everything they need to know: trademarks, model numbers, distinguishing features, and condition. Your job, as a seller of collectibles, is to include as many photos as necessary to fully illustrate what you have to sell.

I'm not going to go into every last technical detail about how to take and post photos on eBay. You can read my books *How to Do Everything with eBay* and *How to Do Everything with Your eBay Business* for that. Rather, I want to focus on the aspects of photos that apply to collectibles. The following sections present you with some suggestions.

## Find a Cheap Photo Host

You shouldn't have to worry about how much you are going to be charged to post photos of the collectibles you have to sell. Try to include three or four or more, if you can. eBay Picture Services is a convenient option. eBay provides all sellers with the ability to *upload* (a computer term that describes the process of moving a file from a computer to a server on a network) photos easily onto its own servers right from the Sell Your Item form. The form even gives you an interactive way to crop and reorient images (see Figure 8-5).

Many sellers choose not to use eBay Picture Services because it can be expensive: Suppose you put 25 items up for sale each week, and each sale has five photos. That's 125 photos, 100 of which cost a total of $15. Spread that over 50 weeks or so, and you've paid $750 annually to eBay for photo hosting.

You may already have an option available to you: storage space on a server where you can host your images. If you have an account with America Online, you

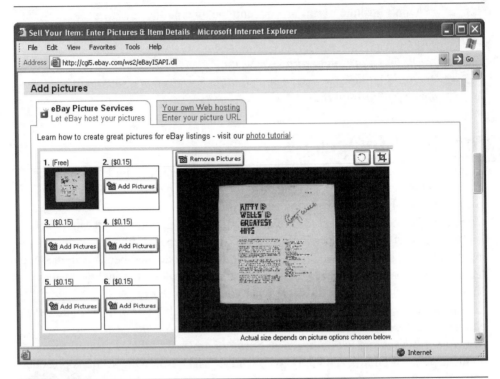

FIGURE 8-5
eBay Picture Services is convenient but charges 15 cents per photo after the first photo, which is free.

can create up to seven user names, and each of those user names is entitled to 2MB of space for web pages and photos. Virtually all ISPs provide web server space to their customers along with their Internet access. You don't have to pay anything for this storage space. Ask your ISP what's available to you.

**COLLECTOR'S NOTE** *A few web sites specialize in providing space where eBay and other auction users can publish auction images to accompany sales listings. Deadzoom.com (http://www.deadzoom.com) costs $5 per month for 10MB of server space, which is more than enough for hundreds of auction images. A few free services also exist. Auction-Images (http://auction-images.com) gives you 1MB of space for free. (eBay Motors images are not allowed on either of these sites, however.)*

## Include Multiple Photos

Once you have found a site where you can host your photos inexpensively, you can feel less reluctant to publish many different images of your merchandise. You have probably seen auction sales that include six or more photos of something, taken from different angles. Did you feel like you were seeing too many images? Chances are you scrolled through the images available and didn't get tired of looking at them.

TIP    *Be sure to include a gallery photo with your regular auction listing photos. Gallery photos are added to your auction titles when those titles are listed in search results or when people browse through categories in which your sales are listed. Gallery images cost an extra 25 cents, but they're worthwhile, if only because so many others include them: if you don't, your sale is less likely to get attention.*

8

## Provide Good Lighting and Presentation

Collectors like to inspect fine details. They want to know just how many cracks and blemishes there are before they bid. Give them all the help they need by lighting your merchandise adequately. Don't use normal incandescent house lamps to light your objects. Take them outside on a sunny day and let Mother Nature provide you with the lighting. Or go to the local hardware store and find some halogen work lights, which provide very bright and accurate light. Get at least two lights and point them at the object from different angles so you don't get shadows.

If you sell frequently on eBay, consider creating a small photo studio that includes a table or stand for your merchandise; several solid-colored blankets or cloths that you can put underneath and behind the objects being photographed; and mannequins or jewelry stands that will help you display the items professionally. A system that you can use repeatedly will help you if you sell the same kinds of things on a regular basis.

## Get a Good-Quality Camera

It took me a long time to realize that cheaper doesn't necessarily mean better. I purchased a digital camera for about $100 at the local pharmacy, but I got what I paid for: I don't use the device now because it produces images that are so poor in quality. It's worth spending some extra money to buy a really good camera.

You can find them inexpensively on eBay itself. You don't have to get a 6- or 7-megapixel version just for posting photos on eBay (3 or 4 megapixels is probably good enough), but if you do, you can use your digital camera for everyday family photography as well.

## Trade Talk

For digital images, resolution is usually described in terms of pixels per inch (ppi) or dots per inch (dpi). You've probably heard the term *megapixel* used to describe the quality of a digital camera. Megapixel means a million pixels. A camera that has a 5-megapixel capacity has the ability to squeeze 5 million pixels into a single image—a resolution so sharp that it rivals the quality of many single lens reflex (SLR) film cameras.

## Keep Your Images Small and Portable

Those digital cameras that take high-resolution photos are great if you plan to print out your own photos and save them in an album. But don't use the highest quality setting for your eBay photos. If you are selling books, magazines, or other printed materials, a scanner will work best. But you don't have to scan an image at the highest resolution available. When you take such an image and save it to disk, it can easily be 2MB or more in file size. For the Web, photos should ideally be 50K or less in size. That's a huge difference. If your photos are to be taken for the Web, take them at a low resolution.

You can reduce an image's file size by opening the image in a program like Adobe Photoshop Elements or Paint Shop Pro and editing it. The easiest form of editing is cropping: cutting out unnecessary details and keeping a certain area of the image on which you want to focus. It makes the image size smaller so that the photo fits better in a web browser window. By making the image smaller, you also make the file size smaller. An image that's, say, 12K appears onscreen much faster than one that's 100K.

In virtually every graphics program the process of cropping works the same: Click the cropping button. Position your mouse pointer just above and to one side of the image. Click and hold down your mouse button and drag your mouse to the opposite corner of the image. Release your mouse when the subject of your photo is outlined with the marquee box (see Figure 8-6).

**FIGURE 8-6**   Cropping is an easy and effective way to make an image smaller.

# Designing Your Description

When collectors hunt, they are in a hurry. I know when I hit an antiques mall or flea market, my eyes are darting all over the place. I barely pay attention to what's around me; I am looking for anything that vaguely resembles the type of collectible I happen to be interested in at the moment.

On eBay, collectors shop with the same sort of frenzy, but they don't have so many objects to peruse at a given time. They can only browse for sales on a page-by-page basis, and there may be "only" 20 or 30 sales listed in a page full of search results. Nevertheless, it's important for you to present your sale in such a way that it can be scanned quickly by eager shoppers. A description that is difficult to read in some way will turn shoppers off and possibly send them to another auction listing. Remember that there are always other listings on eBay at least a little bit similar to yours, and shoppers can click away from your sale and move to another description at any time.

## Avoid Obvious Turnoffs

Some of the qualities that make a description easy to read are well known to anyone who has worked in an editorial capacity. Of course, few of the sellers listing on eBay have such experience. You frequently see obvious mistakes that someone doing layout for a newspaper or magazine or for a printed book wouldn't allow. Here are some examples:

- **Don't center everything.** It's OK to center a line or two or even a short paragraph for emphasis, to make it stand out from the surrounding text. But some descriptions have every line centered, and this makes it far harder to read.

- **Don't use distracting backgrounds.** Once you learn a little bit of HTML, it's tempting to add background images to your auction descriptions. *Resist the temptation to do this.* A simple black or white background (black background with white type, or vice versa) is easier to read.

- **Don't use animations.** A few listings have been known to employ a little animated mouse that seems to follow your mouse pointer around the screen. These are among the most unpopular auction listing features around, and are sure to send a potential buyer hurrying off to another description for relief.

- **Don't overuse ALL CAPS.** A few capital letters go a long way. While it's okay to emphasize a word or two with caps, you occasionally see listings that are entirely in capital letters, which makes them especially difficult to read.

**WATCH OUT!** *It's not clear to me why anyone would want to include background music with an auction description, but it happens occasionally. It's a surefire way to turn off visitors and drive them to other people's sales: avoid background sounds at all costs.*

## Use a Template

You don't have to reinvent the wheel when you are creating auction descriptions on eBay. Instead, you can come up with a template for your auction sales. A template is a predesigned web page—not a complete web page, mind you, but the framework for a web page that you can fill in with your own content and customize to suit your needs. A template is commonly used to prepare a publication that appears periodically, such as a newspaper or a magazine. It's a preformatted set of items that appears the same from issue to issue. A template saves time, and it lets readers know what to expect. After a while, they use the standard elements in the template to process information more quickly.

A web site designed especially for those who buy and sell antiques, Antique Central, provides a set of eBay auction listing templates to its visitors at http://www.antique-central.com/tips1.html. As you can see from Figure 8-7, the eZ Auction Template is simple and tasteful.

TIP    *eBay's own free software for listing multiple auctions at once, Turbo Lister, also provides you with templates for creating descriptions quickly, as does Seller's Assistant, which is available for a monthly subscription fee. See Chapter 13 for more information.*

8

**FIGURE 8-7**    A template provides you with the structure for an auction listing; you add photos and descriptions.

It's easy enough to copy a template from this or another auction site. Once you have copied the page to your computer, you type in your text, paste in your photos, and save it with a new name. Then you post the document online and start your sale.

If you have already created your own web pages and are comfortable with HTML, you can make your own auction template. Typically, the template is a simple web page that contains the name of your business (if you have a business, and if that business has a name, of course); your shipping and payment options; and any other statements that apply to all of your sales. The nice thing about templates is that they are half-completed before you even start filling in your content.

Some auction templates (or other auction descriptions, including those that are created without the aid of templates) make use of an HTML feature called a table. Tables are structural containers for web page content. They allow web pages to be arranged in the form of rows and columns. Tables are for organizing the contents of web pages and controlling how they turn out. You don't have to work directly with HTML to create your own table. One web page creation programs that's easy to use and free of charge, Netscape Composer (which is part of the Netscape browser package) lets you create your own. In Figure 8-8, I have opened Composer, chosen Insert | Table, and am about to create a simple table that contains one column and two rows and is centered on the web page.

It's easy to add images and format text with software like Composer. If you choose Insert | Image from Composer's menu bar, then locate a logo you have prepared earlier (see "Creating a Logo," coming up next), you can add that to the top row of your template. You then type your description beneath (see Figure 8-9).

**FIGURE 8-8**   A web page creation tool can streamline the process of creating a table so you can design auction listings.

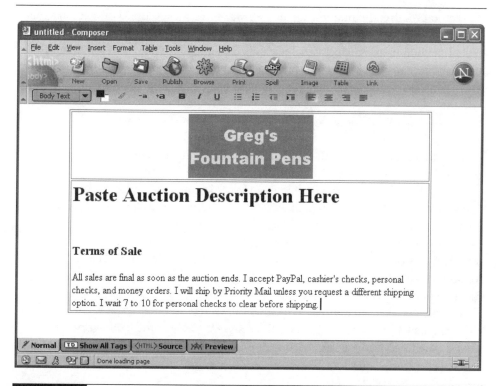

**FIGURE 8-9**   A simple template formatted with a web page creation tool.

*Bob Bull (user ID: bobal) is a frequent contributor to the Photos/HTML board who has made a name for himself by being helpful to others and providing lots of useful tips. His list of links to sites that provide eBay members with auction templates is located at http://www.zoicks.com/ auctiontemplates.htm.*

## Create a Logo

A *logo* is a graphic image that helps give a business or individual an identity. A logo helps "brand" a business by making its name a visual object that can be moved from one location to another. Logos make a business credible, even if that business is only one or two people working out of a garage or basement. Buyers don't need to know that you have been selling on eBay for only a matter of weeks. A logo makes you look more credible, and credibility is something you want when you begin to sell collectibles on eBay, just because competition is so fierce.

If you are already an antiques dealer and have a logo that you use on your stationery, your truck, or your brick-and-mortar store, it's worth adding the image to your auction listings. Most logos use only text and don't take up a lot of computer memory (perhaps less than 50K). First, you post the logo on a web server. Then you make a link to the logo in the body of your auction description, using this format:

```
<img src="http://www.url.to.host.com/account/logo.jpg">
```

Be sure to replace the URL shown in the preceding example with the actual one for the hosted image file.

If you don't have a logo yet, you can hire a designer to create you one. You'll find plenty of graphic designers in a marketplace that is affiliated with eBay called Elance (http://www.elance.com). Elance is a place where contractors (freelancers) can find jobs and companies and individuals can post jobs. One of the most popular types of jobs posted on Elance is for people who want to do design work for others—creating logos or web sites. To get started, first think up a short and catchy name for your collectibles business. It can be something as simple as Jo's Collectibles or Tom's Treasures. Once you have settled on an idea, go to Elance, click Elance Online, and click the Web Design & Development category. You should be able to find a designer to create a logo for you for $150–$300.

## Collecting Step-by-Step

If you're the type who likes to do things yourself or you have some experience with graphics software, you can easily create your own simple text-only logo. A text-only logo is one that consists primarily of words and that uses colors. You don't actually have to draw objects to create such a logo, you make use of your graphics software's text tool.

You can use a graphics program such as MacPaint, Super Paint, or Paint Shop Pro to create a logo. But perhaps the simplest way is to make use of one of the many web sites that enable people to create banner ads for free. A banner ad is a simple, rectangular text advertisement. Even though the purpose is different, you can use them for logos as well. One utility that I'm familiar with, CoolArchive's Logo Generator, is described here:

1. Go to the Logo Generator page (http://www.coolarchive.com/logogen.cfm) and read the instructions in the box near the top of the page.

2. Fill out the options in the Settings box. The nice thing about using a free utility like this is that you can try out different options before deciding on the one you want. So feel free to experiment. But there are some choices that make the most sense for a text-only logo:

   ■ Format: Choose GIF, which is best for line art; JPG is preferable for photos.

   ■ Size: Approximately 72 pixels are contained in one inch. There is no standard size for logos, but it's generally a good idea to keep yours smaller than 2 inches in height and 3 inches in length. Consider starting with a height of 100 pixels and width of 200.

   ■ Font settings: Don't pick any special effects to begin with. Antialiasing produces a blurry-looking typeface; I suggest you uncheck this option to begin with.

3. Select colors for the type and for the background. Make sure the type contrasts well with the background so it has maximum readability.

4. Click the Submit button at the bottom of the form. In a few seconds, your logo appears.

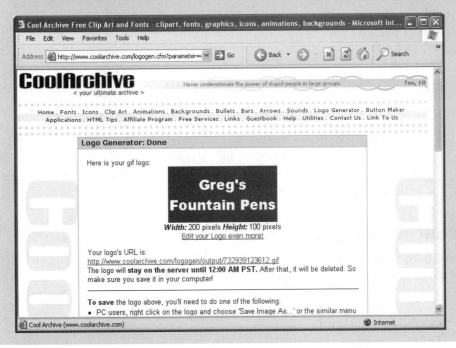

5. Chances are you won't get your logo just right the first time. You'll probably want to make the typeface heavier or lighter or change the type or background color. You have two options for editing your image:

■ If you want to return to the same form you just used and reuse the same controls, click your browser's Back button. Change the values you entered, and click Submit again to see the new version.

■ Click the link Edit Your Logo Even More, which appears just beneath the logo you previously created. You go to a new web page, where you can edit your logo in a more complex way, adding special effects or cropping or flipping the image.

6. When you are satisfied, copy your logo from the remote web site to your hard disk. If you use a Macintosh, hold down your mouse button and choose Save Image As from the shortcut menu. On a Windows-based PC, right-click the logo and choose Save Image As from the shortcut menu. The Save As dialog box appears so you can save the file on your computer.

Once you have the logo file on your computer, you can post it on the space your ISP gives you for hosting web pages and other files or with a photo hosting service if you have one.

**WATCH OUT!**    *It's free to use CoolArchive to create your logo, but the site requires you to make a link back to the CoolArchive web site. This is a reasonable request for a useful utility, but be aware that eBay prohibits you from including links in your auction listings. If you use a free utility such as CoolArchive, make sure you post the logo on your About Me page or your own web page (as described in the section that follows), and make a link back to the logo generator site from that page.*

## Create a Web Page

If you have been on the Web for a while, the chances are good that you've already got a web page out there somewhere in cyberspace. Maybe you use it to talk about yourself and your hobbies or to show off photos of your family or your pets.

You can also use the Web to talk about your hobby and what you like to buy and sell on eBay.

If you've already created auction listings and completed transactions with satisfied customers, you've done much of the work involved in creating a business web site. You only need to take one more step: creating a set of web pages devoted to your commercial activities. You've got plenty of options for creating pages: you can create a simple About Me page on eBay; create an eBay store; or launch your own full-fledged web site. As an entrepreneur, you owe it to yourself to take the next step and create web pages that boost your eBay sales even further.

## Create an About Me Page

If you sell collectibles on eBay, you should strongly consider creating an About Me page. About Me is a feature that eBay offers to all of its participants that helps people get to know and trust one another.

By taking a little time to create a simple page that tells people a little about you, you increase the chances that people will bid on your merchandise. Not only that, but you get another cool icon placed next to your user ID as it appears on your auctions. If shoppers click your Me icon they'll be taken directly to your About Me page.

As the name suggests, an About Me page is a place where you talk all about you personally—why you use eBay, what you sell, what you're interested in, or where you live. You can use an eBay Store or a web site to focus on your business rather than your personal side. Of course, these aren't firm dividing lines: You can use About Me to promote your business and your eBay Store to promote yourself and your business. No matter how you use these resources, however, they give you another way to point shoppers to your auction listings and the all-important Place Bid or Buy It Now buttons.

Before you start to create your About Me page, you just need to gather a little information. The amount of detail you provide depends on how active a seller you are, how many different kinds of items you sell or collect, and whether your page is about you personally or just about your auction activities. The best way to find out what to say on your About Me page is to search the About Me pages of other sellers. Unfortunately, there's no eBay page that gathers all the About Me pages in one set of links (you'd probably have tens of thousands of links in one place, which wouldn't necessarily be helpful). Rather, you find a seller who's reputable and presents sales items in a professional manner, and click that seller's About Me link.

Once you have gathered some basic information about what you want to present on your page, you only need to log in to eBay and go to the About Me

8

starting page (http://members.ebay.com/ws2/eBayISAPI.dll?AboutMeLogin). Click the Create or Edit Your Page button, and then follow the steps presented on subsequent pages to create your page.

> **TIP** *If you have more to tell the world about your hobbies, your family, your business history, or your thoughts about society in general, place a link on your About Me page that leads visitors to a web page that contains more information. You'll learn how to create such pages in the following sections.*

## Publish Your Own Web Site

About Me pages and eBay Stores (see Chapter 10) are easy ways to promote your business. But the really effective way to promote trust is to create your own set of interconnected web pages—in other words, a web site. On your site, you can talk about yourself and your qualifications in as much detail as you wish. You can also promote your business if you have one.

You don't *have* to provide a web site if you plan to sell at auction. For the most part, it makes sense to take this additional step if one of the following applies to you:

■ You're in a business related to the items you're selling.

■ You plan to make auction sales a significant part of your income.

■ You plan to sell not only through eBay but through a catalog you present on your web site so that all the income from the sale (less sales tax) comes to you and not to your web host.

The first step in creating your auction web page is to decide where your page is going to live online. Your site needs to be hosted on a web *server* (a computer that is connected to the Internet all the time and whose primary purpose is to make web pages available to anyone with a browser) so others can view it. In other words, you need to find a hosting service—a company that functions like a virtual landlord, giving you space on a computer where you can set up shop. This is only the first step of a three-step process:

1. You pick your web host.

2. You create your web pages using either your host's online tool or template or web page creation software that you purchase and install prior to designing your pages on your own computer.

**3.** You get your pages online. If you create your site using your host's online tool, you'll use another tool provided by that same host to move your files to the web server, where they can be seen by everyone. If you create your web pages yourself, you need to move the files from your computer to the web server. Sophisticated web page tools like Macromedia Dreamweaver and Microsoft FrontPage include a file transfer utility. Otherwise, you have to use a special file transfer protocol (FTP) program to do the moving.

It's worth taking some time to pick the right host because where your page is located can affect how you create it and how it looks. When it comes to finding a home for your web pages, you have several options:

■ **A free hosting service**    There aren't too many free web hosts around anymore, but you can use Yahoo! GeoCities.

■ **Your own ISP**    If you have an account with a company such as America Online (AOL) or EarthLink, they'll usually give you space to create a simple web site as part of your monthly Internet access fee.

■ **A company that specializes in hosting web sites**    Businesses that host web sites provide lots of handy tools and help for creating sites.

8

Your choice of host also has an impact on how you create your web pages. If you aren't technically minded and have no interest in the technical aspects of designing web sites, you'll enjoy using a simple forms-based web site creator provided by AOL, Yahoo! GeoCities, or Tripod: you fill out a form, and your web pages are created and automatically placed online. If you want to be in control and make everything look just the way you want, you'll probably prefer using a web page creation tool like Dreamweaver or FrontPage and publishing your page yourself with your ISP or a web hosting service.

When you use an ISP for web hosting, you save money, And you don't need to necessarily go with the ISP's free web editor, either. You can easily download and install the web page creation tool of your choice. The advantage of creating your own hosted web site is control: you can design your page by selecting your own colors and page layouts and adding as many images as you want. Creating and launching your own web site is complex, but the results can be worth the effort: you create a web site that looks professional and that can be the foundation of an eBay business that can bring you a regular source of income, too.

## Links for Collectors

| Web Site | Address | What's There |
| --- | --- | --- |
| National Auctioneers Association | http://www.auctioneers.org | Information on how to become a certified auctioneer, and a Find an Auction feature |
| Auction Listings discussion board | http://forums.ebay.com/db1/forum.jsp?forum=102 | Questions, answers, and comments about creating or reading auction descriptions |
| Auction-Images.com | http://auction-images.com | A photo-hosting site that offers 1MB of eBay hosting space for free |
| Elance | http://www.elance.com | eBay's marketplace for finding contract jobs or posting jobs |
| Logo Generator | http://www.coolarchive.com/logogen.cfm | An online utility that helps you create your own graphic logo |
| About Me starting page | http://members.ebay.com/ws2/eBayISAPI.dll?AboutMeLogin | A page where eBay members can create a new About Me page or edit an existing page |

# Chapter 9

## Strategies for Serious Collectors

## In This Chapter You'll Learn...

■ The importance of focusing on the best things to collect or sell on eBay

■ How to do research, both on eBay and off, to learn more about what you collect

■ Ways to take advantage of promotions and links on category opening pages

■ Gathering tips and statistics in eBay's Seller Central clearinghouse

eBay has dramatically changed the way collectibles are bought and sold. It's taken away some opportunities and at the same time provided new ones. Buyers are less likely to find the "good stuff" at estate sales and antiques malls because they're being sold on eBay. Sellers won't find as many buys in those traditional real-world venues, either. They've got to start selling on eBay in order to stay competitive.

eBay has also provided a wealth of new information about collecting. Along with the invaluable data about completed sales, you gain access to the tips and opinions of other collectors who post messages in the community venues or write essays for one of eBay's publications. In addition, eBay itself provides information about what's popular in selected sales categories. This chapter points you to some resources that are of special interest to serious sellers—ones you might have to look long and hard to find otherwise.

# Deciding What You Want to Collect

I probably don't need to tell you that most collectors don't collect just one type of object. Doll collectors might collect dollhouses, collectors of women's purses might also collect jewelry, and so on. On eBay, it's tempting to try to indulge all your obsessions at the same time. It's so easy, in fact, that you can easily start selling too many different types of things. The "clean out your garage" approach to selling on eBay works on a limited basis: once you have cleaned out whatever space you need to clear, you are faced with the challenge of what to sell on an ongoing basis. Most sellers who want to do business on eBay for any length of time—say, weeks or months, if not years—do their best to focus on what people are most likely to buy and what is likely to be most profitable. The following sections suggest strategies for choosing the best type of sales merchandise for you.

## Scouring Price Guides

The price guides you have read through in years past should not be thrown out simply because you are on eBay. Those guides have been compiled by collectors who often have many years of experience. They give you a good idea of what is valuable in a particular category and what is not. They also provide you with model numbers and, hopefully, photos of objects that are especially rare and precious and that you might not recognize otherwise.

Price guides often have a lot of useful information about condition: how to grade a certain item and what qualities to look for when evaluating whether something is to be described as "good," "very good," or "mint," for instance. Sometimes, information in price guides can help you write eBay sales descriptions. The citation "as depicted on p. ___ of the price guide" is not an uncommon one on eBay. Price guides are a good starting point for deciding what you want to buy and sell and what to collect.

Price guides also provide background information on the material you collect and sell. For instance, the *Old Magazine Identification and Value Guide* lists publishers and dates for the publications it covers. The *Comic Book Price Guide* provides material on the history of the publishers, beginning and ending issues of comic book titles, and detailed artist and author information. The *Baseball and Sports Publication Price Guide* not only gives detailed historical information on the publications it covers, but it also provides a listing of cover appearances of various sports stars.

On top of that, such guides do contain useful pricing information. Prices on eBay change faster than an annual guide can keep up with, but these publications allow you to see value relationships between similar items. For instance, if you are offered an Indianapolis 500 program that is valued at $1000 in a guide and another that is valued at $50, you'll know which one to buy right away. The relationship of values between similar items can help eBay sellers have the knowledge to properly price all their items. Many sellers will start their opening bids at $9.99 or less because they don't have the experience selling a particular item and do not want to start at a high opening price. Such lack of knowledge can play into the hands of collectors. A collector might be very happy to pay $100 for an item, but if he or she sees it on eBay with an opening bid of $9.99 and no one else is looking for that item during that week, then the collector gets it for a $9.99 bargain. If the seller had started the item at $99.99, the same buyer would have bought it and still would have been happy. Price guides can help prevent such losses.

9

The obvious place to find guides is in a real, live, brick-and-mortar bookstore. They are also available at the many collectors' shows or conventions that take place throughout the year. These shows also provide excellent firsthand research experience if you are trying to determine what to sell on eBay.

You can also find some guidebooks online, such as the venerable Kovels line of books about many different types of collectibles. Kovels Online (http://www.kovels.com) also maintains a searchable database of antiques. Krause Publications (http://www.krause.com) publishes a wide variety of collectors' magazines and newspapers such as *Comics Buyer's Guide, Toy Shop,* and *Goldmine.* The well-known TIAS.com site (shown in Figure 9-1) includes a monthly newsletter (http://www.tias.com/newsletter/merchant-assists-tiasstuff/) that focuses on the antiques business and that regularly includes a "Hot List" of popular antiques.

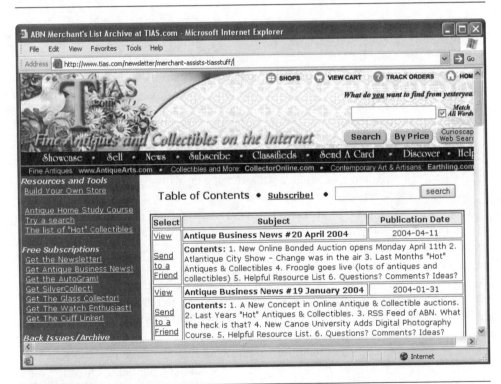

FIGURE 9-1    TIAS.com's free newsletter includes lists that can help you focus on a type of collectible.

# Drawing Up a List

Draw up a list of the types of items you want the most. You can narrow down your list according to two basic criteria: quality or quantity. If you just want something that is usable and that you can enjoy in your day-to-day life, you make trade-offs. I might buy a pen that is damaged because I know I am primarily interested in keeping it and using it, for instance; I can do some basic repairs and get it in good enough shape to write with on a daily basis. If you are looking to resell, you should focus either on quality items that will attract bidders or on items that you can get very cheaply at wholesale and that are sure to turn a profit, even if you only sell a handful of them.

## Buying Quality

If you have a whole converted schoolhouse in which to live and store your collection (as the antiques TV show host Harry Rinker revealed about himself in an interview on eBay Radio), you don't have to worry about how many things you collect. But if you have only a basement, attic, extra room, or garage, you have to be selective. To keep the collectibles from piling up all over your storage and living space, focus on high-quality items.

For example, in the world of watches, there are many different brands. But a few are guaranteed to have resale value:

- Rolex
- Gruen Curvex
- Breguet
- Omega
- Movado
- Tiffany
- Baume and Mercier

Not only that, but specific types of watches, such as chronographs, are very desirable. If you focus on the most desirable brands, you will spend more at the outset, but you are less likely to go through an auction without getting any bids.

## Buying Quantity

If you are looking to build up quantity (and hopefully get some measure of quality as well) you can buy wholesale lots of things very inexpensively. You can give away some of the extras when you sell, or as gifts, or you can resell them. On the other end of the spectrum, to continue the watch example, you might be able to find a box or a lot of Swatch watches. Some of these can be valuable, some not; however, they are widely collected and you probably won't have much trouble finding someone who wants to purchase them.

# Researching What You Have to Sell

Doing research may sound like an obvious idea, but evidently it's not. Many people put objects up for sale on eBay that are far more rare and valuable than they ever imagined. For buyers, that's a great thing. If you're a seller, it might be good too: you might be astonished at the number of bids you receive and how high they go. Still, it's to your advantage to know what you have and do research about it: that way, you can mention any key selling points in the title or subtitle and provide documentation in your auction description that builds trust and confidence in a prospective bidder.

Sometimes, doing extensive research about an item and detailing your research in your merchandise can overcome the "quality" issue mentioned in the previous section—the fact that, in most categories, there are several models or brands that will always sell well and many that are less desirable. Figure 9-2 shows an example. I've looked at a lot of listings for bass guitars since I took up the instrument. This sale contains one of the longest and most detailed descriptions I have ever seen. Less than half of it is shown in the figure.

In this description, the seller explains that this brand of bass, Acoustic Control, is hardly as well known as other quality brands like Fender and Gibson. However, a few of these guitars were manufactured by a company called Mosrite that is well known among musicians and that is no longer in existence. In great detail, the seller provides evidence that this bass may actually have been one of the few rare ones produced by Mosrite. He also provides photos of the serial number and other distinctive details. He concludes that, while he can't prove without a doubt that this is one of the rare instruments, it may well be. His research produced bids on a model that otherwise might not have drawn much attention.

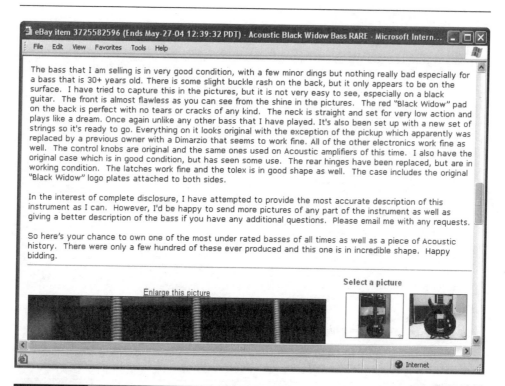

The bass that I am selling is in very good condition, with a few minor dings but nothing really bad especially for a bass that is 30+ years old. There is some slight buckle rash on the back, but it only appears to be on the surface. I have tried to capture this in the pictures, but it is not very easy to see, especially on a black guitar. The front is almost flawless as you can see from the shine in the pictures. The red "Black Widow" pad on the back is perfect with no tears or cracks of any kind. The neck is straight and set for very low action and plays like a dream. Once again unlike any other bass that I have played. It's also been set up with a new set of strings so it's ready to go. Everything on it looks original with the exception of the pickup which apparently was replaced by a previous owner with a Dimarzio that seems to work fine. All of the other electronics work fine as well. The control knobs are original and the same ones used on Acoustic amplifiers of this time. I also have the original case which is in good condition, but has seen some use. The rear hinges have been replaced, but are in working condition. The latches work fine and the tolex is in good shape as well. The case includes the original "Black Widow" logo plates attached to both sides.

In the interest of complete disclosure, I have attempted to provide the most accurate description of this instrument as I can. However, I'd be happy to send more pictures of any part of the instrument as well as giving a better description of the bass if you have any additional questions. Please email me with any requests.

So here's your chance to own one of the most under rated basses of all times as well as a piece of Acoustic history. There were only a few hundred of these ever produced and this one is in incredible shape. Happy bidding.

Select a picture

Enlarge this picture

**FIGURE 9-2** Extensive research can increase value in an otherwise little-known brand.

# Getting an Online Appraisal

You don't have to do all the work yourself when it comes to researching items you want to sell. In cases where you don't have time to do the work, or the item you are interested in selling could be especially valuable, it might be worth your while to spend $19.95 to get an online appraisal. On its Collectibles category opening page, eBay points visitors to the Collecting Channel site (http://www.collectingchannel.com/ata), shown in Figure 9-3.

Along with a web page that appraises your object, you get a link to some HTML code that you can paste into your eBay auction description. If viewers click the link, they can view the appraisal, which will hopefully induce them to bid on the item.

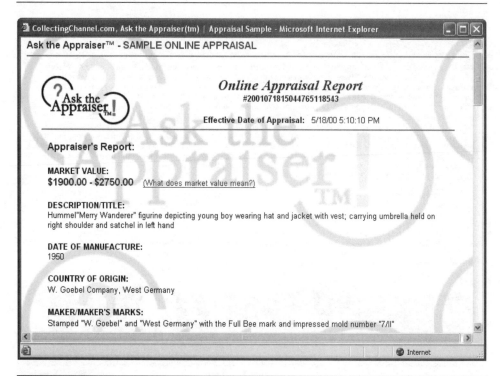

FIGURE 9-3     For $19.95, you can get an appraisal if you submit photos and a description to this web site.

## Consulting an Authority in Your Category

Some eBay sellers are especially well known in their area of interest. They are frequently very generous with advice and will be more than happy to advise you on how to tell if something is valuable or not. They may not be willing to go out on a limb and do an actual appraisal, but they can probably tell you what sorts of identifying marks to look for and where to locate them. The question is, how to you locate the experts? You can check in a number of places:

- Look up the web site for the collectors' association for your hobby, such as the Train Collectors Association (http://www.traincollectors.org), the Antique Fan Collectors Association (http://www.fancollectors.org), the Automobile License Plate Collectors Association (http://www.alpca.org), and so on.

- Look through past issues of The Chatter (http://ebay.com/community/chatter), eBay's newsletter, for collectors who have written articles there.

- Look through the Seller Central newsletters for articles by or about collectors.

It's always a good idea to scan the discussion forums and Answer Center for postings by particularly active members. As described in the following section, you can also look for threads that have been highlighted as particularly valuable for both buyers and sellers.

## Discussion Threads for Collectors

A *thread* is a set of messages posted on a discussion board about a single topic. Some threads on eBay's discussion boards last only a day or two and are replaced as new topics are posted. But others stay online indefinitely; they are given a standing position at the top of the board's messages so that they won't be replaced over time. These threads have been judged as being of interest to both buyers and sellers of collectibles. To save you some clicking around, I have listed some of them below:

9

- The Antiques discussion board (http://forums.ebay.com/db2/forum.jsp?forum=13) contains "The Official 'What Is It?' Thread" and "Repair Shop" near the top.

- The Booksellers discussion board (http://forums.ebay.com/db1/forum.jsp?forum=4) has "Ask Any Question About Any Book."

- The Hobbies & Crafts discussion board (http://forums.ebay.com/db2/forum.jsp?forum=27) has a Quilting link (one of many) in the right-hand column. Click it, and you go to a thread called "Quilter's Questions, Answers & Tips."

- The Sports Card, Memorabilia & Fan Shop discussion board (http://forums.ebay.com/db2/forum.jsp?forum=83) has "Top Ten Tips for Selling Cards" and "Questions About PSA grading."

TIP

*To avoid typing these lengthy URLs (with all the question marks and equals signs), from the eBay home page, click Community | Discussion Boards (under Talk), choose your topic from the list under Category Specific Discussion Boards, and scan the list for the thread you want. You may also want to look at the column on the right for threads and articles of interest.*

# Category Opening Page Promotions

If you have an area of special interest, either as a collector or because you want to sell, it's a good idea to visit its category opening page. These pages often contain special promotions you won't find elsewhere that eBay conducts with well-known companies. You'll also find links of interest to sellers. For instance, when I visited the Collectibles category page, Disney was offering Harmony Kingdom toys at special reduced rates. The Antiques category page (http://antiques.ebay.com) contained links to the Antiques area of eBay Live Auctions, as well as these useful links for those who want to sell antiques on eBay:

- **Antiques Newsletter**   eBay's category-specific newsletters are a gold mine of tips for sellers and feature profiles of others who sell a particular type of merchandise.

- **Popular Searches**   This brief list of five words toward the bottom of the page is important for sellers: it indicates the most frequent keyword search terms in a category. You should try to work those keywords into your own descriptions to increase the frequency with which your sales turn up in search results. For instance, if a category tells you that the most popular terms include "oriental" and "primitive," you should work them into your descriptions if they apply.

- **Top 10 List**   This list identifies the most popular items in the category in question.

- **Category Community Links**   Visit one of these links to view comments, ask questions, and just gab with other buyers and sellers who are interested in this category.

COLLECTOR'S NOTE   *Each of the category opening pages has its own URL, with links to subcategories within the category. But if you always navigate eBay by searching for terms, or if you click category links that you see on a page of search results, you won't reach the category opening page. You can only find a category opening page if you have bookmarked it, added it to your browser's Links bar, or clicked the category link from the site map or home page.*

# Looking for eBay Exclusives

Huge groups of collectibles are bought and sold all the time that are not old, not "vintage," but brand new. They are limited editions, and they are created by well-known companies in controlled quantities. Some of these editions are offered on eBay for a limited time. You can find the ones currently available and ones that will be for sale in the near future on the eBay Exclusives page (http://www.ebay.com/exclusives), shown in Figure 9-4.

# Scanning Top 10 Lists and Popular Searches

"What's the best thing to sell on eBay?" Even experienced collectors ask this common question once in a while. You can try selling a variety of objects by hit-or-miss, of course. But you'll save time and trouble by referring to eBay's own lists of popular search items, which are part of every category opening page.

9

**FIGURE 9-4**   Some collectors' items are offered in limited editions only on eBay.

## Trade Talk

In May 2004, eBay held a contest to choose five enthusiastic collectors from among its members. The five were given free passes to attend the eBay Live conference in New Orleans. Look for similar contests to be held each year in the spring: talking about what you collect just might make you a big winner, too.

Just connect to the page you want and scroll down to the Popular Searches and Top 10 List headings (see Figure 9-5).

Both Popular Searches and the Top 10 List are drawn from the same source: the search terms people enter when they look for something on eBay. The Top 10

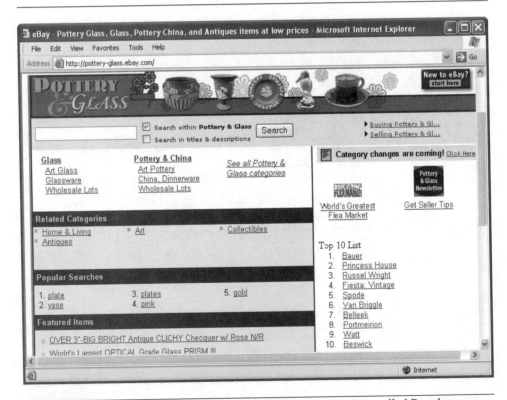

FIGURE 9-5    eBay suggests the most popular items in a category called Popular Searches and in the Top 10 List.

List focuses on the most popular brands that turn up as a result of searches; the Popular Searches list shows the actual keywords that shoppers enter when they are looking for something in a category.

## Industry Resources

Collecting might not be an industry as such, but many fields such as numismatics (that's coin collecting) or philately (stamp collecting) have programs and publications for their members. Many of these resources can help you decide what the best products are to sell on eBay and how valuable your own merchandise is, or simply to find out more about what you have. Sandafayre, the stamp auction service based in the U.K., maintains an online library of stamps from around the world (http://www.sandafayre.com/gallery/gallery.htm), shown in Figure 9-6.

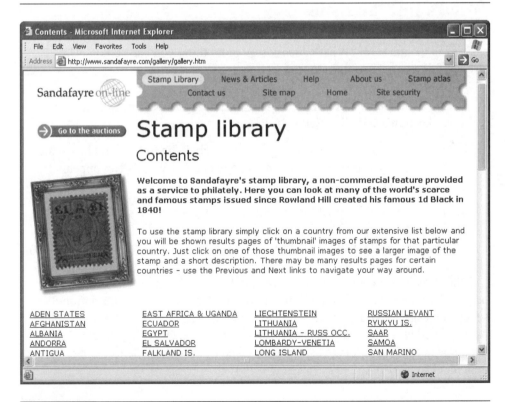

FIGURE 9-6    Merchants and associations related to a popular hobby frequently post reference materials online.

The Train Collectors Association mentioned earlier maintains a list of grading standards at http://www.traincollectors.org/standards/grading.html. Toy collectors Bob and Gayle Olson have articles about dolls, kites, and other collectibles at http://toyscollectibles.allinfo-about.com.

# Exploring Advanced Resources in Seller Central

Seller Central is like that useful resource you keep in the glove compartment of your car and refer to only rarely—it's called the owner's manual. Seller Central is like a seller's manual for eBay—a resource that is overlooked until you run into a problem or have nothing better to do with your time. If you're looking for some advanced resources for sellers, though, this is the place to turn. Some of its tools are described here.

## "What's Hot" Statistics

Buried within all the links on the Seller Central site is a most valuable resource for answering the question "What's the most popular thing you can sell on eBay?" Use the following these steps to find it.

**1.** Go to the Seller Central home page (http://pages.ebay.com/sellercentral/index.html) and click Sell by Category.

**2.** When the Sell by Category page appears, click the In Demand link under the category you're interested in. A page entitled What's Hot appears (see Figure 9-7).

**3.** Read the list of Top 10 Picks, which lists items that have sold well in this category recently. The Top Buyer's Searches list, farther down the page, indicates what potential buyers have been looking for recently in this category.

The What's Hot pages contain more detailed lists than the category opening pages mentioned at the beginning of the chapter. It's the sort of information that sellers are eager to know about—the most popular searches within a particular category and what items are the hot ones within the category. If you click one of the items in the Top 10 Picks list, you are taken to the current sales listings for that item on eBay.

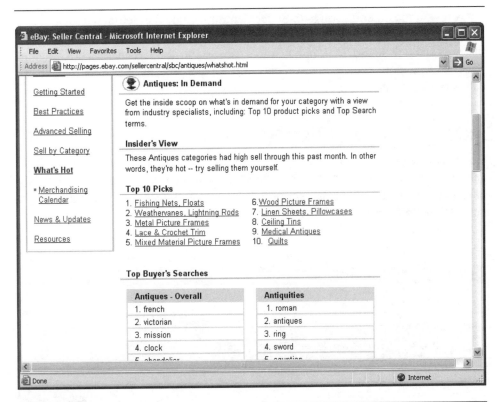

**FIGURE 9-7**    Seller Central provides lists of the most popular items in a category.

# Getting the Seller's Edge

If you go to the Seller Central page and click the Seller's Edge link under the category you want, you get a newsletter devoted to that area of business. The Seller's Edge newsletters present you with news about developments in the category as well as tips and trends culled from eBay sales. You might find that textbook sales are growing at a rate of 230 percent per year and that textbooks sell for a higher price than most other trade books.

If you click In the Field, you get a profile of a seller who is doing a good job of building a business in that category. You learn how the seller began on eBay and how he or she has built the business over time.

A few of the other offerings in Seller Central include the Selling Guide link, which provides you with detailed instructions for how to get started as a seller in that area and how to turn your hobby into a part- or full-time business. The Clothing, Shoes & Accessories category has such a link, for example, as does the Collectibles category (see Figure 9-8).

# Collecting Tips on eBay Radio

Collectors are used to hunting for treasures that are buried within pages full of eBay sales listings. It shouldn't be a great leap, then, to scrounge past the commercials and chatter that clutter up eBay's own radio station and uncover some tips and suggestions from insiders who are experienced collectible dealers.

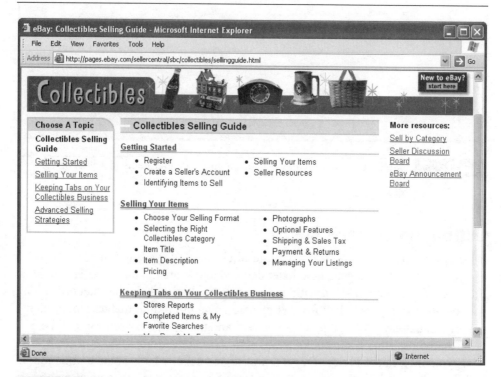

**FIGURE 9-8**    If you can find a Selling Guide in Seller Central, you'll get a jump start on creating an eBay business in that area.

In case you're wondering what Internet radio is, here's a quick explanation: Most web page content is posted by the page's creator, and the page's contents stay the same until revisions are made. Internet radio, in contrast, uses content that is posted continuously to a web server. (The term used to describe the continuous downloading of this content is *streaming*.) To listen to such programming, you need an application that is designed to process and play streamed audio, such as Real Networks' RealPlayer or Windows Media Player.

## Trade Talk

RealPlayer or Windows Media Player is needed for listening to eBay Radio. If you have a PC, Windows Media probably came with your version of Windows so you don't have to install it. RealPlayer comes in two versions: one that is free to download and use, and a premium version that you have to purchase. To find the free version, go to the RealNetworks home page (http://www.real.com), and click the Download RealPlayer button. When the download page appears, click the link for the version you want to download. Both versions let you listen to Internet radio stations; the premium version has additional controls for watching video online, and for burning your own CDs. I suggest that you start with the free version and upgrade to the premium version if you want the additional features.

9

eBay Radio is scheduled for live broadcast every Tuesday at 11 A.M. Pacific time. To hear the live broadcast, once you have RealPlayer installed on your computer you go to the web site that hosts eBay Radio, wsRadio.com (http://www.wsradio.com), and click on the eBay icon at the right time.

I strongly suggest, however, that you skip the live version, which is plagued by seemingly endless ads and irrelevant small talk, and focus instead on the specific interviews that pertain to collectors and that have been archived—in other words, the original broadcasts are saved as files that you can download and listen to at any time, not just during the live broadcast.

## Collecting Step-by-Step

Another good feature of the archived files is the ability to search them by topic. You'll find a whole page full of links to archived discussions about collectibles and antiques by following these steps:

1. Go to the home page for eBay Radio (http://www.wsradio.com/ebayradio).

2. Click Audio Archives to go to the archived versions of eBay Radio broadcasts.

3. Click the Archives by Topic link.

4. Under Special Interest Topics, click the Antiques and Collectibles link.

A page appears that contains a list of recent interviews conducted with antiques dealers and authorities who buy and sell collectibles on eBay. When I visited, these included an interview with price guide author Judith Miller, coin collector Troy Thoreson, *Collector Inspector* TV show host Harry Rinker, and vintage-chandelier seller Tom Stone. You're likely to find many more interviews available when you visit the page.

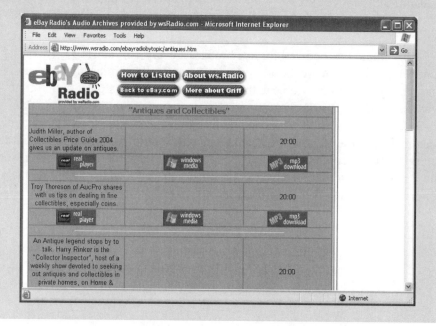

When you listen to an archive show, you can skip ahead so you don't have to listen to the commercials. (The first three or four minutes of an eBay Radio program are ones you can safely skip over, for instance.) You can drag the progress bar or click the "fast-forward" buttons; RealPlayer's controls are shown in Figure 9-9.

**TIP**    *eBay Radio is also saved on the archives as an MP3 version; you can download it to your iPod and play it just as you would any other MP3 music file.*

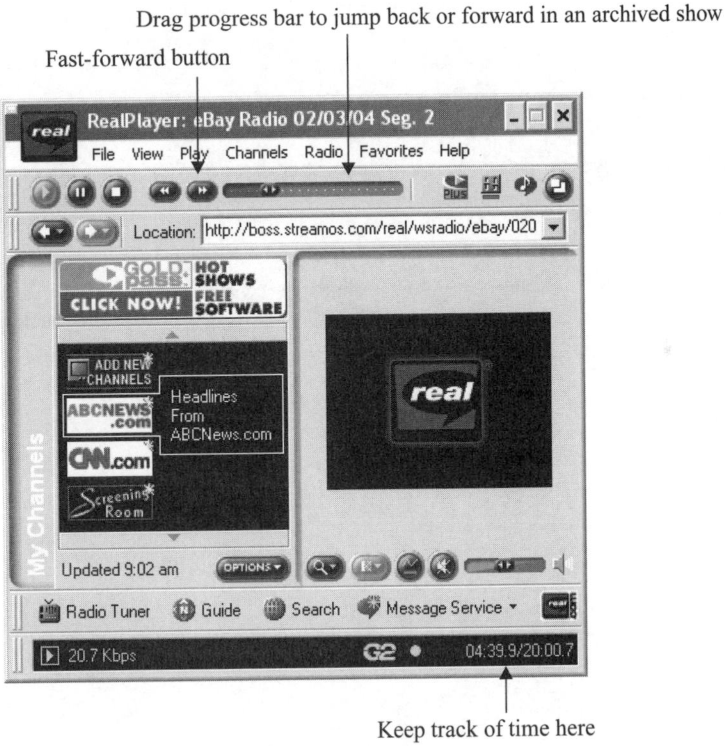

Drag progress bar to jump back or forward in an archived show

Fast-forward button

Keep track of time here

**FIGURE 9-9**    You can control what you hear when you listen to an archived file online.

## Links for Collectors

| Web Site | Address | What's There |
|---|---|---|
| Kovels.com | http://www.kovels.com | Web site for a well-known line of price guides that contains a searchable database so you can check prices |
| TIAS.com Antiques Business Newsletter | http://www.tias.com/newsletter/merchant-assists-tiasstuff/ | Monthly online publication that tracks trends in "hot" collectibles |
| Collecting Channel online appraisal service | http://www.collectingchannel.com/ata | A service that offers online appraisals for a $19.95 fee |
| The Chatter | http://pages.ebay.com/community/chatter | eBay's community newsletter |
| eBay Exclusives | http://www.ebay.com/exclusives | Current and upcoming sets of limited edition collectibles offered solely on eBay |
| Seller Central | http://pages.ebay.com/sellercentral | Tips, statistics, and instructions for eBay sellers |

# Chapter 10

## Expanding Your eBay Sales Options

## In This Chapter You'll Learn...

- How to boost your income by selling for other people

- Strategies for expanding your antiques or collectibles business with eBay Live Auctions

- Ways to sell at fixed price as well as at auction

- How to build trust and attract bids by becoming a PowerSeller

- Methods of earning extra money by becoming an eBay affiliate

- How to link your eBay sales to your web site

There's more than one way to skin a cat, and there's more than one way to make money on eBay, too. After you've gotten some experience conducting auctions, you can expand your options for making money through a variety of approaches. You can sell on consignment or through live auctions. You can offer your merchandise at fixed price as well as to the highest bidder. If you become either a PowerSeller or an eBay affiliate, you can find new ways to make money and attract customers. eBay's diverse opportunities for making money outside of traditional auctions are described in the sections that follow.

# Selling for Other People

Like so many things having to do with eBay, the process of selling for other members as a regular source of income probably started by accident. In my book *How to Do Everything with Your eBay Business*, I profiled a young Canadian who started selling on eBay when a serious illness forced him to quit his job for a while. He sold so many sports trading cards that he gained the attention of friends, who asked him to put their own collectible items up for sale. Before too long, his "secondhand sales" business grew to be a regular source of extra money. Now, eBay has formalized the process by creating the Trading Assistants Program, in which sellers can advertise their services as consignment dealers.

The fact is, many people want to sell on eBay but they lack the time and technical expertise to get the job done. Things that experienced sellers take for granted, like digital cameras, scanners, photo hosting, and file transfers, leave many beginning sellers scratching their heads. You can make a few extra dollars by helping them out—as long as you don't give yourself any extra headaches you don't need.

# Selling on Consignment

Lots of people sell things on eBay on behalf of other individuals. The owner presents them with one or more items, and the consignment seller handles the photography, creates the seller description, posts the sale online, answers questions from prospective bidders, and does the packing and shipping after the sale ends. The seller and owner then divide up the revenue based on a formula they've agreed upon beforehand.

If this sounds like just as much work as selling your own possessions, it is. Don't go into consignment selling with the idea that it's "easy money." The only difference between selling for yourself and for someone else is the fact that you don't have to find the object in the first place. Other than that, the amount of work is the same. In fact, it might be more work: if customers ask questions that you can't answer and you have to ask the owner for an answer, for instance, that's an extra step you wouldn't have if you were selling something you owned yourself.

Whenever you decide to sell something for someone else, you have to answer a number of basic questions, such as:

- Will you charge the owner a percentage of the final sale price or a flat fee?

- How much will you charge for your time and effort—the time spent in packing, hauling the package to the shipper, buying and applying postage, and so on?

- What happens if the item doesn't sell? Will you automatically relist the item? Will you charge a service fee anyway, or just give the item back and not charge anything?

You may also need to educate some new sellers who come to you with consignment merchandise and a desire to have you sell for them on eBay. They may only be aware of eBay in passing due to news stories or word of mouth and may have unrealistic expectations. They may expect to receive a certain amount for what they sell and to have you guarantee that they will make that amount. You'll have to explain that it's totally uncertain how items will sell on eBay, and that they rarely attract prices as high as those listed in well-known price guides.

You may have to turn down sellers who have rigid views and who have items that you know won't attract a lot of bids and probably won't sell on eBay. You don't want to put merchandise up for sale that won't generate revenue for you—it just wastes your time and can be counterproductive.

**WATCH OUT!** *Make sure you sell for consignors who have material that complements what you already sell and doesn't duplicate what you have to sell. Selling the wrong items can actually detract from your own regular sales, which will reduce your income.*

## Trade Talk

How much should a consignment seller charge for his or her services? I consulted my eBay friend Jo Stavig, who does consignment sales for a mutual friend as well as for others.

For close friends, I've kept my commission lower and included the eBay fees as part of my "take" of 25 percent or 30 percent of the final price. However, as I've been doing more preparation work recently to get something ready to sell (such as research, cleaning, and repairing) I've decided that doesn't cover my costs adequately, so I've been taking 50 percent, but also including eBay and PayPal fees, so it's effectively considerably lower as a percentage.

I've sold a few higher priced items on a flat-fee basis and kept the eBay fees as a separate charge. I sold a Jeep ($4000) recently for a friend this way, and it worked out quite well. They got a buyer from St. Louis who undoubtedly wouldn't have seen a local newspaper ad but was willing to drive here to pick up the car on a Saturday.

For items that don't sell after two listings, I would still charge a "kill" fee to cover my time and charge separately for the eBay fees. I don't think I've had this happen, though.

There are lots of different ways to get these questions answered. Some consignment sellers simply purchase the items outright from the owner; they can then sell the items as their own and not be a middleperson at all. Others charge a flat fee for each sale, to cover the time and effort involved. Others charge a percentage of the sales fee. The important thing is to not shortchange yourself when it comes to your time: the time you spend selling for someone else could be spent shopping for merchandise or putting your own items up for sale, after all.

## Becoming a Trading Assistant

Plenty of budding sellers need a jump start when it comes to selling on eBay. If you are comfortable with creating descriptions, taking digital photos, and fielding e-mail questions, you may want to sell on consignment. Selling on consignment means that an owner gives his or her item over to you so you can handle the sale on eBay for that person—for a fee, of course.

You can become a consignment seller in two different ways: as someone who puts items up for sale "on the side" but who doesn't have any formal designation, or as someone who has been admitted to eBay's Trading Assistants Program. Either way, the general idea is the same: you handle the photography, description, and management of the sale. Your consignment customers are likely to be someone you know or a friend of a friend. When the item sells, you both share in the sale price. You don't make as much money as you would if you did everything yourself, but you don't have do the finding and researching of what's being sold, either. And you don't have to spend any of your own money, either. In fact, being a Trading Assistant can help you learn about merchandise you might want to buy and sell yourself in the future. It might open your eyes to collectors' items you would never have considered otherwise.

Once you get a few consignment sales under your belt, you might consider becoming a Trading Assistant. You can find out about the program at http:// pages.ebay.com/tradingassistants/learnmore.html. At its annual conference in summer 2003, eBay estimated that there were 20,000 Trading Assistants around the world. In order to join the program, Trading Assistants must have a feedback rating of 49 or higher and more than 97 percent positive feedback.

10

Once they are certified, Trading Assistants get a logo they can add to their eBay store home page, like the one shown here.

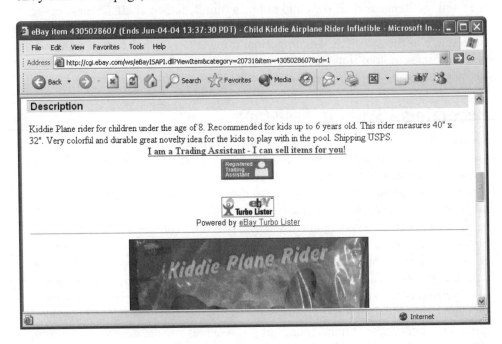

Trading Assistants have the ability to set their own terms of sale and to specialize in certain types of items they already know well. You might charge as much as 10 to 15 percent of the purchase price or high bid, as well as a fee for packing and shipping. Some Trading Assistants charge $1 per listing plus 4 to 5 percent of the final sales price; others might charge 25 percent of any high bid. If you are lucky enough to sell off an entire catalog full of items, you can charge an even higher percentage as a commission.

# Selling at Live Auctions

If you already buy and sell antiques or collectibles for a living, or if you are conducting an estate sale or other sale with a licensed auctioneer, consider moving beyond traditional eBay auction sales by becoming a dealer on the eBay Live Auctions site. This option is especially good if you sometimes are called upon to liquidate someone's estate and you have a large number of items from a single collection (and you expect the collection will fetch thousands of dollars, thus making it worth paying the $1500 insertion fee). Such batches of objects are frequently offered for sale on Live Auctions.

Being a Live Auction seller lets you do some things you can't do on the regular eBay. You have the option of specifying that you want to manually approve bidders before you allow them to bid on your sales. You can set up your sales catalog months before the sale is scheduled to occur. You can also tell prospective bidders that they have to verify their identity by placing a credit card on file or by going through eBay's ID Verify process. Plus, you can accept bids not only from the Internet but also from real, live bidders on an auction house floor, if you decide to conduct your sale with a licensed auctioneer.

Even if you already sell at auctions on eBay.com, you need to apply to be a seller on the Live Auctions site. Follow these steps:

1. Go to the Live Auctions home page (http://www.ebayliveauctions.com), shown in Figure 10-1.

2. Click Sign Up as a Seller.

3. Read the instructions on the Selling on eBay Live Auctions page, and then click the Apply link for more information or use the link provided to go directly to the application form (http://cgi3.liveauctions.ebay.com/aw-cgi/ eBayISAPI.dll?LAApplicationForm).

4. Click Submit to send the application to eBay.

There is no application fee to sign up; you do, however, have to provide the name of the licensed auction house you'll be using, or your own company's address, logo, and web site's URL, if applicable.

Before you sign up, make sure you are going to be able to generate enough revenue from your sales to justify the fees associated with selling on Live Auctions. First of all, you have to sell a *lot*—a group of associated items. Each lot costs $1500 to list. On top of that, you pay a Final Value Fee of 5 percent on each item sold to an Internet bidder. This explains why Live Auctions lets people include as many as 10,000 separate items in a lot: it can take that many sales to pay eBay, pay the auctioneer, cover your expenses, and give yourself a profit as well.

**10**

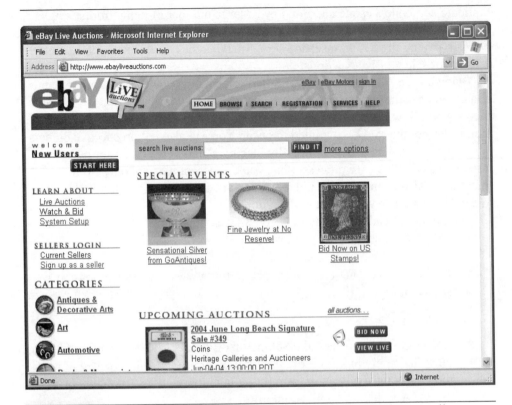

**FIGURE 10-1** You need to be an established dealer or use an auctioneer to sell on Live Auctions.

# Becoming a PowerSeller

As you learned in your college days, the more degrees you have after your name, the more attractive you are to employers, and the more you are likely to earn. Until eBay comes up with a Master's degree in Auction Selling (don't laugh; it'll probably happen some day), the closest thing you can get is the title of PowerSeller.

A PowerSeller is someone who has met eBay's rigorous standards for selling proficiency. That doesn't mean the seller has to have a large feedback number. You are likely to find PowerSellers with feedback in the 200 to 500 range, as well as those in the 2000 to 5000 range. The criteria has more to do with maintaining a steady number of sales each month plus a high degree of customer satisfaction.

To become a PowerSeller, you don't have to fill out a form or pass a test. It's much harder than that: you have to be a really good and active seller for a number of months. You can't nominate yourself for PowerSeller status, either. eBay automatically evaluates your sales and feedback and invites you to become a PowerSeller if you are deemed worthy. Requirements include:

- eBay membership for a minimum of 90 days.

- A feedback rating of at least 100.

- At least 98 percent of your feedback must be positive.

- Maintain average gross sales of $1000 for three months.

It's this last requirement—sales revenue that averages $1000 per month—that can be difficult, particularly if the collectibles you sell are small and don't fetch high prices. For instance, if you sell postcards for $5 to $10 each, you would have to sell 100 to 200 per month to attain the required income. That's an average of anywhere from 20 to 50 per week. Of course, if one or more of your items sells for $100 to $500, you can reach the PowerSeller minimum much more quickly. But anyway you slice it, you need to find a steady supply of desirable stock and turn around sales with maximum efficiency.

For all that work, you would expect to get some benefits, and you do. For one thing, you get more bids and purchases on what you sell, because buyers feel an extra degree of trust (buyers know that you aren't likely to risk PowerSeller status by failure to deliver what you sell, for instance). You get better access to technical support from eBay, by a toll-free number or other means. You get to place free ads on eBay. You get merchandise with the PowerSeller logo that you can give your customers as gifts to build goodwill. Perhaps best of all, you and your employees get access to health insurance coverage.

The most important long-term benefit for many, whether they work on their own or sell on eBay as part of a traditional brick-and-mortar business, is an increase in sales—to put it simply, by selling more and putting a premium on customer service, you end up selling even more. If you want to get an idea what is involved in becoming a PowerSeller, look at sales figures for a few over a period of a week or two. Here are examples for three PowerSellers I profiled in *How to Do Everything with eBay* for the period May 24 to May 31, 2004.

| User ID | Feedback | Items for Sale | Items Sold | Gross Sales |
|---|---|---|---|---|
| venusrisinglimited | 1084 | 42 | 5 | $1,065.16 |
| Roniheart | 1076 | 56 | 35 | $1,195 |
| morning-glorious | 2024 | 48 | 19 | $277.25 |

TIP    *You can view more details about the benefits gaining the PowerSeller icon at http://pages.ebay.com/services/buyandsell/welcome.html. Click the How Do I Qualify for PowerSeller link to find out more about the requirements for gaining this coveted designation.*

# Selling at Fixed Price

When you decide to sell something new at a fixed price, you have an advantage: you can look up the retail price on a search service like Froogle (http://froogle .google.com). Or you know that if you bought the item from a wholesaler for 75 cents you need to put a fixed price of $2 or more on the item to cover expenses. But selling collectibles at fixed price can be tricky, because most items aren't new at all. The value might well depend on intangibles like the demand, the state of the economy, the value of similar items, and so on. Make very sure that the fixed price is a reasonable one so that you don't cheat yourself. After all, you never know if bidders would drive the price up higher than your fixed price.

COLLECTOR'S NOTE    *For items that cost hundreds or even thousands of dollars, or if you suspect something is rare and valuable but you don't know for sure, get an appraisal. The auction house Bonhams & Butterfields offers appraisals to individuals who send in a photo and a detailed description of an item. Find out more at http://www.butterfields.com/services/appraisals/ appraisals.html.*

When you are deciding whether to offer a Buy It Now price on an item, you also need to determine how the BIN price will interact (if at all) with bids. Ask yourself the following:

- Should you offer an item only at a fixed price or at a fixed price along with auction bids?

- If you want to make both the bids and a fixed price available, do you want to protect yourself even more with a reserve?

There's no straightforward answer to these questions. The pros and cons of each are explored in Table 10-1.

Keep in mind that eBay shoppers like to feel that they have some degree of control. If you specify a BIN price, you assert control, and you might turn some bidders off.

| BIN Price | Auction | Pros | Cons |
|-----------|---------|------|------|
| Yes | No | You can sell the item instantly at any time. | You might have received more money through bids. eBay members like competition. |
| Yes | Standard | Someone who wants to pay a fixed price can do so immediately, and you get instant profits. | The BIN price disappears when a bid is placed, so bids can be placed low just to "kill" the BIN price. |
| Yes | Reserve | The BIN price stays available as long as bids do not meet your reserve. | The reserve price might discourage bidders who know the item may sell at any time until reserve is met. |

**TABLE 10-1**    Combinations of BIN Fixed Prices and Auction Bids

# Buy It Now

Buy It Now (BIN) prices can be an especially good option for sellers who are offering collectibles that are highly sought after. By their nature, BIN prices appeal to people who see something they are knowledgeable about and have been seeking for a while. Avid collectors who see a reasonable BIN price will be inclined to click the Buy It Now button in order to avoid competition from other bidders.

10

For sellers, BIN has other advantages, such as the ability to receive income from an instant purchase without having to wait 5, 7, or 10 days for an auction to end. If you choose the often-overlooked Buy It Now with Pay Now option in the Sell Your Item form, you can receive payment instantly: by clicking Buy It Now, the buyer automatically deducts the purchase price from his or her PayPal account and transfers it to yours. You add this option by checking the Require Immediate Payment box when you get to the Enter Payment & Shipping page of the Sell Your Item form (see Figure 10-2).

The question is, what's a reasonable BIN price? The best way to determine this is from your research in collectible price guides and the like. You can also try Andale's BIN service: if you subscribe to Andale, you can add a feature to your auction descriptions that tells potential buyers that your BIN price is a good one, compared to previous sales on eBay. (An example is shown in Figure 10-3.) The feature is called In-Ad Price Compare, and it comes as part of Andale's Lister software. You can find out more about Lister as well as other Andale software at http://www.andale.com/setup/auctiontool_quickstart.jsp.

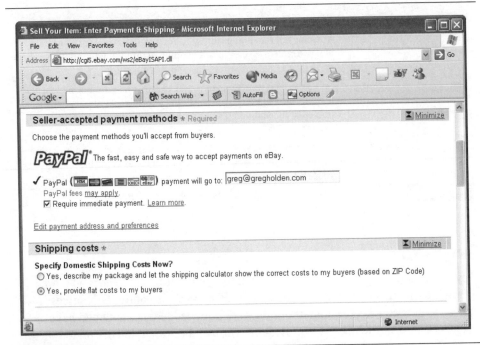

**FIGURE 10-2**   For instant results, consider having PayPal buyers immediately send you payment.

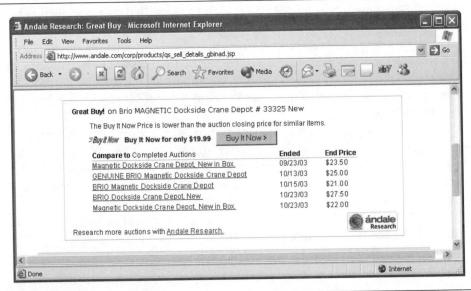

**FIGURE 10-3**   When you use Andale software to create listings with BIN prices, you can add this feature to the description.

## eBay Stores

In order to make the most profit on eBay, you need to get maximum exposure for your merchandise. One of the best ways to increase exposure is to open an eBay store. An eBay store is a web site that eBay lets you establish and where you can sell items at a fixed price. The cost is only $9.95 per month for a basic subscription, plus nominal listing fees. In contrast, setting up your own online web-based store with a web hosting service might cost $50 a month or more.

**COLLECTOR'S NOTE** *You need a minimum feedback of 20 and an ID Verify listing to open an eBay store. The fees include the $9.95 per month charge, a listing fee of 2 to 8 cents per item (depending on how long you want the item to appear in your store), and a Final Value Fee of 5.25 percent for items priced at $25 or less. Find out more at http://pages.ebay.com/help/stores/store-fees.html.*

For collectors, eBay stores are a great way to sell lots of identical items that are created by well-known manufacturers like Ty, Hummel, and Lladró. Everything in a store is offered at a fixed price, so knowledgeable buyers who already collect what you sell are likely to make the purchases. Once you've decided what you want to sell, go to the eBay Stores Welcome page (http://pages.ebay.com/storefronts/seller-landing.html), and click the Sign Up Now! button.

**10**

## Collecting Step-by-Step

You can start up an eBay store at any time but, as with any web-based business, you'll get better results if you tend and regularly update the site. (To edit a store you have already created, go to the eBay Stores Welcome page mentioned in the preceding paragraph and click Manage Your Store.) Whether you are creating or editing a store, the Create or Edit Your Store page appears. Log in to eBay with your password, if you aren't logged in already, and click Sign In. When the Build Your Store: User Agreement page appears, read the statement that says you are subject to the same user agreement that governs your auction sales. Then click Continue to connect to the Select Theme page, where you begin to create your store.

On the Select Theme page, you have to choose a graphic design for your store from the examples supplied. If you don't want to use a theme, you can delete or change it later on. Click Next, and you go to the Provide Basic Information page. The Store Content page presents you with a form that you fill out to locate your store and describe it to potential customers.

1. Enter your store's "brand name" in the Store Name box.

2. Write a short (300-character-or-less, including blank spaces between words) description of your store in the Store Description area. (You add more information in step 9 if you run out of space.)

**WATCH OUT!** *You don't get much room to sell your store—each field in the Store Content page is limited to a small number of characters. If you really want as many words as you need to create your own store, opt for your own web site instead. Otherwise, type your content in Microsoft Word and count the number of characters using the program's Word Count feature (it's on the Tools menu).*

3. Choose a logo for your store, or click the button next to Do Not Display A Logo.

4. Click Continue. The Review & Subscribe page appears. You choose whether you want to open a Basic Store for $9.95 a month (this is the preferred option for beginners), a Featured Store for $49.95 per month, or an Anchor Store for $499.95 per month. Click the button next to the option you want (or send e-mail to anchorstores@ebay.com if you prefer that option) and click Start My Subscription Now.

5. After you have created a store, you enter the types of sales categories in which your merchandise will be sold. You also specify your payment methods, ship-to locations, and your sales tax specifications. In the Store Customer Service & Return Policy box, type in any money-back guarantee, customer service numbers, return policies, or Square Trade memberships you can boast.

Give yourself a pat on the back: you've created your store and now you can start selling on it.

**TIP** *You can always change your store's category or description by clicking the Seller, Manage Store link on your store's home page.*

## List Your Sales Items

Once you've made the decisions needed to create your eBay store, you'll probably find listing items for sale a breeze, especially if you are already adept at putting up items for auction on eBay. Plus, you don't have to worry about setting reserve prices or starting bids. You also don't have to worry about monitoring bids as they are placed. There aren't any bids at all; rather, you set a fixed price and the item is listed at that price for 30 days.

The challenge lies in driving customers to your store: you really have to "push" and promote your store or you may not have any sales. Be sure to add a link to your store to all e-mail correspondence and to include a link to the store when you send notifications to winning bidders. Make it easy and natural for the buyer to purchase additional items from you.

**WATCH OUT!** *There are downsides to selling with an eBay store. For one thing, the items you sell aren't retrieved by users who use eBay's popular search page. They only appear in response to a seller search. There's also no guarantee you'll get enough business to make the store worthwhile, and it takes work, time, and commitment. If you're already spending 10, 20, or 30 hours a week on your auctions, expect to add several hours more for your store. You've got to put new items up for sale regularly and ship items out quickly, just as you do with auctions.*

10

# Advertising Your eBay Sales on Your Web Site

eBay doesn't let you link your web site within your auction sales descriptions. However, you can make up for this by including links to your eBay sales on your web site. While these aren't "sales," technically, they are additional ways for you to generate income as a result of the sales listings you create. You have two options for how to do this:

- **Do-it-yourself**   If you want to add details about your sales, you can paste links to your individual auctions one by one into your web page—a tedious and time-consuming process if you have lots of sales going on at the same time.

- **Let eBay do the work**   You use eBay's Editor Kit or Merchant Kit to "pull" your current auctions from eBay's database whenever someone views your web page. That way, you can be sure they are up-to-date whenever someone views them.

The manual option is impractical, especially since eBay sales are changing all the time and you might have sales ending and starting on different days. It's more efficient to use one of eBay's software kits to display the auction links automatically, as is described shortly. But to use any of the kits, you first need to join the eBay Affiliate Program.

## Drumming Up Affiliate Sales

By joining eBay's Affiliate Program you gain the ability to earn some money when someone clicks a link you have placed on your web site and your visitor goes to a page on eBay's web site as a result. If you already have a web site and you advertise or sell your creative works or your collectibles on it, it's well worth the effort to add some links. You gain a 5 cent commission when someone places a bid on eBay as a result of your links. If someone registers to become a new eBay user after clicking one of your links, you earn a $5 commission. To join the Affiliate Program, follow these steps:

1.  Go to the eBay Affiliate Program page (http://affiliates.ebay.com), shown in Figure 10-4.

2.  Click Join Now.

3.  When the Join and Become an eBay Affiliate page appears, read the details, and then click the link Join Now under the link CJ.com. The Publisher Sign Up page appears.

 *CJ.com stands for Commission Junction, a company that works with eBay to make the Affiliate Program possible.*

4.  Choose your country and preferred currency, and click Next.

5.  Read the Warning message that describes the kinds of links you can make on your web site, and then click Close.

6.  Read the rules on the Publisher Application page, check the three boxes near the bottom of the page, and then enter the name, URL, and a description of your web site. Fill in the required information about your business.

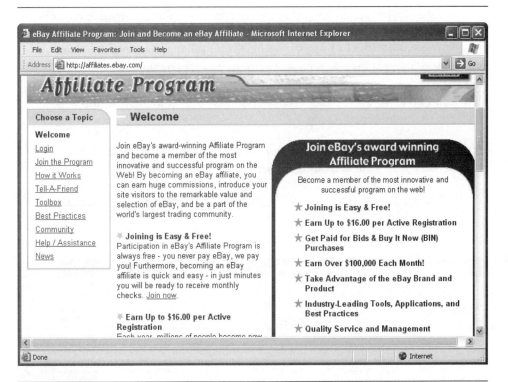

**FIGURE 10-4**   You need to join eBay's Affiliate Program before you can use the Editor Kit or Merchant Kit.

At the bottom of the page, choose your desired method of receiving payment from the drop-down list under the heading Payment Information. You can choose to receive checks from eBay, for instance. If you choose direct deposit, you have to provide checking account information so eBay can send you commissions.

7. Click Accept Terms. In a few minutes, check your e-mail. You'll see messages from Commission Junction and eBay. Open the one from Commission Junction and make note of the user name and password contained in the body of the message.

8. Go to the Commission Junction home page (http://www.cj.com), and log in to the Advertisers section. A page appears where you can pick out banners to add to one of your site's pages so that you can earn commissions.

10

It's not a bad idea to add an eBay link or two to your site; someone may click one and you might earn a commission. You can make a link from your site to a specific page on eBay. For instance, suppose you sell antiques and you want to link to eBay's Decorative Arts page. Go to the page, copy the URL from your browser's address bar, and paste it into the Flexible Destination Tool form shown in Figure 10-5. The page containing this form is located at http://affiliates.ebay.com/tools/linking/.

**COLLECTOR'S NOTE** *The Flexible Destination Tool is only one of a variety of links you can make from your web site to eBay to earn money. Others include Dynamic Landing Pages, SmartLinks, and Content Links. Find out more about the complete Affiliate Program toolbox at http://affiliates.ebay.com/tools.*

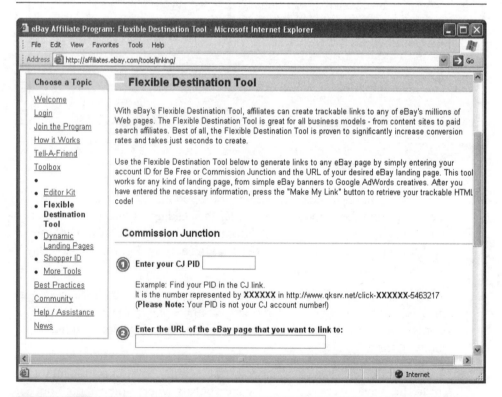

**FIGURE 10-5** You can earn money by making links from one of your web site pages to a related page on eBay.

## Editor Kit

If you're just starting out with your web site and don't have an eBay store, the Editor Kit is a practical option. The Editor Kit is software that enables you to make "live" links to any current sales you have on eBay from your personal or business web site. If people visit your site, they see a list of current items you have for sale; they can click on any of the links to those sales and view them immediately so they can place bids and make purchases. This package (in contrast to the Merchant Kit described next) only lists auction titles on a web page and isn't able to list sales on eBay stores. The Editor Kit is free to install and use.

To start using the Editor Kit, click the Get Editor Kit Now button on the Editor Kit page: http://affiliates.ebay.com/tools/editor-kit. Then sign in with your eBay user ID and password. After reading the license agreement for using the software, click I Agree. Then fill out the form shown in Figure 10-6.

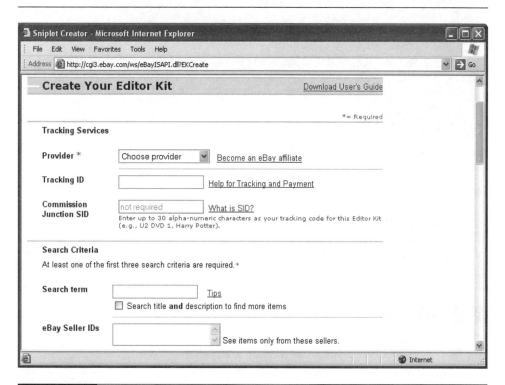

**FIGURE 10-6**   Fill out this simple form to download and install eBay's Editor Kit.

When you have filled out the form, click Preview to view a block of JavaScript code. You need to highlight this code and press CTRL-C to copy it. Then paste it into your web page where you want the search results to be displayed.

The kit allows businesses to sell both on eBay and on their own web site at the same time. For example, the Nomad Trader collectibles site (http://www.nomadtrader.com) has an eBay Marketplace page along with other pages. This page presents links to the company's current auctions of vintage postcards on eBay (see Figure 10-7).

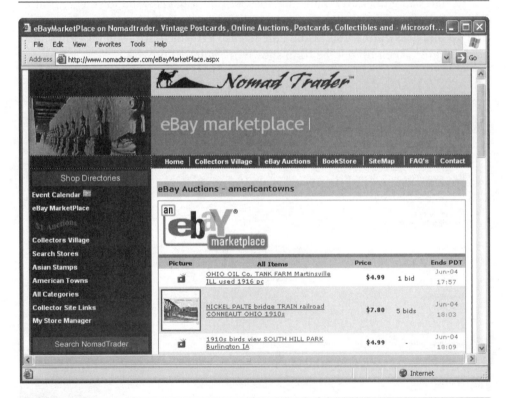

FIGURE 10-7    The Editor Kit gives you another way to sell collectibles on your web site.

## Merchant Kit

If you sell through your own eBay store and through your web site, you are a true online merchant. That's why you need to take a step up from the Editor Kit and install eBay's Merchant Kit. The Merchant Kit works in a similar way to the Editor Kit: you go to the Merchant Kit home page (http://pages.ebay.com/api/merchantkit.html). You fill out a form, get a snippet of JavaScript, and add it to the web page on which you want your eBay sales to be listed. But the Merchant Kit presents categories full of sales listings from your store and the rest of eBay. The Ritz Camera web site (http://www.ritzcamera.com), shown in Figure 10-8, gives you an example of how the marketplace looks: it's similar to the Editor Kit presentation, but the listings are drawn from many categories on eBay.

**FIGURE 10-8**   The Merchant Kit lets you link to fixed-price sales in an eBay store as well as auctions.

## Links for Collectors

| Web Site | Address | What's There |
| --- | --- | --- |
| eBay Trading Assistants page | http://pages.ebay.com/tradingassistants/learnmore.html | Information on how to become a Trading Assistant, as well as a link to a searchable database of assistants around the country |
| eBay Live Auctions | http://www.ebayliveauctions.com | Home page for the live auctions site, with links for prospective buyers and sellers |
| PowerSeller program information | http://pages.ebay.com/services/buyandsell/welcome.html | Requirements for joining the PowerSeller program and a list of benefits to PowerSellers |
| eBay Stores Welcome page | http://pages.ebay.com/storefronts/seller-landing.html | eBay Stores page with link for members who want to open a store |
| eBay Affiliate Program home page | http://affiliates.ebay.com | Information about how to become an eBay affiliate and make extra money |

# Chapter 11

## Acquiring Collectibles: Payment and Shipping

## In This Chapter You'll Learn…

- ■ Options for accepting payment for the collectibles you sell on eBay

- ■ How to obtain a merchant account so your customers can pay with credit cards

- ■ Ways to securely pack your fragile collectibles

- ■ How to ship your collectibles conveniently and securely

Shopping on eBay is fun. Winning an auction is downright exciting. But the process turns into serious business when it comes time for a collector to pay up and have the precious cargo shipped. Collectibles tend to be fragile and are almost always valuable, if not in terms of dollars and cents, then in terms of their meaning for the people who want them. Buyers are the ones who need to pay up, and shippers perform the important function of making sure the package reaches its destination safely. But it is the seller who is primarily responsible for ensuring that all the details of wrapping up (no pun intended) the transaction go smoothly.

Often, the things you buy or sell on eBay are one-of-a-kind things. When museums borrow priceless art treasures for a special exhibit, they employ a tremendous amount of care when it comes to packing and shipping, complete with security guards and specially designated trucks. You, too, need to take care when you ship. Although it can be intimidating if this isn't something you do every day of the week, the job is not impossible. You can follow the example of the millions of sellers who have spread goodwill and boosted their income by handling this part of a transaction smoothly. With a little extra care and thoroughness you, too, can complete a sale so that both you and your customer are satisfied.

# Accepting Online Payments

Authenticity and condition are of utmost importance when it comes to collectibles. Suppose a bidder is ready to put down a thousand dollars on a piece of pottery that has only been seen online. The seller claims that the artist is one who is not well known to the general public but very desirable in the outsider specialty. The potential buyer wants a reasonable degree of assurance that the piece is genuine and not a fake. In the brick-and-mortar world, the collector either would be buying from a reputable auction house or could obtain his or her own appraisal. Perhaps an arrangement could be made for the seller to put the credit card number of the buyer on file or accept a deposit while the object was appraised. Only when the customer was absolutely sure the item was genuine would he or she be compelled to part with cash.

In the world of eBay auction payments, there are no such certainties. There are remedies and recourses in case someone actually defrauds you. But when it comes to handing over money, there isn't any foolproof, absolute protection of the sort that collectors like to have. Yes, longtime sellers who want to build up good feedback ratings know they can ruin their reputation by defrauding a single person. Yes, credit card companies have "zero liability" clauses on purchases made online using their cards. But when the moment comes when you have to pay, there is always a certain level of trust you need to place in the seller. It's not unreasonable to have a nagging uncertainty until the item you have purchased actually shows up on your doorstep and you can verify its authenticity.

I wish I had a magic solution to offer you, but in all honesty I have to say that auction payments for pricey collectibles on eBay have come down to a number of methods, none of which gives the buyer a foolproof level of protection. eBay's own payment service, PayPal, has been the subject of complaints by some eBay users who have run into fraud and who contend that the service has done little or nothing to help them. Hopefully, you'll go through lots of auction sales and never run into trouble. Many users of PayPal and eBay pay for items and have them shipped and delivered with no trouble at all. Chances are you'll be among them. In case you aren't, it pays to know your payment options and alternatives, which are summarized in the sections that follow.

## Spelling Out the Terms of Sale

One of the important aspects of receiving online payments and handling shipping of merchandise purchased on eBay is the description of the terms of sale. The *terms of sale* is the section that comes at the end of the auction description that

11

## Trade Talk

When I first started using eBay, there were companies that called themselves escrow services providing buyers and sellers alike with a real sense of protection. An escrow service is a company that facilitates payments between buyers and sellers who are unable to meet in person. The services would hold the buyer's money until payment had been received, and then the seller would ship the item being purchased. The escrow company would wait until the buyer received the shipment and approved it before releasing the funds to the seller. eBay's payment service, PayPal, does provide fraud protection for buyers who either don't receive what they have paid for or who receive items that aren't as they were originally described. But it doesn't function like the aforementioned escrow services, which went out of business because, in part, PayPal was so popular.

spells out what forms of payment you receive, how you will ship, and what your policies are on specifics like checks or requests for returns. There is no single set of requirements you have to fulfill or an approach you have to take: like many aspects of eBay's operation, the details are up to you, the individual seller. While you don't have to take one particular approach when you sell collectibles, you do have to make sure you spell out several essential details clearly. These include:

- What forms of payment you will accept.

- What forms of payment you will not accept.

- Any restrictions on payment. For instance, if you accept personal checks, you need to make it clear that you will wait a suitable period, such as a week to 10 days, for the check to clear before you will ship.

- Your shipping options.

- Shipping and handling charges.

- Your returns policy. You may not allow customers to return any items for any reason, but if that's the case, you need to state so clearly in the terms of sale.

You can take a hard-line approach to your terms of sale, or go easy on your customers and provide them with a variety of options, putting the emphasis on making the customer satisfied. The important thing is that you provide your prospective bidders and buyers with as much information as possible. On the Web, information builds trust and encourages purchases. Make sure you let buyers know approximately how long it will take to ship their item and let them know if there are any times when extended periods will be required for shipment to be made. For example, there may be certain periods each year when you or your staff are on the road for one to two weeks attending collectors' conventions. Or you may be out of town during part of the auction sale. Even a delay of a couple of days can make shoppers uneasy, so make sure buyers know this in your terms of sale.

**COLLECTOR'S NOTE** *Shipping details don't always have to go at the very end of an auction description. Nancee Belshaw, who was profiled earlier in this book, puts a shipping note before her description, at least for the new celluloid collectibles she sells. That way, the shipping information actually serves as a sales incentive: "Shipping: $5 Priority Mail (box) includes delivery confirmation. Multiple celluloid animal purchases will be combined at $1.25 additional charge!"*

## The "Customer Is Always Right" Approach

If you want to be extra nice to your customers, your terms of sale will emphasize the number of payment and shipping options you provide and mention the possibility of a return, like this:

- Shipping: All shipping is done by USPS Priority Mail, but if you want to upgrade to Express Mail, I will be happy to do so for the appropriate additional shipping charges. I will e-mail you a delivery confirmation number once the package has been shipped. Insurance is available for an extra $1.30 and is highly recommended for all collectibles.

- Payment Options: I accept personal checks, cashier's checks, money orders, and PayPal. For cashier's checks and personal checks, allow seven days for the check to clear before shipping.

- Customer Service and Returns: Returns are handled on an individual basis; I will be happy to accept returned items if you feel they have been grossly misrepresented in the auction listing. If you want to return simply because you are unhappy, I will provide you with a refund, less shipping costs.

- Multiple Items: I will be happy to provide you with a single shipping charge if you want to combine multiple items.

Combining multiple items is always a good way to boost sales, especially when you sell items that are similar, such as lines of new collectibles or objects that are part of a series.

## The "Do It My Way" Approach

Some sellers (particularly those who have been "burned" by buyers who failed to pay up or who complained that their items arrived damaged or that they were not what they expected) are hard-nosed about auction descriptions. Their terms of sale might sound like those in the preceding section, but with differences of emphasis like the following:

- Payment: PayPal is strongly encouraged. Checks are held for 10 business days before shipping. I reserve the right to refuse any PayPal payments if the buyer does not have a confirmed PayPal address. If I do not hear from the buyer in 10 days the item will be relisted and negative feedback will be left.

- Shipping: Buyer pays all shipping and handling charges, including insurance when requested. Delivery confirmation is used. I ship only USPS Priority Mail, not UPS or FedEx. I do not ship internationally. Shipping is only done on Wednesdays. Any claims for lost or damaged merchandise must be handled by the post office, and shipping fees are nonrefundable.

- Returns: All sales are final. I do not grant returns for any reason, so be very sure you have gotten any questions answered before bidding.

- Feedback: Bids from members with zero feedback will not be honored.

You are well within your rights to set restrictive sales terms; the clearer and more specific the rules you set, in fact, the fewer disputes or questions you'll encounter. But keep in mind that, if you do offer refunds, you'll encourage repeat business. You might not make any money off the first transaction, but you'll make profits when the same customer returns to you over and over again.

## Proceeding Smoothly After the Sale

What happens after a sale ends depends on how much time you have and how many transactions you need to process. If you sell only a handful of objects at a time, you can afford to send out a personal notification e-mail to each of your high bidders or buyers. If you sell a dozen or more items at a time, though, you'll probably want to create a template with fields that you customize. You don't have to rewrite the letter completely for each sale. Just create an end-of-sale message that covers the most important points: the item number, the shipping cost and method, the payment method options, your address, and the date by which you expect to receive payment:

It is my pleasure to tell you that you are the high bidder for eBay item #998664432, the 1959 Hasbro space action figure. I look forward to a smooth transaction that results in positive feedback for both of us.

My preferred payment method is PayPal, but I also accept personal and cashier's checks as well as money orders. Please send the following:

Winning bid amount: $59.95

Shipping (Priority Mail): $8.95

TOTAL: $68.90

Insurance is also available for an additional $1.30. I do ship with delivery confirmation. If you want to ship by Express Mail, please let me know and I will calculate a new total for you. Payment should be sent to:

Jane Eyre
1885 Example Street
Springfield, IL 60668

If you pay by personal check, your order will ship after a 10-day waiting period.

Thank you for your bid, and I look forward to providing you with a smooth transaction.

Best wishes,
Jane Eyre

As an alternative to sending out an end-of-sale notification yourself, you can use eBay's Checkout option. When the sale ends, eBay sends you its own end-of-sale notification (see Figure 11-1). If you click the link Create and Send an Invoice, you go to a sign-in page, and then to the Send Invoice to Buyer page. This page enables you to use eBay's own automated Checkout feature, which saves you the trouble of sending your own e-mail to the buyer.

As you can see, the e-mail from eBay contains the basic information you need: the item number, shipping information, and totals, as well as links to pages that encourage you to trade safely.

## Accepting Traditional Paper Payments

As an eBay seller, you have an advantage. You can receive many different forms of payment, and you don't have to ship until you are sure the payment is in your bank account. Your big worry is a buyer or high bidder who turns out to be a headache, either through complaints about damaged or fraudulent items, through a bounced check, or through a fraudulent credit card number. However, the overwhelming number of transactions proceed without a hitch.

 *If you are dealing with international buyers, be sure to specify that they pay in U.S. funds. It's much easier if they do the currency conversion rather than putting the burden on you.*

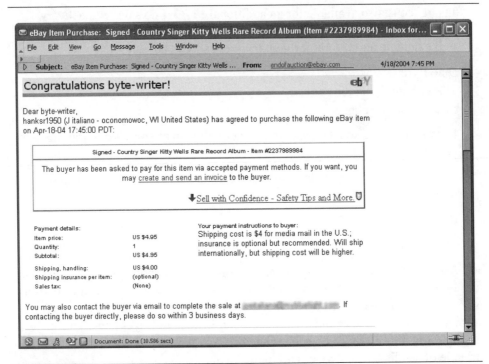

FIGURE 11-1   eBay's notification to sellers includes a link to its automated Checkout feature.

## Checks and Money Orders

The simplest form of payment you can accept is one with which collectors are sure to be familiar—a check or money order. It's comforting to receive a paper check in the mail. When you're just starting out, you should definitely include these methods of payment. Many sellers start out accepting checks and money orders, move up to PayPal or another payment service, and a few move on to accepting some sort of credit card payment directly.

To make sure you have checks and money orders listed in your auction description as forms of payment you receive, you need to manually check these options when you get to step 4 of the Sell Your Item form (shown in Figure 11-2). That's because the option for PayPal is checked by default, but the options for checks and money orders are not—at least not the first time you use the Sell Your Item form. (On subsequent visits, the form "remembers" your previous settings.)

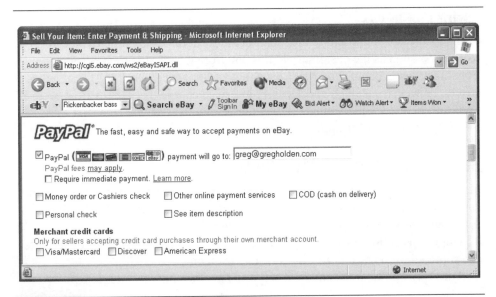

FIGURE 11-2    Make sure you check the options for "paper payment" if you want to receive checks or money orders.

**COLLECTOR'S NOTE** *One of your goals as an online businessperson should be to make life as easy as possible for your customers. Personal checks give customers another payment option, and they are also less likely to "bounce" than you might think. You should consider accepting them, while setting stringent conditions for your bidders.*

## Trade Talk

On previous occasions when I've written about eBay, I have usually taken pains to discourage sellers from accepting cash. Then one of my own buyers insisted on sending me cash, and the transaction turned out all right. I don't usually recommend that you accept cash from your buyers because of the danger that it can be stolen from the mail. If something happens and payment is lost, it becomes your responsibility to explain to the customer that the money never arrived, which can easily lead to a dispute. On the other hand, if a buyer insists that they have to send cash, just tell them that if the payment is lost or stolen in the mail it's the buyer's responsibility to send payment again.

11

## Cashier's Checks

Cashier's checks are probably the most secure form of payment that you can receive. As soon as the customer obtains one from a bank, the money is debited from his or her account. You don't have to wait for such a check to "clear" when it arrives. However, cashier's checks carry a service charge that ranges from $3 to $5. You can't blame your customers if they don't want to send you a cashier's check. Be sure to provide other options as well.

# Becoming a PayPal Merchant

Many sellers and buyers alike prefer to have a middleman accept the money and pass it along, and sellers don't mind having the service subtract a fee for doing so. A payment service like eBay's own PayPal (http://www.paypal.com) does just that: it functions as an intermediary between someone who provides goods or services and someone who pays money in exchange for them.

For eBay transactions, payment services have two big advantages:

- **Security**    Payment is no longer a matter of trust when you use a payment service. The buyer knows they're going to get the money, rather than having to trust a shipper. The seller knows the payment is going to be received—and quickly, without having to wait for the mail to deliver it. (PayPal also offers fraud protection for its members.)

- **Credit card purchases**    Payment services like PayPal enable customers to pay you with a credit card even if you don't have a merchant account with a bank, a point-of-sale (POS) terminal, or payment gateway software. The payment service deducts the purchase price from the customer's credit card account and transfers it to you. You become an instant credit card merchant!

PayPal isn't perfect, but it is eBay's own payment service, and it works well for millions of transactions every month. So many buyers use PayPal that you are well advised to sign up as a PayPal merchant so you can accept payments from buyers who have also signed up for the service. For sellers, PayPal is exceptionally easy to use: signing up for a PayPal seller's account can be done in a matter of minutes.

Even if you have a user ID with eBay, you still have to register with PayPal to accept payments once your first payment comes in. Registration is free, however. When you register, you'll need to choose one of two accounts: a Personal Account or Premier/Business Account. As a seller, you definitely want the Premier/Business Account because Personal Accounts cannot receive credit card payments. To receive credit card payments, sellers are charged either a Merchant Rate or a Standard Rate. To qualify for the lower merchant rates, one of the following must apply:

■ You have been a PayPal member in good standing for the past 90 days and received an average of $1,000 in payments per month over the previous 90 days.

■ You have received a competitive offer from an established merchant account provider such as First Data Merchant Services or Metavante Corporation.

■ You have proven yourself to be a long-standing eBay seller who deals in high volume, and you include your eBay user ID and password on your Merchant Rate application.

To keep yourself qualified for the Merchant Rate fees, you need to maintain a volume of $1,000 a month with PayPal and keep your account in good standing (that is, you have no unresolved chargebacks due to customers' using credit cards fraudulently). The difference between the Standard Rate and Merchant Rate fees at this writing is shown in Table 11-1.

*Keep in mind that PayPal's fees change from time to time and may be different by the time you read this. You can get the current fees at http:// www.paypal.com/cgi-bin/webscr?cmd=p/gen/fees-receiving-outside.*

Once you sign up for a PayPal account, you'll receive e-mail asking you to verify your account. Verification is important because it gives those with whom you do business an extra assurance that you are who you say you are. PayPal accounts, like eBay accounts, can be "hijacked" by unscrupulous individuals who try to impersonate someone else in order to make unauthorized purchases or receive money for items they don't actually have to sell.

## Credit Cards

Collectors who purchase sought-after items on eBay or elsewhere want to have those items in their possession as soon as possible. They want to put that doll on the shelf, that antique rifle above the fireplace, or that old convertible in the garage. Credit cards are the fastest way for collectors to pay up; depending on the seller, they can

| Currency in Which You Are Paid | Standard Rate | Merchant Rate |
|---|---|---|
| U.S. dollars | 2.9% + $0.30 | 2.2% + $0.30 |
| Canadian dollars | 3.4% + C $0.55 | 2.7% + C $0.55 |
| Euros | 3.4% + €0.35 | 2.7% + €0.35 |
| Pounds sterling | 3.4% + £0.20 | 2.7% + £0.20 |
| Yen | 3.4% + ¥40 | 2.7% + ¥40 |

**TABLE 11-1**   Premier/Business Account Rate Fees

send payment and have the merchandise shipped within a day or even a matter of hours. One of the biggest advantages of using PayPal, for sellers, is that it enables them to accept credit card payments from buyers. PayPal handles the processing of the payment, and the seller doesn't have to take out a merchant credit card account.

*One especially nice feature of PayPal is that it accepts credit cards such as Discover and American Express that can be hard to accept with a conventional merchant account. Normally, even if you obtain a conventional merchant account through a bank or other financial institution, you have to make arrangements through those two credit card companies separately to be one of their merchants.*

### eChecks

The big thing in electronic payments these days is not credit card or debit card payments but making deductions directly from a consumer's checking account. This is the method used to make online bill payments. PayPal allows buyers to make payments by deducting from a checking account; it calls this "paying with an eCheck."

*Some eBay users love PayPal for its convenience. Others dislike it for various reasons: the main one is cost. PayPal's fees aren't inconsiderable. Other services specifically advertise themselves as having fees that are lower than PayPal's.*

## Turning to Western Union Auction Payments

If you are used to receiving traditional paper payments for the antiques or collectibles you sell, Western Union provides a popular and safe alternative to electronic payments. Buyers send a credit card or other payment to Western Union; the company then issues a paper money order and sends it to you, the seller. Only when you receive payment are you obligated to ship the merchandise to the customer.

As a seller, using Western Union Auction Payments (http://www.auctionpayments .com/) is especially simple. Sellers don't have to register with Western Union to receive money orders using the service. (Although registered sellers can set up accounts where they can review records of past orders and have their address verified by Western Union Auction Payments.) However, buyers *do* need to register with the service so they can send you money orders. They use the web site to choose a credit or debit card in order to make payment. They add any shipping fees you have specified to the amount of the money order. They also pay transaction fees as shown here. (You'll find a full table of fees at http://www.auctionpayments.com/ PurchaseMO.asp.)

| Face Value of Money Order | Transaction Fee |
| --- | --- |
| $10 or less | $1.95 |
| $10.01 to $30 | $2.95 |
| $30.01 to $50 | $3.95 |
| $50.01 to $100 | $4.95 |
| $100.01 to $1,000 | $4.95 + 2.25% of the face value of the money order |

Western Union Auction Payments uses the U.S. Postal Service to send you its money orders. Once you get a confirmation e-mail from Western Union saying that the money order has been sent to sellers by first-class mail, and the cost of postage is included in the Western Union Auction mailed to you, you have the option to either ship the merchandise immediately or wait until the money order actually arrives.

Money orders are shipped to sellers by first-class mail, and the cost of postage is included in the Western Union Auction Payments fees. However, buyers who are in a hurry to receive their merchandise can send you a money order by Priority Mail for an extra $8 or by Express Mail for $15.

If you become a registered Western Union Auction Payments seller, you can add a mention in your auction description that you accept Western Union to your auction listings as shown below. But you need to add this information to your description after you post the sale on eBay; the Sell Your Item form does not have a space for Western Union (this is not surprising, since it's a competitor to eBay's own PayPal.

11

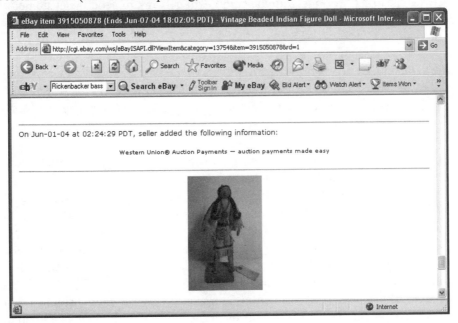

# Obtaining a Merchant Account

As you may know if you already run an antique store or other brick-and-mortar business, the other way in which you can accept credit card payments from a buyer over the Internet is to become a credit card merchant. This isn't a terribly complex process, but it can take several weeks and involves application fees, so it is beyond the scope of this chapter to explain fully. The following is only a brief overview of what's involved. (See my book *How to Do Everything With Your eBay Business* for more detailed information.)

Suppose you are starting from scratch and need to obtain a traditional merchant account, which is the type of account needed in order to accept credit cards. The traditional way to obtain a merchant account is through a bank or other financial institution. You apply to the bank and provide documents that show that you are a legitimate businessperson. You also pay an application fee, which can amount to $300 or more. The bank's officers review your request for several weeks, after which time they hopefully grant you approval. You then purchase an input device that lets you send your customers' credit card numbers to the credit card network. This might be a point-of-sale terminal that lets you do "card swipes," plus a printer that can print out the receipts your customers sign. You can find inexpensive versions of such terminals on eBay for less than $50 (see Figure 11-3).

After you set up the hardware or software processing, your financial institution processes the order, working with the credit card network to debit the customer's account and credit yours. Along the way, the financial institution charges fees for the processing.

> *Banks tend to be more expensive than companies that specialize in providing merchant accounts to online merchants. Companies like 1st American Card Service (http://www.1stamericancardservice.com) don't charge an application fee. But they do charge Internet fees, discount fees, and so on.*

In the online world, you don't need a hardware terminal to submit credit card purchase information to the financial network that does the processing. Instead, you use a software program that functions as a *gateway* to the network. One program that I'm familiar with is called GO Authorizer by Go Software (http://www.gosoftware.com/index.htm). GO Authorizer functions as a payment gateway: it allows you to add a "Pay Button" to one of your web pages so that customers can send their payments to you. This means you need to set up a web site with a payment form where your auction customers can go to pay for what they've purchased. If you already have an online store, and you want your customers to be able to make purchases there as well as on eBay, this is a convenient way to do it.

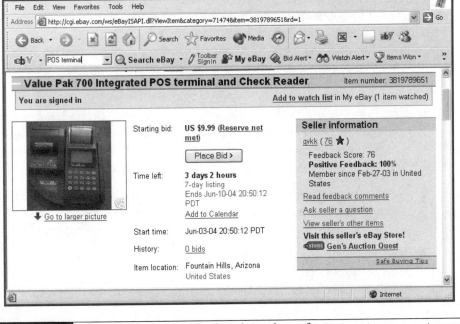

**FIGURE 11-3**    You need hardware like that pictured or software to enter your customers' credit card data.

11

## Verifying Addresses

If you accept credit card payments only for Internet-based transactions, you don't need to purchase and set up a POS terminal to communicate with the credit card network—after all, people aren't going to be sending you their actual credit cards to swipe, and you aren't going to be printing out receipts for them to sign. Both of these things—receiving the actual credit card and having the customer sign the charge slip in front of you so you can compare his or her signature to the one on the card—are safeguards for you, the seller. They enable you to verify that the person making the purchase is actually the cardholder and not someone who has stolen the card.

How do you process transactions and verify the cardholder's identity in an Internet transaction? You're at a disadvantage because you never see whom you're dealing with and you don't get a signature to ensure someone's identity. In that case, you need to use credit card processing software to do the verification for you. The software compares the cardholder's billing address to the shipping address that the customer gives you. A program called ICVerify (http://www.icverify.com) performs such verification and processing.

## Keeping Your PayPal Account Secure

PayPal is used by many eBay members—so many, in fact, that PayPal accounts are tempting targets for hackers and con artists who try to get legitimate user names and passwords. As I was working on this chapter, PayPal sent an e-mail warning to its customers, notifying them of fraud problems that had been reported recently. Clients were advised to:

- Connect to the PayPal home page by using a secure URL (https://www.paypal.com) rather than the regular one (http://www.paypal.com). A secure URL connects to a web server that uses encryption to protect any information that is exchanged by browser and server.

- Never give out PayPal account information or other critical details such as bank account numbers or Social Security numbers in response to e-mail inquiries from anyone.

- Not respond to any requests to download software in order to make their account work; such e-mails, which may claim to come from PayPal, are probably fraudulent.

- Pick a secure, unique password (not a word in the dictionary, and not a proper name), and change it every 30 to 60 days.

These security tips, of course, apply equally well to your eBay user account as to your PayPal account.

## Paying Fees

Credit card merchants are required to pay a variety of different fees for the ability to process their customers' credit cards. Such fees typically include the following:

- **Discount rate**    This is a fee charged by banks or merchant account companies of 1 to 4 percent for each transaction.

- **Monthly premium**    Every month you may be charged $30 to $470 for maintaining your merchant account.

- **Per transaction fee**    You'll probably have to pay 10 to 30 cents per each transaction to the merchant account company or bank. For transactions conducted over the Internet, some institutions charge an additional 2 to 3 percent.

In addition, most merchant account companies charge you a fee if you process a purchase that turns out to be fraudulent because someone was using a stolen credit card number.

Besides credit card fees, you'll need to pay your final value fee to eBay, as well as any extra fees for highlighting, selling in a second category, or other added features. You don't really have to manually send a check to eBay, however; instead, you'll receive an e-mail invoice like the one shown in Figure 11-4, stating that the required fees were already deducted from the credit card or checking account number you provided to eBay when you signed up for a seller's account. Be sure to look the figures over to make sure you actually paid for what you are being charged; if you see a discrepancy, contact eBay by logging on to eBay's web site and clicking Help in the navigation bar to connect to the eBay Help pages. Then click sequentially Contact Us, Ask About Selling, and finally Billing and Fees.

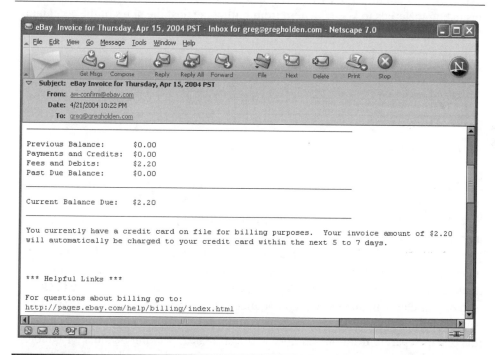

**11**

**FIGURE 11-4**   eBay automatically deducts seller's fees, but you should make sure they are accurate.

# Packing Your Merchandise

Think about what happens when a package finally arrives (it always seems like too long, when an eagerly sought-after item has been purchased) at the buyer's door. Then the collector eagerly unpacks it, makes sure all the pieces are in place, inspects for any damage, and compares cracks and blemishes to what was mentioned in the description.

*You'll find a good set of tips for packing collectibles on the Holt Howard Collectibles web site (http://www.geocities.com/holt_howard/holthoward/ shipping_hints.html).*

## Obtaining Packing Materials

Your packing materials don't have to be new, but they do need to be reasonably sturdy. When collectibles are concerned, you can't use too many insulating materials. When you do obtain a box, whether it is new or recycled, remember to stuff it with insulating materials to keep the item from rattling against the sides of the container. Commonly used "cushioners" include:

- Packing peanuts
- Newspaper
- Bubble wrap
- Foam insulation

Besides these materials, which are primarily intended to keep collectibles from bouncing against one another or against the box, you should also keep an eye out for such materials as corrugated dividers and pressure-sensitive or nylon-reinforced tape.

I say "keep an eye out" because it doesn't matter where you find your packing materials, whether you buy them on eBay, at an office supply store, or "recycle" them by picking them up from alleys or behind various stores. If you are packing something that contains more than one piece or component, be sure to wrap it separately in bubble wrap or newspaper, and tape it with packing tape. Then keep the pieces separate from one another with cardboard, packing peanuts, or bubble wrap. Make sure you have a layer of insulating material on the bottom of the box and one on top before you seal it.

If you sell the same type of items over and over, you can order custom-made shipping supplies that are specially created to fit them. For instance, various manufacturers fashion custom boxes and cardboard pads that are made to fit comic books and magazines. If you do a big volume, you will save time and effort by having shipping supplies tailor-made to suit your needs. On the other hand, if you need a variety of sizes of shipping boxes, visit an office supply store like Office Depot each day and get their cartons before they are crushed and trashed. Make friends with store managers so they will save boxes for you, and greet them in a friendly way every time you go in to buy your other supplies.

**TIP**   *If you decide to use a recycled box, be sure to use one that is in good condition, or the U.S. Post Office may not allow it. If you do re-use a box, cover the labels and markings with a black marker or other adhesive labels. After you seal the box, be sure you mark it "Fragile." You might even consider adding "Fragile—Collectibles" or "Fragile—Antiques."*

## Including an Extra Gift

Few things are guaranteed to build goodwill with your customers like an extra touch you can add to your item(s) when you ship them out. I've interviewed a number of PowerSellers and other longtime sellers over the years, and many of them throw in something extra along with what's shipped. It might be a coupon for a household item, or a coupon of your own offering 10 percent off on the next purchase if it is made within the next 30 days. It might be a postcard or an extra trinket. It's the thought that counts. Even just a short handwritten note wishing the buyer well (and possibly directing them to your web site or eBay Store) and encouraging them to buy from you in the future will end the transaction on a good note and virtually guarantee positive feedback.

11

## Trade Talk

This book's technical editor, David T. Alexander, says he has been offering discount coupons for nearly 30 years. "Coupons give buyers a reason to keep looking at your eBay About Me page or your web site," he comments. "Since I sell comic books, I have had various comic book artists draw a sketch for my own coupons. These have become quite popular and have generated additional sales. Over the years the coupons have become collectors' items themselves. I recently sold a 20-year-old coupon with a drawing of Richie Rich on it for $8.99 on eBay."

# Shipping Your Collectibles

Shipping safely, quickly, and reliably is one of the keys to being a successful eBay seller. Yet new sellers tend to underestimate the amount of time and care required to pack and ship effectively. One seller I interviewed told me that it takes an hour to prepare, photograph, list, pack, and ship an item from start to finish. Scout the nearest postal facility and private mail stores. If you have such a facility right around the corner and there's a convenient parking lot, you might prefer to travel there for shipping. If your post office is small and parking is a problem, it might be better to set up an arrangement with United Parcel Service or Federal Express to provide pickup service. The following sections briefly compare the shippers used by most eBay sellers.

 *Is the collectible item you want to sell really suitable to ship? Suppose you have a Tiffany lampshade worth thousands of dollars. Do you think you could trust it to any of the "Big Three" shippers listed below? If you are in doubt, perhaps you should try selling through an auction house or antique store in your area and not doing the shipping yourself at all.*

## The Big Three Shippers

Most eBay sellers have a post office within walking or driving distance or are on a FedEx or UPS pickup route. That's the primary reason they choose one of these three shipping options over the other two: convenience. Pick the shipper you find easiest to work with to make your sales activities proceed more easily. If you can get a shipper to do a pickup at your home or business, for instance, you save a lot of time that you can spend building up inventory and putting up more items for sale.

### United States Postal Service

One of the big advantages of using the United States Postal Service is convenience: they have offices all over the country, they are inexpensive, and you can find supplies there as well. In fact, many sellers choose to ship Priority Mail because it's not only fast but the USPS gives you free envelopes, boxes, and tape that you can use for packing (the free packing materials are available only for Priority Mail, however).

As any USPS customers can tell you, waiting in line at the post office is an all-too-common experience. But it doesn't have to be that way. You can order the Priority Mail shipping materials on the USPS's Postal Store (http://shop.usps.com). And you can order postage from Stamps.com (http://www.stamps.com), a USPS-authorized service that enables you to print postage from your computer. Just hand the window clerk your packages and you are on your way. Stamps.com also gives you the option of hiding the postage amount. This prevents complaints from buyers who can tell if you charge a fixed fee for shipping that is higher than the actual postage cost.

TIP
*If you sell books or records or tapes, the post office offers the Media Mail option, which used to be called Book Rate. You can use it to send a very heavy book very inexpensively.*

## Federal Express

If you are looking for a good, low-cost alternative to the USPS, consider FedEx Ground and FedEx Home Delivery. Both are good options for sellers and buyers who don't mind five- to seven-day shipping. And packages up to 150 lbs. each for Ground service and 70 lbs. for Home Delivery are allowed.

For faster shipments, FedEx is generally more expensive than USPS. On the other hand, once you sign up for an account with FedEx, you can obtain free shipping materials at your home, do your packing there, and have FedEx pick up from your door on their regular route.

## United Parcel Service

UPS is a fast and reliable shipper, and you can open an Internet account (http:// www.ups.com/bussol/solutions/internetship.html) so you can print out your own shipping labels at home. However, UPS charges an extra fee of $7 to $16 per week to make a pickup at your address.

COLLECTOR'S NOTE
*You can use a variety of online calculators to quickly determine the most economical way to send your package. A USPS online calculator is available at http://pages.ebay.com/usps/calculator.html. The UPS Service Center online calculator is at http://www.servicecenter.ups.com/ebay/ ebay.html#qcost. FedEx's Rate Finder is at http://www.fedex.com/ ratefinder/home?cc=US&language=en.*

11

## Delivery Confirmation

Where collectibles are concerned, it's essential to make sure what you ship actually reaches its destination. For an extra dollar or so, you should get delivery confirmation: a paper that the shipper sends back to you when the item is delivered. This protects you against claims that are occasionally made by a few (not many) buyers, who say they never received an item and demand a refund. It also prevents disputes with the shipper over whether something was lost in transit and actually delivered or not. It's well worth getting this extra service, which you can add as part of the handling fee that you charge to your buyers.

## Insurance

Insurance is more important with valuable collectibles than with easily replaced household goods. The reasons should be obvious: The collectibles are hard to find and replace, if not one-of-a-kind. They may well be fragile. The condition is critical to their value. All of the popular shippers (FedEx, UPS, and USPS) offer insurance, but you might save some money by buying insurance separately from Universal Parcel Insurance Coverage (http://www.u-pic.com).

You can even order a complete insurance policy that covers your collectibles in your home or store from Collectibles Insurance Agency (http://www.collectinsure.com). This protects your inventory in your home r store or when you travel with merchandise to sell at a show. If you are a Trading Assistant, such insurance protects you from having to pay off a consignor if your home or business is burglarized or damaged by fire. This policy can optionally insure all the packages you ship.

## Tracking and Shipping Notices

Tracking is especially important where collectibles are concerned. When you ship, be sure to get a tracking number from the shipper. You can then transmit this tracking number to your customer when you send out a shipping notice. There is no rule that says you are required to send out a notice to a buyer stating that their item has been shipped to them, but it builds goodwill and calms the nerves of collectors who are anxiously awaiting their new possessions. Also ask the buyer to let you know when the item has been received and whether he or she is satisfied with the transaction. Such a note encourages the buyer to leave positive feedback for you after the item is delivered. It never hurts to remind buyers to leave feedback for you.

 *Be sure to leave positive feedback for the individual after the transaction is complete. You don't need to receive feedback from someone in order to leave feedback for that same individual, of course. But if you want to build up your positive feedback rating, a reminder e-mail asking specifically for feedback can help.*

# Links ^for^ Collectors

| Web Site | Address | What's There |
|---|---|---|
| PayPal | http://www.paypal.com | eBay's electronic payment service |
| PayPal Seller's Fees | http://www.paypal.com/cgi-bin/ webscr?cmd=p/gen/fees-receiving-outside | A table that indicates how much PayPal will charge you for accepting payments using its service |
| Holt Howard Collectibles | http://www.geocities.com/holt_ howard/holthoward/shipping_ hints.html | A page full of useful shipping tips for sellers of collectibles |
| USPS Online Calculator | http://pages.ebay.com/usps/ calculator.html | Forms and tables you can use to calculate United States Postal Service shipping costs |
| UPS Service Center online calculator | http://www.servicecenter.ups.com/ ebay/ebay.html#qcost | United Parcel Service shipping calculator |
| FedEx Rate Finder | http://www.fedex.com/ratefinder/ home?cc=US&language=en | Federal Express shipping calculator |
| Stamps.com | http://www.stamps.com | Buy postage and print it out from your computer |
| Collectibles Insurance Agency | http://www.collectinsure.com | Insurance for a wide variety of collectibles whether they are stored in your home or business or you are traveling with them |

11

# Part IV

## Advanced Collectors' Options

# Chapter 12

## Appraising Your Collectibles on eBay and the Web

## In This Chapter You'll Learn...

- Different ways to discover what items are in demand in an eBay category

- How third-party auction companies provide software that analyzes eBay sales

- Where to find easily overlooked reports on especially "hot" eBay categories

- Where to get your collectibles appraised, either through eBay or experts on the Web

"How much is that thing worth?" This is a question every collector asks at least once in a while. The short answer is simple: It's worth what someone will pay for it at the time you put it up for sale. It's impossible to predict that purchase price exactly, but knowing your collectible's approximate value can help you set reasonable reserves and starting bids. The answer to that question can usually be found on eBay. eBay, more than price guides or the opinions of appraisers, provides real-world information about what people actually pay for items similar to yours.

Even if you don't want to buy or sell that precious object in your display case or on your shelf, eBay can serve as a useful resource. The trick is finding the right items and doing research in the places where you can find items that are similar to yours. Then, too, there is another question other than what something is worth, and that is "Should people actually pay what they pay on eBay?" That question is best answered by experts in the field, and this chapter covers where to find them, too.

# Discover What's "Hot" in a Category

One of the most common questions new eBay sellers ask goes along the lines of "What do people like to buy or bid on?" or "What are the most popular things I can sell on eBay?" In years past, eBay used a special "lighted match" icon to designate items that were particularly "hot"—in other words, that had attracted 20, 30, or more bids. They don't mark such items anymore. But you do have a couple of options for tracking with lists of items that are in high demand, as described in the sections that follow.

## Revisiting a Favorite Category

One of the best ways to discover what's popular is to pick a category full of objects you know and love and follow it carefully. If you have collected comic books since you were a kid, you already have an idea what the rare issues are and which series people tend to collect. On eBay, the demand might be slightly different. Logging on to eBay on a daily basis and browsing through the items for sale can tell you what's hot at a given moment; doing so over several weeks can be time-consuming, even tedious, but it will give you a better idea of what you should try to sell. Go to the category in which you want to sell and choose Price: Highest First from the Sort By drop-down list. The list of items currently for sale in that category refreshes, and the items with the highest prices appear at the top. The category Collectibles : Comics has some amazing and highly priced books right on the first page (see Figure 12-1).

Of course, simply because a seller puts a $22,000 Buy It Now price on a set of Amazing Spider-Man comic books doesn't mean they are actually worth that much. But the high-priced items that have attracted 10 or more bids are ones that are obviously in demand. When you browse through categories regularly, you also learn what's involved in advertising items, too. You learn that for the rarest comics,

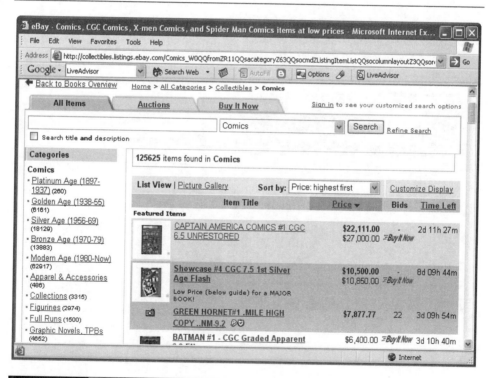

**FIGURE 12-1**   Sorting by price can give you an idea of what's rare and valuable in a category—according to sellers, at least.

such as Batman #1 or early Spider-Man issues, it's important to grade the condition of the book on a scale of 1 to 10, with 10 being mint. The most valuable issues are typically graded by someone who belongs to the Comics Guaranty Corporation (CGC). In fact, eBay has an affiliation with the CGC, and eBay's Pop Culture category opening page has a link to the organization; you can send your own comic books there for grading (see Figure 12-2).

When you click the link to the CGC, you discover that you get a 10 percent discount for being an eBay member and that the fee for grading and mounting the book in a plastic sleeve, frame, or other protective container runs anywhere from $11 to $79. But for a truly valuable comic book, such handling and certification is essential.

If you are already a collector, you probably have several price guides and reference books that cover your areas of interest. And if you are not a collector but want to sell specific types of collectors' items, be sure to obtain a reference book or two covering material you hope to sell. These books may or may not have contemporary pricing information, but they are invaluable for determining grading

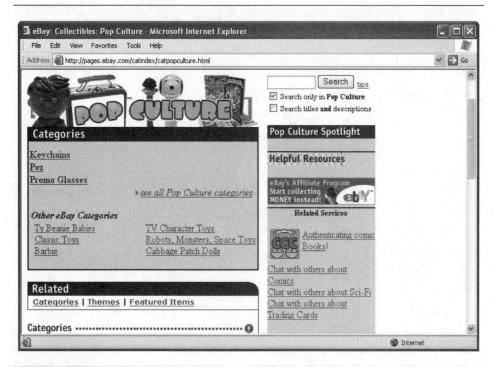

**FIGURE 12-2**   Make sure you grade valuable collectibles and describe them in a way that collectors will understand.

and description standards. Besides that, they help you understand the collectors' nomenclature. If you are able to understand and use the accepted terminology in a given field, it gives potential bidders a feeling that you know what you are talking about, and that builds trust.

> COLLECTOR'S NOTE *It would be nice if you could sort category listings and search results by the number of bids, but at present, eBay doesn't provide this functionality.*

## Scouring Seller Central

eBay's Seller Central contains plenty of useful information for sellers that is made available free of charge and can help you evaluate what's in demand. Going to the Seller Central home page (http://pages.ebay.com/sellercentral) and clicking the What's Hot link takes you to a page of the same name. Click Hot Items by Category, and you are taken to a document called the Hot Items Report, which is prepared every month. The report doesn't describe all of eBay's categories, only those in which demand is growing faster than available supply. In fact, categories are further divided into "degrees of hotness":

- *Super Hot* categories are those in which the number of bids is growing at least 35 percent faster than the number of listings.

- *Very Hot* categories see the number of bids growing 15 to 35 percent faster than the number of listings.

- *Hot* categories have a bid-to-listing growth difference of up to 15 percent.

> COLLECTOR'S NOTE *It's easy to overlook the Merchandising Calendar link on the What's Hot page. The calendar lists seasonal promotions that are planned for the coming months; eBay will give special attention to certain categories during those promotions. (Usually, on the eBay home page, links to those categories are prominently displayed within a promotional ad.) For example, during the Dads & Grads promotion in early June, sports, electronics, watches, and other categories are featured. If you are able to obtain wholesale or collectible merchandise in those categories and put them up for the sale during the promotion, you're likely to get more bids.*

Naturally, if you are able to provide Very Hot or Super Hot items for auction or for fixed-price sale on eBay, you are likely to get bids on them. Many of the items listed as

Super Hot or Very Hot in May 2004 didn't fall into the category of collectibles, however. The list included APS film, Nikon digital cameras, industrial paper folders, Dell computers, and the like. But plenty of collectibles were listed, including:

- **Coins:** Coins from Israel and Poland

- **Entertainment Memorabilia:** Press kits from television shows or movies from the decade 1970–1979, as well as autographs of operatic performers

- **Miscellaneous Collectibles:** This meta-category includes everything from comic book collections, Mars Attacks or Angel trading cards; to This Little Piggy collectibles, Marlboro cigarette memorabilia, and Mountain Dew advertising items

- **Musical Instruments:** Kramer electric guitars and blues and jazz sheet music

- **Pottery and Glass:** China and dinnerware by Midwinter, Copeland, and Crown Ducal, and art pottery by Camark Pottery and Coors Pottery

It's not a bad idea to print out selected pages or the entire report and take it with you the next time you hit a big flea market or go on a garage sale expedition.

COLLECTOR'S NOTE    *The Hot Items Report is not formatted as a web page but in Adobe Acrobat's Portable Document Format (PDF). You need to have the Adobe Acrobat Reader plug-in for your browser to be able to view PDF files. If you have the plug-in for your browser, the file will open automatically. If not, you'll need to download the plug-in from Adobe's web site (http://www.adobe.com).*

You can also find items that are in vogue on the Sell by Category page in Seller Central (http://pages.ebay.com/sellercentral/sellbycategory.html). Click the In Demand link beneath one of the categories shown, and you go to a page full of information about what buyers want in that part of eBay: Top Buyer's Searches, Top 10 Picks, and a short description of trends within the field (see Figure 12-3).

When you have a collectible item to sell that you think is in demand, there's nothing wrong with notifying your own previous bidders of what you are selling. Most of them will probably find your items through their own searches, but you might create an early demand by directing interested collectors to your items.

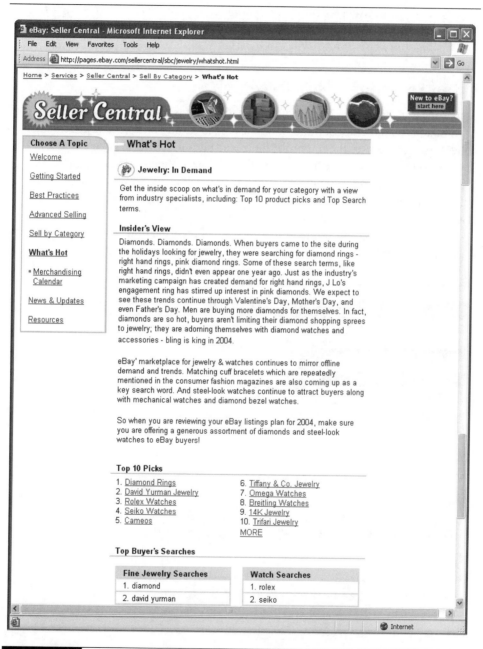

**FIGURE 12-3**    In Demand pages give you an insider's view of a category and lists of what buyers are looking for.

TIP

*The auction service provider Andale offers a product called What's Hot that tracks in-demand items on eBay. The service costs $3.95 per month; find out more at http://research.andale.com/hotreport/hot_quickstart.jsp.*

## Using Someone Else's Research

Sometimes, if you are lucky, you will find someone who actually tracks eBay sales in a particular category and publishes those results online. These dedicated collectors provide useful content for their web sites and information about what's in demand that can help both them and their fellow collectors. For example, the folks who run the Badgerland web site in the UK (http://www.badgerland.co.uk/help/charity/examples.html), which is devoted to anything badger-related, list a few examples of objects that have been sold on eBay (see Figure 12-4).

It's not easy to locate such sites or such sales records, however. Even if you can find some examples of eBay sales, you don't know how recent or reliable they

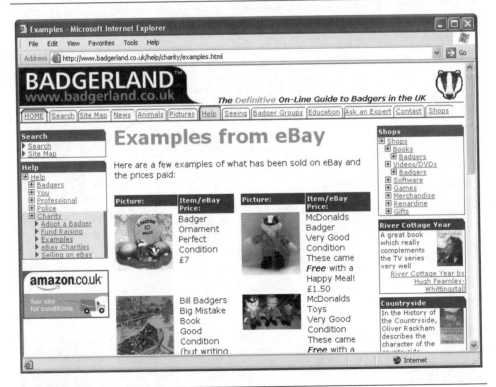

FIGURE 12-4    If you're lucky, you'll find a web site that tracks collectors' items on eBay.

really are. You depend on the site's owner to provide you with a representative and accurate sampling of eBay sales. And the sites you find tend to be very narrowly focused on a single type of collectible. Here are some examples:

- The Roycroft Copper Online Price Guide lists some eBay sales of this particular line of collectibles at http://www.roycroftcopper.com/other.htm.

- A few rare antique pickle bottles that sold on eBay for as much as $44,100 are described at http://www.antiquebottles.com/pickle.

- Sandy's Vintage Tonka Vehicles web site (http://www.fortunecity.com/business/turn/1370/tmaps.htm) lists several rare Tonka pieces that have sold on eBay.

**COLLECTOR'S NOTE** *An article on the Real Estate Journal web site entitled "Should You Buy or Sell a Home Through eBay?" reported on the sale of high-priced celebrities' homes on eBay and interviewed a couple of regular folks who bid on or made real estate purchases through the site, but pointed out that eBay doesn't keep track of completed real estate transactions, so detailed conclusions can't be reached about sales in this part of eBay.*

## Tapping into Completed Sales Yourself

In "the good old days," a few years ago, you could search eBay's completed auctions using Advanced Search and get several weeks' worth of previous sales. Over time, eBay has reduced the amount of completed auction data available on its site. These days, a Completed Items Only search turns up about two weeks worth of completed data. Not only that, but eBay requires you to log in with your user ID and password. Still, despite the limited nature of the results, Completed Items Only can be of value. Suppose you want to search for completed comic book sales in past weeks. You could enter the name of a specific type of comic book, such as "Incredible Hulk," and you would get results specific to that series.

On the other hand, if you enter the general term "comic," you'll get a whopping 52,000-plus listings that have the term "comic" in the title. Click Price: Highest First, and you discover that a dealer attempted to sell a million (that's 1,000,000) comic books all at once, received a high bid of more than $200,000, and that this did not meet the reserve price! If you choose other criteria, such as Ending Soonest, you get more everyday sales, such as Bugs Bunny comic books that sold for $35 and others that sold for less than $10. But you have to laboriously click on each completed sale's description to find out more about each item, and you have to draw your own conclusions about trends in the category or in the industry. For more detailed research information, you need to turn to an auction service company other than eBay.

## Searching eBay with Andale's Free Research Tool

In Chapter 3, you were introduced to the auction service Andale, and how it can help you estimate the value of items you have for sale. You can find Andale's free research tool right on Andale's home page (http://www.andale.com/corp/index.html, shown in Figure 12-5). Enter the name of an item you want to research, click Search, and you get an extensive set of data based on recent eBay sales.

Besides the research box on its home page, Andale also offers a search on its Price Finder page. Price Finder is Andale's service that studies the prices sellers attract for completed transactions. Enter a keyword or words, click Search, and you get a summary of a month's worth of sales on eBay. The summary includes the average sale price, examples of typical sales, and a chart that indicates how many items were sold compared to the number of items listed (see Figure 12-6). Like most of Andale's other services, this one costs $3.95 per month.

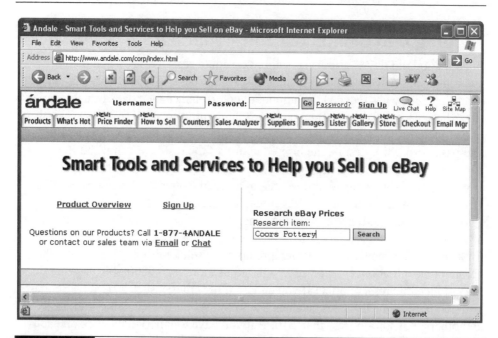

**FIGURE 12-5**    Andale's free search box could be a good alternative to eBay's search tools.

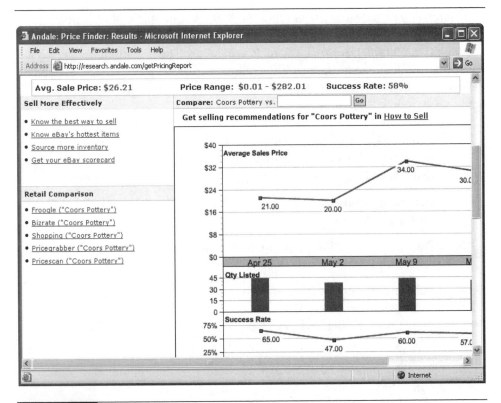

**FIGURE 12-6**    Price Finder reports on a month's worth of sales on eBay.

Andale's Price Finder can provide you with results that are far more detailed than the ones eBay provides. The following compares the results of an eBay Completed Items Only search for Coors Pottery sales with a search done using Andale's free search tool:

| Source | Number of Completed Sales | Dates Reported | High Price | Low Price |
|---|---|---|---|---|
| eBay Completed Items | 91 | May 26–June 10, 2004 | $103.51 | $3.99 |
| Andale Price Finder | 163 | April 25–May 22, 2004 | $282.01 | $0.01 |

# Mining eBay for Data with DeepAnalysis

Research on eBay is free, but results are limited, and you have to draw all your own conclusions. With Andale's Price Finder, you download software that lets you search completed auctions on eBay for $3.95 per month. A 30-day free trial fee (and a $179 purchase price if you decide to keep the software) lets you try out another research tool, DeepAnalysis by HammerTap. The big difference between DeepAnalysis and other programs is the ability to search eBay's current auction database and generate reports about what's up for sale. To install and run the application, follow these steps:

1. Go to the DeepAnalysis download page (http://www.hammertap.com/deepanalysis/DownloadDeepAnalysis.html), read the system requirements, and download the version of the program that is right for your computer.

2. After you download the software, run the setup wizard to install the files on your hard disk.

3. When the program first starts up, it prompts you to check the HammerTap web site for updates. Click Check for Updates.

4. After the check has been completed, another window opens, prompting you to enter your license key if you have purchased the software. For the 30-day trial period, click Evaluate. The DeepAnalysis main window opens (see Figure 12-7).

5. Enter the number of the category you want to search in the eBay Category Number box.

**TIP** *If you don't know the category number, click Category List near the top of the window. You will then go to eBay's All Categories window, where you can scan the list of categories and note the number of the one you want. For this example, let's use Collectibles : Comics (category 63).*

6. Click Current Auctions or Completed Auctions, and then enter the number of items you want to analyze from the Analyze drop-down list (during the evaluation period, the software will analyze only 2000 auctions; if you register, you can analyze up to 5000).

7. Click Start Analysis. A window appears reminding you that this is an evaluation copy of the software. Click Continue.

8. If you are searching completed auctions on eBay, you'll be prompted to log in with your user ID and password. If you are not already logged in on eBay, enter this information, and click Sign In. An eBay window appears with search

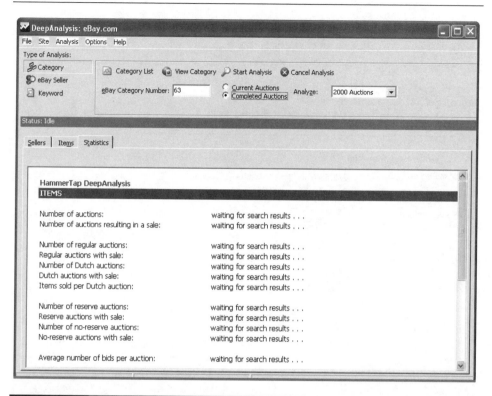

FIGURE 12-7    DeepAnalysis provides detailed information on current eBay sales—not just completed items.

results that you could not get otherwise: a set of completed auction results for the entire Comics category without a keyword having been entered. You get a whopping 200,000-plus results for this search (see Figure 12-8).

**9.** Look over the search results, and then click the button at the bottom of the window labeled "I have logged in." Continue the search. The eBay search results window closes and you return to DeepAnalysis, where a progress bar informs you of the status of the search. If you have decided to search through 2000 items, the analysis of the data will take several minutes, even if you have a broadband Internet connection.

Once DeepAnalysis's work is complete, you can view some really detailed search results for a huge number of sellers. Many of the statistics on sales (the

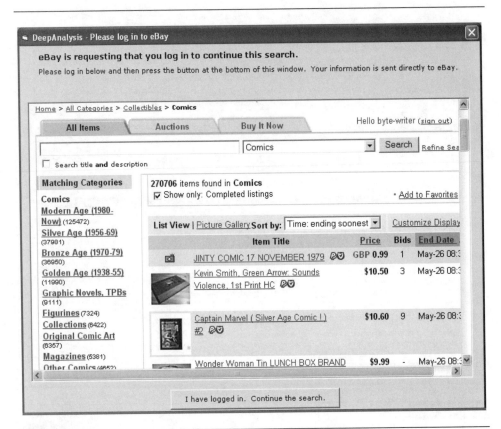

**FIGURE 12-8**   DeepAnalysis lets you search entire categories without entering keywords.

percentage of Dutch auctions, for instance) are available only to registered users. But the information on sellers is really interesting: you learn about sellers who sell nearly everything they put online, for instance. Some of the conclusions reached about our example search include:

■ Of the 2000 completed comic book auctions on eBay, 932 (or 45.51 percent) resulted in a sale.

■ Those 932 sales resulted in a total purchase price of more than $21,000.

If you click the High Bid column heading in the Items tab of the search results (see Figure 12-9), you sort the sales by price. But perhaps the biggest benefit of the results is that there are so many of them: you can scan through them and are

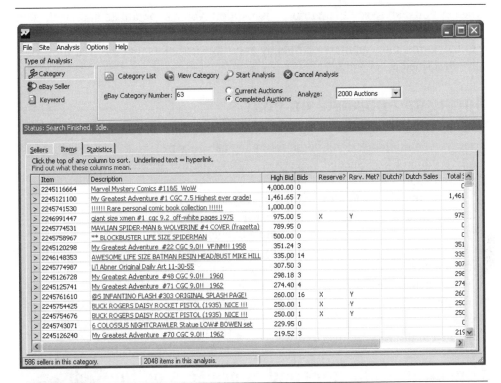

| Item | Description | High Bid | Bids | Reserve? | Rsrv. Met? | Dutch? | Dutch Sales | Total S |
|------|-------------|----------|------|----------|-----------|--------|-------------|---------|
| > 2245116664 | Marvel Mystery Comics #11&5  WoW | 4,000.00 | 0 | | | | | C |
| > 2245121100 | My Greatest Adventure #1 CGC 7.5 Highest ever grade! | 1,461.65 | 7 | | | | | 1,461 |
| > 2245741530 | !!!!!! Rare personal comic book collection !!!!!! | 1,000.00 | 0 | | | | | C |
| > 2246991447 | giant size xmen #1  cgc 9.2  off-white pages 1975 | 975.00 | 5 | X | Y | | | 975 |
| > 2245774531 | MAVLIAN SPIDER-MAN & WOLVERINE #4 COVER (frazetta) | 789.95 | 0 | | | | | C |
| > 2245758967 | ** BLOCKBUSTER LIFE SIZE SPIDERMAN | 500.00 | 0 | | | | | C |
| > 2245120298 | My Greatest Adventure  #22 CGC 9.0!!  VF/NM!! 1958 | 351.24 | 3 | | | | | 351 |
| > 2246148353 | AWESOME LIFE SIZE BATMAN RESIN HEAD/BUST MIKE HILL | 335.00 | 14 | | | | | 335 |
| > 2245774987 | L'l Abner Original Daily Art 11-30-55 | 307.50 | 3 | | | | | 307 |
| > 2245126728 | My Greatest Adventure  #48 CGC 9.0!!  1960 | 298.18 | 3 | | | | | 298 |
| > 2245125741 | My Greatest Adventure  #71 CGC 9.0!!  1962 | 274.40 | 4 | | | | | 274 |
| > 2245761610 | @5 INFANTINO FLASH #303 ORIGINAL SPLASH PAGE! | 260.00 | 16 | X | Y | | | 260 |
| > 2245754425 | BUCK ROGERS DAISY ROCKET PISTOL (1935)  NICE !!! | 250.00 | 1 | X | Y | | | 250 |
| > 2245754676 | BUCK ROGERS DAISY ROCKET PISTOL (1935)  NICE !!! | 250.00 | 1 | X | Y | | | 250 |
| > 2245743071 | 6 COLOSSUS NIGHTCRAWLER Statue LOW# BOWEN set | 229.95 | 0 | | | | | C |
| > 2245126240 | My Greatest Adventure  #70 CGC 9.0!!  1962 | 219.52 | 3 | | | | | 219 |

**FIGURE 12-9**   DeepAnalysis reviews up to 2000 sales during the evaluation period, and 5000 if you register the product.

more likely to find something that matches what you have than if you only get results for a few hundred completed auctions, for instance. You can also do some sorting of the data to find the top ten sellers by sales, the top ten by the number of auctions offered, and many other criteria.

 *DeepAnalysis runs on Windows 95, 98, ME, and XP (Windows 2000 is apparently not supported as it is not listed in the system requirements on the HammerTap web site). It requires you to have 32MB of RAM and 5MB of free hard disk space.*

# Researching the Value of What You Have to Sell

Using eBay to search for what's in demand and which sort of items tend to fetch the most bids and the highest prices in a category is one type of research you can do. You can also use eBay to determine the value of the collectibles you own, whether you plan to sell them or not. In addition, you can obtain an appraisal, such as the comic book certifications mentioned earlier and the ones commonly used for baseball cards, that can increase bids by assuring customers that the condition you have described is accurate.

## Buying an Appraisal on eBay

eBay itself, under the Everything Else category, auctions off appraisals at a fixed price for certain items. Look in the following category tree:

Everything Else : Specialty Services : eBay Auction Services : Appraisal, Authentication

Be careful when you browse these listings, however. Make sure the people who offer them are reputable. In some categories, such as trading cards, there are appraisers who are respected in the field and who overshadow other appraisers (baseball cards certified and mounted by an organization like Professional Sports Authenticator tend to have more credibility, for instance).

In particular, be wary of listings that offer to provide you with reports on how much items similar to yours have sold for on eBay recently, and which categories are likely to bring in bids for what you have to sell. You can do that yourself, as described in the sections that follow.

## Consulting Collectors and Appraisers on the Web

The many experts who make a living from grading, pricing, and writing about collectibles in print publications know which way the wind is blowing. They realize that they have to develop a presence on the Internet in order to maintain their credibility. Not only that, but their web sites have to be useful: they need to attract return visitors by making their pricing information searchable on the Web. But the amount of data provided by such experts differs, as does the difficulty of actually finding what you want. Shop around, and you can find collectible price information that serves as an alternative to eBay.

### Kovels' Online Price Guide

One of the most valuable and extensive resources for collectors of all sorts has to be the Kovels' Online Price Guide, a database containing as many as 450,000 items gathered from 12 of Ralph and Terry Kovel's well-known books on antiques and collectibles.

Actually searching for something in the database can be an adventure, simply because there are so many items and they are broken into so many different categories.

For instance, my mother has a Jerusalem Bible with illustrations by Salvador Dali that she wants me to sell on eBay. I decide to get an idea how much the Bible might be worth in order to set a reasonable reserve. I do the following:

1. Go to the Kovels' store on the TIAS.com web site (http://www.tias.com/stores/kovels).

2. Click the Kovels' Online Price Guide link on the left-hand side of the page.

3. Enter **Jerusalem Bible** in the Search for a Specific Item box, and click the What's It Worth? button. A page appears containing a lengthy list of categories, with links to each one. The categories seem to have nothing to do with the printed book: they range from Chalkware to Cookie Jar to Roy Rogers, in fact. I click on the category that seems closest to the printed Bible: Paper. I get a set of four results for Bibles, none of which is a Jerusalem Bible, and all of which date back to the 19th century.

Other searches in the price guide were just as involved. Then, when you find something you really want, you discover that you have to be a member of the site and enter a registered user ID and password to see a price.

## Other Collectors' Web Sites

ArtBusiness.com, a web site devoted to art services and appraisals, includes a page full of articles on collecting and appraising at http://www.artbusiness.com/collectors.html. A regular feature called Art Picks from eBay takes a piece of art that was listed on eBay and analyzes the sale. As the newsletter author Alan Bamberger points out:

> eBay does not actively police their auction offerings, but rather depends on emails from dealers, collectors, experts, buyers, and potential buyers to notify them of problems relating to particular works of art. Any seller can describe any work of art in any manner that he or she chooses, and as long as no one complains, that art sells to the highest bidder. As a result, eBay and similar online auction sites are risky places for uninformed or inexperienced collectors to buy original art.

I couldn't say it better myself, except to add that this comment applies to all kinds of collectibles, not just art. As a potential bidder, you need to observe the time-honored principle of *caveat emptor* (let the buyer beware). As a seller, you need to do some research to find out exactly what you have and what it might be worth—not only to preserve your own reputation, but to protect your customers as well. In his eBay Picks articles, Bamberger critiques art that has sold on eBay and comes up with some alarming observations. For instance, the painting shown in Figure 12-10 sold for $18,000 in June 2003 after attracting 35 bids.

Bamberger reports that he consulted with a leading authority on the artist, Martin Johnson Heade, at the Fogg Art Museum of Harvard University. The expert stated that the painting was not included in the Yale University Press *catalogue raisonné* for Heade—the definitive list of the artist's work. This catalog is supposed to list all currently known Heade paintings. Of course, it's possible that the eBay seller (who had a 100 percent positive feedback rating) had a previously unknown Heade painting. But as Bamberger commented, "One wonders if the 35 bidders knew about the Heade catalog of paintings and were aware before they bid that the painting was not listed in the 'official' catalogue raisonné?

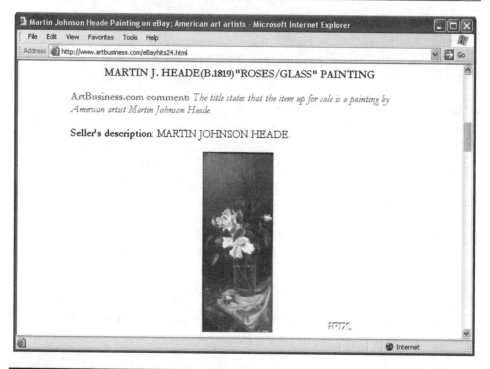

**FIGURE 12-10**    This painting sold for $18,000 but was unknown to an expert on the artist who had cataloged all his known paintings.

They would not have learned about this fact from the seller's description."
Bamberger's recurrent complaints about such sales descriptions include:

- The seller does not provide documentation or cite experts when claims are made that a work of art is authentic. Documents establishing provenance aren't provided, and experts in the field aren't named. Claims are simply made without any proof.

- Art sales are frequently conducted as private auctions: bidders' identities are kept secret, and this prevents communication between eBay members.

The important thing for you as a seller to realize is that, in the field of collectibles, there are many experts all over the Web, and you should make an effort to consult them and do your research before you put something up for auction. When you get an opinion, appraisal, or certificate establishing the worth of what you have for sale, be sure to include it in your auction description.
Other expert sites that provide you with opinions and appraisals include:

- **Great Old Cars** (http://www.greatoldcars.com/eBay_listings.htm) will appraise your vehicle and put it up for sale for you for $149.95.

- **Petroleum Collectible Appraisal Service** (http://www.oilcollectibles.com/appraisal.html) will appraise your gas- or oil-related collectible for $25 per item.

- **Ceramic Restorations of Westchester** (http://www.swiftsite.com/hummel-preciousmoments/appraisals.html) will appraise Hummel, Precious Moments, and other figurines; the cost is $15 for the first item, and $5 for each thereafter.

- **Banknotes.com** (http://www.banknotes.com/evaluate.htm) will appraise from 1 to 10 bank notes for $25.

TIP

*Don't overlook eBay's community of collectors for finding knowledgeable individuals who will give you appraisals, either informally or for a fee. Find out more about the collectors' community in Chapter 4. Also see Appendix C for a selection of organizations that provide online appraisals or collectors' price guides.*

12

## Consulting eBay's Appraisal Partner

In 2002, eBay partnered with CollectingChannel.com to provide an "Ask the Appraiser" service to its members. The program makes CollectingChannel.com authorities available to eBay members to appraise items in more than 170 different categories. To get feedback on the value of their items, you pay a $19.95 fee, fill out an online questionnaire about the item you want appraised, and then upload digital pictures to the Ask the Appraiser site (http://www.collectingchannel.com/ata). You receive a detailed appraisal within three days.

In addition to delivery via e-mail, the appraisal is posted on a web page that eBay users can link to from their auction descriptions, helping to authenticate the value of the items they are selling.

## Trade Talk

The Ask the Appraiser site is hardly the only resource on the Internet that provides appraisals. There's also Instappraisal (http://www.instappraisal.com/antique_appraisals.asp), which charges $17.95, and EmailAppraisals.com (http://www.emailappraisals.com), which charges $9.95. You may get perfectly good results with online appraisals, but they bother me for a couple of reasons: The appraisers never get to see your object in person. The appraisal depends on the quality of your photos and the number of images you send in. And do you really know who the appraiser is and what his or her level of experience is? If you never meet the appraiser in person, this can be hard to judge, too. Finally, the appraiser might be able to tell you what he or she thinks an item should fetch on eBay, but that person cannot predict exactly what the demand will be on a given day. Keep all these things in mind before you put down your money. Taking the time to do your own research and cite your own sources may be the best way to go.

You can also contact several dealers in the field to determine what they would offer you for the item. Many dealers will also offer you the service of selling your material on eBay with a consignment agreement. This will cost you some of the proceeds, but the dealer will know how to accurately categorize and describe your item and usually has long-standing customers. In some cases, the dealer will be able to get a price that is far above what an average collector will receive.

# Asking About.com

About.com (http://www.about.com) functions as a guide to resources on the Web, and it sets itself apart from other directories and search services by emphasizing the services of individuals who are knowledgeable in a particular area. The Experts area of About.com has a page devoted to eBay and other auctions (http://experts.about.com/q/2160/index.htm) where buyers and sellers can ask all sorts of questions about eBay (see Figure 12-11).

Occasionally, sellers ask questions about the value of a piece of Noritake china, an old football program, a celebrity photo—you name it. To my surprise, I discovered that the available experts do handle such questions and provide rough estimates on the value of particular items. If you're in doubt, give it a try yourself.

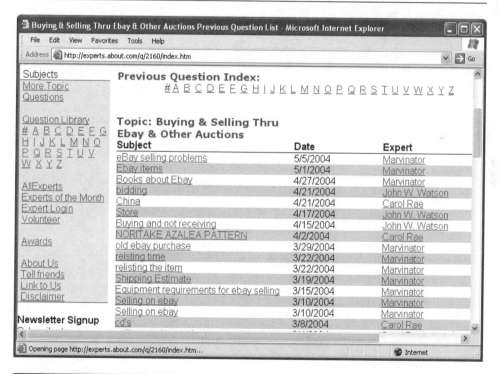

**FIGURE 12-11**   This site's eBay experts occasionally provide opinions on an item's value.

## Links for Collectors

| Web Site | Address | What's There |
|---|---|---|
| Seller Central home page | http://pages.ebay.com/sellercentral | Links to What's Hot Reports and other resources for sellers |
| Sell by Category | http://pages.ebay.com/sellercentral/sellbycategory.html | A page that provides In Demand links for selected eBay categories |
| What's Hot | http://research.andale.com/hotreport/hot_quickstart.jsp | An online service provided by Andale that tracks in-demand items on eBay |
| DeepAnalysis | http://www.hammertap.com/deepanalysis | $179 software program that searches up to 5000 completed or current auctions on eBay |
| Instappraisal | http://www.instappraisal.com/antique_appraisals.asp | Online appraisal service for antiques and collectibles |
| Ask the Appraiser | http://www.collectingchannel.com/ata | Service affiliated with eBay that provides appraisals for $19.95 |
| About.com eBay Experts page | http://experts.about.com/q/2160/index.htm | A web site where you can ask experts questions about using eBay or even for a snap appraisal of an item |

# Chapter 13

## Automating Your Sales

# In This Chapter You'll Learn…

■ Ways to systematize your eBay sales so you can make more money

■ How to find help either within your family or by hiring employees

■ eBay's own software options for creating sales descriptions

■ How to use third-party auction sales management software

The collectibles you sell on eBay might be one-of-a-kind articles, but your sales descriptions don't have to be. The more items you can get online, the more income you'll have, and the faster you'll be able to build up the all-important positive feedback numbers that can boost your reputation and attract more bids. As one eBay PowerSeller told me: "There's a reason why I have the user ID 'bargain-hunters-dream.' I do not sit on inventory—my goal is to move it *fast*. I am successful because I always have new items up, never the same thing week after week."

You may not be a PowerSeller or even have that designation as your ultimate goal, but if you can get 10 or 20 items online in a week instead of one or two—or even if you can get a small number of items online with less time and effort—you'll have more time for treasure hunting. It's a matter of changing your perspective and looking at eBay as a business activity rather than an unusual hobby. This chapter presents some suggestions for how to ramp up your sales by bringing a method to your activities.

# Developing a System

There is a system to your collecting, even though it probably seems haphazard. I think back to my boyhood days as a coin collector. I used to buy the blue books in which the coins were placed; I bought the price guides; I inspected all the loose change I could find. Sometimes, I made an occasional trip to the coin collectors' store to make a purchase when I had some extra pocket money. There was a method to it, and gradually, my collection grew into something of which I could be proud.

If you turn eBay selling into a system instead of a haphazard activity, you'll be more successful. The key is to cut out unnecessary and repetitive steps, and to find people to help so you don't have to do everything all by yourself.

## Preparing a Template with Boilerplate

You can probably fill out the Sell Your Item form in 5 to 10 minutes if you type everything from scratch and are a reasonably fast typist. But what if your descriptions or terms of sale run several paragraphs in length and you aren't a reasonably fast typist? You might spend an hour preparing just half a dozen sales descriptions.

It needn't be that way. Just do what promotional writers have been doing for years and create something called *boilerplate.* Boilerplate is material you repeat from listing to listing, such as your terms of sale. There's no reason why you should retype such information every time you put something up for auction. You can create a standard listing template that combines your boilerplate with some standard items such as a business logo and an introduction you use for each sale.

Figure 13-1 shows an example. Nancee Belshaw, a seller and collector described in Chapter 3, creates all her postcard auction sales the same way, using a template. Her template begins with her web site logo. A single-line title (which is not part of the template) introduces the sale. This is followed by a link to her other eBay sales (this is part of the template). She has created a simple HTML table, which is also part of the template. She fills in the fields in the table with information about the item being sold.

Boilerplate and templates are a great timesaving device that can help you put many sales online in a single day, if you want to.

## Uploading Photos in Bulk

For collectibles, it's especially important to have more than one photo. Often, it's a good idea to have five, six, or even more images so you can show the object from every angle. If you try to put, say, 20 items up for auction in a week, you can easily have more than a hundred photos you need to upload at any one time. eBay offers a program designed to help you get a variety of sales online quickly, as described in the "Turbo Lister" section, later in this chapter.

## Trade Talk

One of the most popular auction photo-hosting services, Marketworks (http://www.marketworks.com, and formerly known as Auctionworks) will host your images and keep each unsold auction posted on its site until it sells. You only pay a fee to Marketworks when a sale is made. "This type of system can have a huge payoff when eBay has a free or discounted listing day," reports this book's technical editor, a collector and eBay seller named David Alexander. "In June, eBay had a 10 cent listing day for their fixed-price format. We were able to transfer 11,457 items (photos and descriptions) from our Marketworks-related web site onto eBay in about 3 hours. The charge from eBay was $1145.70. At their standard costs, the listing fees would have been around $9000. To put it into perspective, that is like getting a car free from eBay. If you aspire to be a volume seller on eBay you need to learn to watch for the discount or free listing days and take full advantage of them."

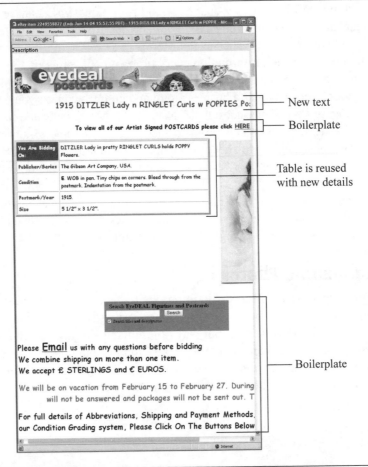

New text

Boilerplate

Table is reused
with new details

Boilerplate

---

**FIGURE 13-1** Create a sales template so you don't have to reinvent the wheel every time you put an item up for auction.

If you select the right hosting service for your images, you can get help there, too. You still have to capture the original images, but you don't have to worry about editing them. For instance, if you are willing to pay a 50 cent hosting fee per image, you can send your raw images straight from your digital camera to Pongo (http://www.pongo.com). Pongo's staff (who have been working with eBay since 1996) will "hand process" the photos—cropping, sizing, and adjusting them so they appear quickly and with good quality. You can simply attach multiple images to an e-mail message you send to Pongo, or pack them in a zip file that you upload using the form shown in Figure 13-2.

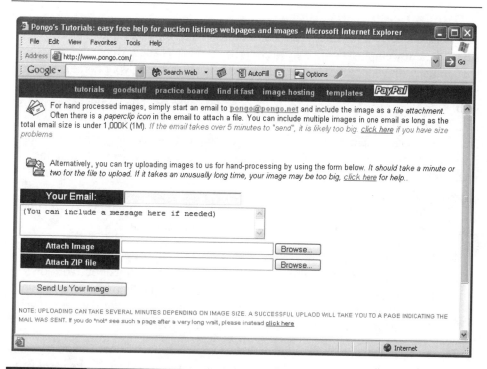

**FIGURE 13-2**  Some image hosting services take a lot of the work out of getting eBay photos online.

# Finding an Extra Pair of Hands

A growing number of eBay sellers have a "good" problem: their eBay businesses are growing so quickly that they can no longer do everything themselves. They need help hauling boxes, moving inventory around, preparing sales listings, or packing and shipping. They are wondering what's involved in hiring someone to help out with a home-based business, and what's different about working with an eBay business compared to a traditional brick-and-mortar store.

Whomever you employ, be sure you prepare a list of the tasks you want that person to prepare: Do you want them to do filing and typing? Manage e-mail with prospective customers? Write out a clear, one-paragraph job description that makes it clear when the employee is supposed to be present and that lists his or her primary job responsibilities. Use the description when you interview the employee.

 *A clear job description can prove invaluable in case of a dispute or when evaluating whether the employee is performing up to expectations. You can refer to the requirements in writing should a problem arise.*

13

## Turning to Family Members

Many eBay sellers turn to their nearest and dearest when looking for help on eBay. After all, family employees are easy to contact; you always know where they are; they are familiar with your "office" and "warehouse" (in other words, your home); and they don't require health or other benefits over and above what you already provide them with. Lots of families get along very well, providing extra income for the young people in the group and giving everyone a new sort of "shared experience." eBay businesses are, in fact, perfect venues for couples: they can help one another when they shop for inventory; they can do the unpacking and organizing together; they can then divide up the other tasks, including answering e-mail, putting photos online, packing, and shipping.

There are, however, some potential pitfalls to hiring your own family, whether just for a rush period or on a regular part-time or full-time basis:

■ Be careful when you are required to order around people who aren't used to being ordered around—especially by you. I'm talking about your own parents, grandparents, aunts, uncles, or other people who are senior to you. Some of them might be retired after years of managing their own employees. Treat them with extra courtesy and ask their advice.

■ Be clear about payment. You might be tempted, if your kids are helping you out, to look on it as a favor. They'll probably be much happier employees if you actually pay them. Some relatives might not want to take money, on the other hand; if so, be sure they receive a small gift or a thank-you note for their help.

■ Treat your relatives with respect. When you're very familiar with people, you tend to let down your guard and be impatient with them. Try to show them the same respect as your other business colleagues. After hours, you can relax again.

■ Don't just work. Your eBay business can grow to the extent that you only work together, and you're always doing something that is part of your home-based business. Get out of the house sometimes and get coffee or lunch together, so you aren't working all the time.

Consider offering your employees, whether or not they are family members, an incentive. If you pay them a percentage of your sales, you'll boost motivation and enthusiasm on their part.

WATCH OUT!    *Some eBay businesspeople get their children involved with their sales operations. Children are particularly good at packing and wrapping merchandise to be shipped. Don't let them work so much that they cut back on their play time or after-school activities. Pay them for their efforts—or make sure you agree with them beforehand that they will get some other kind of reimbursement. Running a business on eBay that involves your children can give them a source of income in the future. The children's participation will ensure that the business will keep running.*

### Looking for Independent Contractors

When you bring "outside" employees (in other words, non-family members) to help out with your eBay business, you have to prepare them for working in your house—and prepare your house for them. Make sure they are OK being around dogs, cats, or other pets if you have them.

Make sure you, too, are at ease with the thought of bringing strangers into your home, and losing some of your privacy. Create boundaries beyond which employees cannot go, so you can separate your home life and business activities as much as possible.

> **TIP** *Entrepreneur.com, in an article entitled "Hiring Employees for Your Homebased Business" (http://www.entrepreneur.com/Your_Business/YB_Node/0,4507,359,00.html), suggests clearly spelling out a home-based employee's job responsibilities as well as boundaries that specify parts of the residence that employees are not supposed to visit.*

# Boosting Sales with eBay's Listing Software

You can find sales management software in a variety of places online. But eBay's own programs have an advantage. First and foremost, the software is designed to keep up with the latest organizational and programming changes on the site. Another advantage is that they are inexpensive—or, in the case of Turbo Lister, free. But eBay provides several different tools whose functions occasionally overlap, which can make it difficult to choose the best application for your needs. You'll find eBay's software on the Seller Tools page (http://pages.ebay.com/sell/tools.html). The pros and cons of each are described in the sections that follow.

**13**

## Turbo Lister

As a collector, you're always looking for a bargain. That probably makes Turbo Lister the right program for you. Turbo Lister is eBay's free (I repeat, *free*) tool for auction sellers who want to format sales without entering HTML manually and who want to be able to get lots of sales online quickly. Turbo Lister may be a bargain, but that doesn't mean it's feature-poor. In contrast, it can perform tasks like the following:

- Scheduling multiple sales so they all start and end simultaneously.

- Transferring groups of sales descriptions from your computer to eBay's servers.

- Helping to create auction listing templates of the sort described earlier in this chapter.

*Turbo Lister does not work on Macintosh systems, only with Windows 98 or later. Macintosh users should consider a program such as eLister by Black Magik Software (http://www.blackmagik.com). To use Turbo Lister, you need a computer with 64MB of RAM, 20MB of free hard disk space, a 256-color monitor, and Microsoft Internet Explorer 5.01 or later.*

Turbo Lister is primarily intended to help you list many sales quickly. It's a good beginning-level tool for eBay sellers who like to do things for themselves and are confident installing their own software. But most eBay sellers who sell in quantity use Seller's Assistant because it has more tools for managing sales.

*Turbo Lister has its own discussion board in eBay's Community area (http://forums.ebay.com/forum.jsp?forum=34). You can turn to group members to see if someone else has encountered the same problem or ask a question if you need help.*

## Installing Turbo Lister

To get started with Turbo Lister, go to the Turbo Lister Download page (http://pages.ebay.com/turbo_lister/download.html).

1.  Click Turbo Lister Web Setup. A small setup application downloads, and the InstallShield Wizard application opens. Follow the steps presented by the wizard to download the full Turbo Lister package.

2.  Once installation is complete, click Finish, and make sure you check the box that specifies that you want Turbo Lister to launch immediately. A dialog box labeled Setting Up Turbo Lister for First Use appears. Turbo Lister opens, and the Welcome to Turbo Lister screen appears, with the heading "What would you like to do?" (see Figure 13-3).

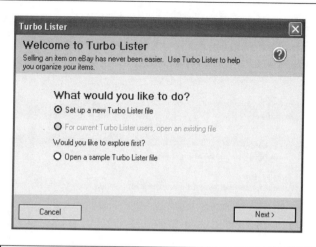

**FIGURE 13-3**   The Turbo Lister welcome screen

## Creating a Sales Listing

1. Click Set Up a New Turbo Lister file, then click Next.

2. In the next screen, enter your eBay user ID and password, and then click Next. When the next screen appears, click Connect Now. Turbo Lister connects to eBay to retrieve your account information.

3. When a Contact Information screen appears, review your information to make sure it is accurate, and then click Next. Once your account information has been retrieved, click Create New, and then choose New Item. The Create a New Item wizard opens (see Figure 13-4).

4. Choose the country you want to sell in, and select a format—an auction, a fixed-price sale, or a real estate listing. Then click Next.

5. Enter a title for your item in the Item Title drop-down list.

6. Enter the category number in the Category box. If you don't have the category memorized or written down, click Find Category and choose a category from the list that appears. Click OK to return to the Create a New Item wizard.

7. Click the Add/Change button in the Specifics section to enter item details if you want to. Then click OK.

13

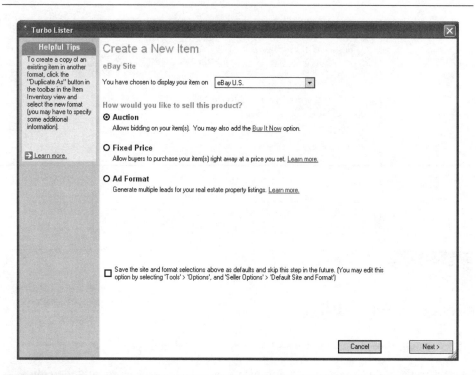

**FIGURE 13-4**    This wizard leads you through the process of creating listings on eBay.

To this point, you have created the framework for the listing. You can now move on to designing your listing's graphic appearance. The Enter Your Description screen of the Create a New Item wizard lets you create a design template for a listing with a user-friendly HTML editor. If you check the Listing Designer box near the upper left-hand corner of the screen, you are given the chance to select a design from a list of graphic themes (see Figure 13-5).

Subsequent screens in the wizard enable you to add photos, type your item description, and preview your layout. Once you are done, when you're ready to start your sales, select them from the list (see Figure 13-6) and click Add to Upload. If you want to schedule your sales to go online automatically, select them, and then click Schedule to Start On, and enter a date and/or time.

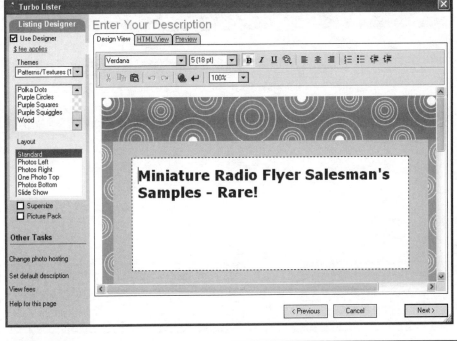

**FIGURE 13-5**   The Turbo Lister wizard makes it easy to select design themes for a sales listing.

## Seller's Assistant

Seller's Assistant, another sales management tool from eBay, comes with 20 different auction templates, as well as a spell-checker you can use before you put your sales online.

Seller's Assistant comes in two versions: Basic and Pro. Another difference between this pair of programs and Turbo Lister is price. Turbo Lister costs nothing, but Seller's Assistant Basic costs $9.99 per month and the Pro version has a monthly cost of $15.99. Both enable you to automate the end-of-sale and other e-mail messages you exchange with customers; the Pro version also lets you put sales online in bulk.

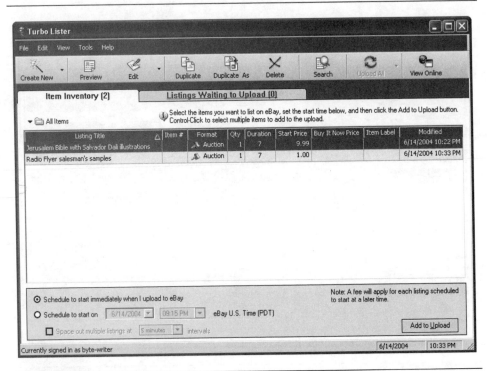

FIGURE 13-6 Turbo Lister lets you select sales descriptions from a list and upload them all at once.

> **TIP**    *You can find out more about both Seller's Assistant Basic and Pro at http://pages.ebay.com/sellers_assistant/index.html. Both Seller's Assistant Basic and Pro have their own discussion areas in eBay's Community area. Basic is discussed at http://forums.ebay.com/forum.jsp?forum=81, and Pro at http://forums.ebay.com/forum.jsp?forum=82.*

In my opinion, the extra cost justifies the purchase of Seller's Assistant Pro rather than Seller's Assistant Basic. The Pro version lets you manage your inventory, relist multiple auctions, and schedule when a sale goes online. Seller's Assistant Basic doesn't cover any of these important tasks.

Keep in mind, though, that both Seller's Assistant Basic and Pro are programs you download and install on your computer and that both consume your hard disk space. The downloaded files for Basic amount to more than 17MB, while the Pro version is 20.5MB. Both programs are Windows-only, and require 40MB of hard disk space, 64MB of RAM, and Microsoft Internet Explorer 5.01 or later. This overhead encourages some sellers to subscribe to the monthly online service Selling Manager instead.

One of the powerful features of Seller's Assistant Pro, for sellers who move many items every month, is the ability to sort information by means of filters and grids. Filters enable you to select only the type of data you want to view, while grids control the way the data is presented. A grid is a set of columns that you can arrange to present what you want to see, such as eBay item number, title, status, and end date.

## Selling Manager

eBay describes Selling Manager Pro as "The Tool for High Volume Sellers." This online service, indeed, is set up to make sales go more smoothly for sellers who have a relatively high weekly or monthly quota on eBay. It's designed to "take your business to the next level," as its eBay developers proclaim. It provides you with a list of the sales you currently have online, as well as those you have completed successfully and those that have not sold and can thus be relisted. Selling Manager keeps track of your buyers' contact information so you can quickly send them e-mails notifying them that they have made a purchase and providing them with payment instructions.

**COLLECTOR'S NOTE** *You can find out about Selling Manager Basic and Pro at http:// pages.ebay.com/selling_manager/products.html. You can also read the archived transcript of the workshop on Selling Manager Pro at http:// forums.ebay.com/db2/thread.jsp?forum=93&thread=1222765.*

**13**

Like Seller's Assistant, Selling Manager comes in two versions: Basic and Pro. But unlike Seller's Assistant or Turbo Lister, which consume a considerable amount of disk space and depend on making a successful connection to eBay's web site, Selling Manager is an online service. You connect to it with your web browser; as long as you are already on the Internet, you don't have any problem accessing the software because it is already on eBay's web site. That probably means you need to sell about 10 or more items each week to justify the monthly fee ($4.99 for Selling Manager Basic; $15.99 for Selling Manager Pro). Alternatively, you could use Selling Manager Basic to manage sales and Turbo Lister to format sales and get them online.

Selling Manager Basic and Selling Manager Pro are two programs provided by eBay to help sellers who conduct a "medium to high volume" of sales. Both programs enable you to automate your e-mail to buyers and prospective buyers, list multiple items at one time, send out automated feedback, and generate sales reports.

If you are going to going to pay a monthly fee for a hosted service, consider moving up to Selling Manager Pro, which includes features such as inventory management, the ability to generate monthly reports, and the ability to print invoices and shipping labels. The full range of eBay's selling tools is summarized in Table 13-1.

| Tool | Main Features | Cost | Pros and Cons |
|------|---------------|------|---------------|
| Turbo Lister | Lets you create multiple listings and put them online at specific times. You can also track your remaining inventory. | Free | Needs 20MB of disk space and at least 64MB of RAM; you either have to download it or obtain a CD-ROM version. |
| Selling Manager Basic | Enables you to relist items but not to create or upload new listings. It lets you track sales online, print labels, and send preformatted e-mails. | Free for first 30 days; $4.99 per month thereafter. | No software to install; you access the service from eBay's web site. Includes relisting and label-printing features that Seller's Assistant doesn't have. |
| Selling Manager Pro | Helps high-volume sellers manage inventory and generate reports, track sales, and relist items in bulk. | Free for first 30 days; $15.99 per month thereafter. | No software to install; automates many features needed to complete sales; relatively high monthly fee. |
| Seller's Assistant Basic | Provides you with 20 templates for designing sales listings. Allows you to upload listings in bulk. | Free for 30 days; $4.99 per month thereafter. | You need to install the software, and you have the ability to upload sales auctions based on other sales. |
| Seller's Assistant Pro | Enables you to create your own macros so you can repeat a sequence of steps. You can also leave automated feedback in bulk and use multiple user IDs. | Free for 30 days; $15.99 per month thereafter. | Many of its features are provided more cheaply (or free) by Turbo Lister or Selling Manager. |

**TABLE 13-1** eBay Tools for Auction Sellers

TIP *You can find out more about Selling Manager's features by going to the program's home page, http://pages.ebay.com/selling_manager. You can take a "guided tour" of the program that lets you see how it works with My eBay, among other features.*

# Finding Sales Software Outside of eBay

There are a variety of reasons why you might choose a non-eBay sales management tool. For example, such programs usually allow you to monitor sales you are watching on sites other than eBay's. Price is also a big consideration: some services are just less expensive than eBay's options. Another is the overall range of features that is made available to you when you subscribe to a service. If you become a member of inkFrog, for example, you get space to host your auction images; a bulk listing program used to format and upload sales descriptions; and management tools for relisting sales, printing invoices, and exporting sales reports to spreadsheet applications. You would have to use two or more of eBay's applications to get all of those services (and you wouldn't get the image hosting space, either). If you choose Andale, you get access to the information that can help you research completed auctions on eBay, as well as hit counters and other features that can add some pizzazz to your sales. A few examples of programs that you might use are listed in Table 13-2.

## SpareDollar's sdLister

If you are a collector, chances are you aren't also a technical whiz. You want auction listing tasks to be streamlined in an inexpensive way so you can focus on shopping for merchandise to resell and providing good customer service. You're better off with a monthly service you access from the comfort of your familiar web browser, rather than a program you install and have to update yourself.

13

| Service | URL | Basic Membership Fee (monthly) | Description |
|---------|-----|-------------------------------|-------------|
| Andale | http://www.andale.com | Varies depending on services used. | Each service requires separate download or subscription, though packages are available; research data is unique and of great benefit. |
| Auction Wizard 2000 | http:// www.auctionwizard2000.com/ | 60-day free trial available; $75 to keep program for first year; $50 for each year thereafter. | A program you download and install rather than a service. Helps you track inventory and send automatic e-mail messages. |
| Channel Advisor | http:// www.channeladvisor.com | $29.95 for entry-level. ChannelAdvisor Pro package includes image hosting, auction creation software inventory tracking, and fixed-price sales. | Enterprise solution works with corporations such as IBM and Motorola; for small businesses, ChannelAdvisor Pro provides a hosted service that helps small-scale sellers keep track of sales and inventory. |
| inkFrog | http://www.inkfrog.com | $12.95 per month. | Easy to use; particularly good range of features for beginning users. |
| Marketworks (formerly Auctionworks) | http://www.marketworks.com | No listing fees; service charges 2 percent on each item sold. | Well-known and popular service when known as Auctionworks. |
| SpareDollar | http://www.sparedollar.com | $4.95 per month. | Includes image hosting, image editing, bulk uploading, counters, templates, inventory tracking, and more. |
| Vendio | http://www.vendio.com | $12.95 to $39.95 for Sales Manager service. | Includes image hosting, scheduled listings, templates, integrated UPS and USPS shipping, and more. |

**TABLE 13-2**    Non-eBay Auction Management Software

## Collecting Step-by-Step

Each of the non-eBay auction management options involves a similar process: You sign up for a free trial, if you wish. You register with a user name and password. Then you either download software or begin to access services using your web browser. With that in mind, the following steps illustrate an inexpensive auction listing program, sdLister, that you get to use when you sign up for the auction service SpareDollar:

1. Go to the SpareDollar home page, and click on the button labeled "30 day free Trial! Register."

2. When the Member Registration page appears, fill out the form, and then click Register.

3. Open your e-mail inbox and retrieve the e-mail message sent to you from SpareDollar. Click the hyperlink included in the body of the message.

4. When the Member Registration page appears, include your user name and the password included in the e-mail from SpareDollar. Then click Activate.

5. When the page entitled SpareDollar - Powerful eBay Seller Solutions appears, click the sdLister tab so you can begin to work with SpareDollar's auction listing application.

6. When the Member Login page appears, enter your user name and password, then click Go.

7. In the sdLister Tasks column on the left-hand side of the page, click Create New Ad.

8. When the Create New Ad page appears, select the type of auction you want, then click Next. The Create New Ad page refreshes, displaying a set of options that closely resembles eBay's own Sell Your Item form,

13

shown here. A Schedule section near the bottom of the page enables you to specify a starting time for your auction.

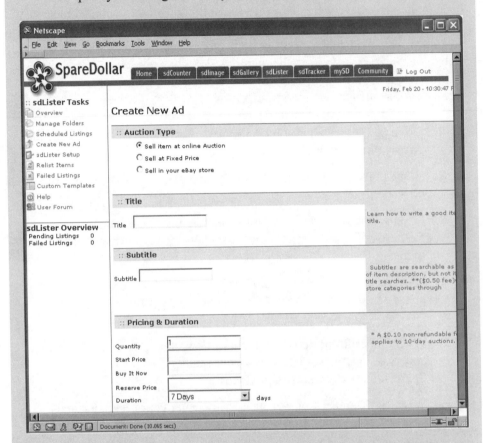

9. When you are done, click one of the buttons at the bottom of the form: Preview, Review Fees, Save Ad, or Save Ad & Launch. Save Ad lets you save the information you filled out in the form so that it remains in the form the next time you access it. You might want to do this if you want to reuse parts of the description, for instance.

By itself, sdLister doesn't represent much of an advantage over eBay's own Sell Your Item form, except in the ability to save listing information. It's the add-on features that are included in the monthly fee—the counters, image hosting tools, and other software—that make such non-eBay management solutions worth considering.

## Links for Collectors

| Web Site | Address | What's There |
| --- | --- | --- |
| Pongo | http://www.pongo.com | One of the oldest eBay photo hosting services, which offers the option of editing images for you |
| Seller Tools | http://pages.ebay.com/sell/tools.html | A page full of links to software for auction management and sales creation |
| Turbo Lister download page | http://pages.ebay.com/turbo_lister/download.html | Page where you can download eBay's free auction creation tool |
| Seller's Assistant | http://pages.ebay.com/sellers_assistant/index.html | Page where you can read about and download eBay's advanced auction management software |
| Selling Manager | http://pages.ebay.com/selling_manager/products.html | Page where you subscribe to eBay's advanced, web-based auction management service |

13

# Chapter 14

# In This Chapter You'll Learn...

■ Responsibilities and benefits of starting your own eBay group

■ How to invite members and create ways for them to interact

■ Strategies for promoting your group to attract members

■ Duties required of group discussion moderators

Some activities depend on word of mouth. Birdwatchers often spot rare species only after getting tips from other enthusiasts in the field. Collectors, too, need to know what's hot, what's available, and where to find it. They also need a place to blow off steam when they lose an auction, or to share their good fortune when they uncover a bargain. eBay groups give collectors the perfect venue for doing all these things.

For sellers, starting an eBay group is one of the most exciting parts of participating in the eBay community. eBay groups enable you to create or join a forum where you can share news and views with like-minded members. eBay groups have less supervision than other eBay discussion areas—on the other hand, they place more of a burden on members to run them closely and manage them so discussions are useful. Groups can be created in keeping with a wide variety of criteria:

■ **Geographic location**   Some groups bring together buyers and sellers who live in a U.S. state or a country, for instance. Many large metropolitan areas have at least one regional eBay group, and some of them are oriented toward specific types of collectibles.

■ **Type of merchandise**   There are collectors' groups for those who love coins, glass, stamps, porcelain, and toys, among other things.

■ **Type of activity**   There are groups on eBay for people who do scrapbooking, who are interested in genealogy, who work from home, and who use Macintosh computers.

eBay groups can be divided into two general categories. Some are public: they are open to everyone who is already a member of eBay. Public groups want lots of members to join up. Others, like the popular Powerchicks Group, are private: they are only open to members who have asked to join and have had their requests approved, or who have been invited. Private groups want to keep the membership low.

If you are looking to make a name for yourself as an authority either in the area where you live or on the type of objects you buy and sell, consider starting your own eBay group. You'll have to put out a lot of effort in terms of advertising your group, suggesting topics for discussion, and the like. But you gain a lot of credibility as well, which can boost your eBay business and make you a more knowledgeable collector.

# Serving as Group Leader

Once you have participated in some eBay groups (which are introduced in Chapter 4) and have a feel for how they work, you can consider starting your own group. The important thing to remember is that starting a group is like throwing a party—a party that keeps assembling on a daily basis. It should be noted that group leadership is not to be undertaken casually. It's not an activity for people who like to set things in motion and then sit back and see what happens. You need to show an interest in your members, answer their questions, and provide them with an interesting mix of activities and topics. To quote eBay member rsvp!, the leader of the Golden Oldies and Group Leaders and Moderators groups:

> Being a leader is a bit of a calling—giving to people should be more important than getting from people. If you only have a few members in your group, show the same effort and enthusiasm each time you visit, as if the group were already established and successful. In the beginning, "seeds" must be planted and you'll find yourself doing most of the watering, feeding, and nurturing, sometimes with no results. Do not become discouraged, though, because one day it will become the vibrant flourishing group you envisioned at first, if you keep giving your all!

Practically speaking, to get the process started (as long as you have the required feedback rating), all you have to do is click the link Start Group near the top of the eBay Group Center page (http://groups.ebay.com/index.jspa), shown in Figure 14-1. But before that, you should join a group called the eBay Groups Information Center (http://groups.ebay.com/forum.jspa?forumID=1254). This group contains all the instructions you need on how to operate a group after you have formed it. After you initiate the process of starting a group, eBay reviews your proposal for a 30-day period to confirm that you are a leader in good standing and that you haven't violated eBay's User Agreement yourself.

14

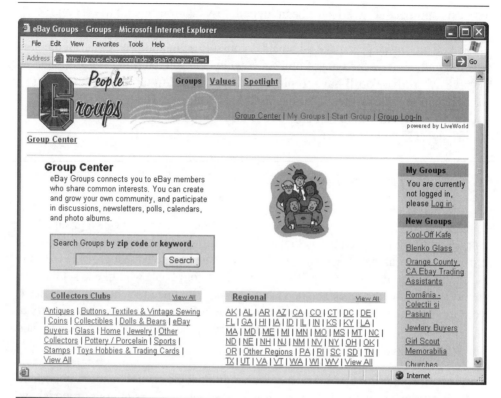

FIGURE 14-1
Whether you want to join a group or start your own, the eBay Group Center page is the place to start.

COLLECTOR'S NOTE

*Even though eBay groups give you the ability to run your own group, that doesn't mean you are ultimately in charge. Group leaders are subject to the authority of the eBay group administrators. Administrators can serve as a resource: if you ever have a question about your group, want to make a suggestion, or run into a problem, you can contact an administrator by clicking the Email Moderators link in the controls section of the eBay Groups Information Center. You can also send e-mail to ebaygroups@ebay.com.*

In order to be successful, a group needs care and tending, just like a web site. You need to develop a schedule of events, and you need to be available to moderate discussions. You might be called upon to handle complaints and disputes between members, should they occur. In order for your group to get off the ground, you might want to invite friends and other members with whom you've done business to join your group. You need to keep interest in your group: if there has been no activity for 90 days, eBay will delete it.

*To start a group, you need to have a minimum feedback of 50 and have been registered on the site for at least 90 days.*

## Developing a Charter

Every eBay group has a charter: a statement of the group's goals and the rules that members need to observe. The charter is especially important because it can provide moderators with a set of rules they can refer to in case they run into a dispute. A charter might read like the following:

> This group exists to bring together buyers, sellers, and collectors of widgets for general conversation, support, exchanging selling/buying tips, or just simply getting to know one other. We're here to help and share and have fun!
>
> Before you post a message, please consider the following: If you are a part of a group (for support, friendship, etc.), aren't you defeating your own goals if you allow emotions or personality differences to interfere?
>
> Keep in mind always that the success of the group depends on the extent to which its members work together and stick together. Do not allow yourself to resent what anyone does. Accept the fact that they mean to be helpful or are simply expressing things as they see them.
>
> Members will make a conscious effort to look for the good in every person in my group. Members will not criticize anyone on a personal basis.

Every group's charter can be accessed from the link Charter on the group home page. But don't expect members to actually click this link and read the charter in detail. You might consider copying all or part of the charter on your group's home page to gain more attention and make sure everyone knows what the group is about and how members are supposed to behave.

Charters aren't the only set of rules that eBay group members need to observe. Everyone needs to be aware of the eBay Groups Guidelines (http://pages.ebay .com/help/policies/group-guidelines.html) as well.

*A charter doesn't have to stay the same all the time. You can edit it to address problems you are encountering, such as profanity or even nonparticipation by members.*

14

## Finding Moderators

One of the nice things about starting your own group is that, no matter how involved and time-consuming it might seem to be, you don't have to do everything on your own. In fact, you might end up doing very little on your own if you select moderators to help you who share your interests and are as involved and conscientious as you are.

There isn't any standard rule to how many moderators you can have, but some of the most active and successful groups get along well with four. Encourage your moderators to act as supporting, helping individuals, and tell them to post subjects that have attention-getting titles.

> **TIP**  *Pay attention to members of your group who seem especially enthusiastic, outgoing, and helpful with their information and tips. They might make great moderators, and they can build your group into an active and useful one.*

## Suggesting Topics

People who spend a lot of time surfing the Web and discussing topics of interest with others are used to seeing new content every day. If a web page isn't updated on a daily (or at least a weekly) basis, people will quickly judge that it is a "cobweb" site whose owner does not tend to it, and they won't revisit it on a regular basis.

By the same token, discussion groups (whether they are eBay groups or other forums) need to have new topics of interest. As a group leader, you need to come up with a list of topics you can post on a daily basis, or suggest to your moderators that they do the same (or both). You might take turns posting topics: "You suggest a new topic on Mondays; I'll do Tuesdays and Thursdays; you do Wednesdays," and so on.

Consider the interests and needs of group members when you suggest topics. In the Group Moderators and Leaders group, the topics that tend to get the highest number of replies are ones that are of universal interest, such as:

■ Designing Group Logos

■ Banning a Member

■ Adding Group Moderators

■ Ideas on How to Increase Your Membership

Ideally, if a group becomes particularly active, you'll get as many suggestions of discussion topics from individual members as you do from your leader and moderators. For a collectors' group, you might be able to suggest lots of topics that can benefit both you and your members. Consider the following topics:

- Where do you find merchandise to sell?

- What's the most amazing thing you found on eBay?

- Are flea markets a dying breed?

- How do you get good close-ups of what you sell?

Your topics don't have to be all that substantive; simply getting people together to talk about collectors' conventions in their area or price guides can keep members posting.

 *At any time, you can choose to leave a group, transfer the leader's role to another qualified group member who wants to assume the responsibility, or hold a group election.*

# Promoting Your Group

eBay groups have taken off, and there are now hundreds of them devoted to many interests. Because anyone with feedback ratings of over 50 and membership in good standing can start a group, new ones are springing up all the time. It's getting increasingly difficult to stand out from the crowd. Anything you can do to promote a group you lead or moderate will help draw members. You can't link to your group from your auction descriptions, but you can mention it in the body of the description, for instance. You can also conduct a "swap meet" day a couple times a year where members bring merchandise to trade or sell to other members.

14

**TIP** *Create a business card devoted to your eBay group and include it when you ship a package to a buyer. Past customers and sellers are good prospects for membership.*

## Inviting Members

One of the most important ways to spread the word about your group is to invite members. This is no time to be a shrinking violet. You need to send as many

## Holding an eBay Party

One of the most intriguing ways to get together with other eBay members and extend the reach of an eBay group is to hold an "eBay Party." This is a real-world gathering that brings together buyers and sellers who live in the same city or the same geographic region. Such parties are easy to get off the ground because everyone present already has a shared interest and a shared activity: eBay.

Members who belong to the regional groups are naturals for eBay parties. If you click on the Regional heading on the eBay Group Center page, you scan an extensive list of international, statewide, and smaller regional groups (there are 22 groups in Texas alone, at this writing). If you or a co-member would like to hand out some basic materials, eBay will send up to 25 pamphlets that can provide an orientation for any new members. (To place an order, send an e-mail message to ebaygroups@ebay.com.)

invitations as you can, and on a daily basis. Go over your auctions and contact anyone who has ever bought anything from you; also contact anyone you have purchased from. Your moderators can also help send out invitations to their own auction contacts.

eBay makes it easy to send out an invitation. You don't need to convince people or "sell" yourself and your group, unless you want to send out individual e-mail messages to eBay members yourself. But if you approach members directly, they might feel offended at receiving an unsolicited e-mail from you. It's safer to use eBay's automatic invitation system to send someone a form message. Here's an example:

```
Dear [User ID],

The eBay user "[user ID]" has invited you to join the group: "!
GROUP LEADERS & MODERATORS CENTRAL"
----------
To join the group, please click the url: "http://groups.ebay.com/
accept.jspa" [URL follows]

This eBay notice was sent to you because someone has invited you to
join an eBay Group.
```

If someone wants to join, they only need to click on the URL supplied to become a member. If they want to find out more about the group, they need to go to the eBay group's page themselves to find out about it (it *would* be nice if eBay's form letter would include a link to the group's description and charter).

> **TIP**  *Whenever you approach prospective members, either through an invitation or through a direct e-mail message, emphasize that you are there to give help—not just to get something from other people, whether it is attention or prestige or knowledge. Emphasize the fact that your group is an exchange and a place for people to share and help one another, and you'll get a better response.*

## Creating a Welcome Image

Once you induce members to join, you need to welcome them. The first thing new members see when they join is your group's welcome page. The welcome page is where you describe your group's purpose and goals, and establish rules of conduct. Group leaders have the ability to customize the welcome page by clicking the Edit link in the top-right corner. (The content of the welcome page is different from the content of the home page.) The Edit Message field will accept most HTML formatting tags and up to 65,000 characters. If you click the Check Spelling button, the system will check the contents of the Edit Message field.

Group leaders also have the option of using an image to create a welcome image that gives their group more pizzazz and illustrates what the discussion is all about. You should strongly consider creating such an image yourself. Suppose someone is looking for a group to join. They do a search and get a page full of results. Most of the groups have flashy images and logos. If your group is listed in the results with a bland, text-only link, you'll easily be overlooked. For example, the Group Leaders and Moderators Group leader rsvp! used some copyright-free clip art to create the attractive image shown in Figure 14-2.

If you use Microsoft Word, you can take advantage of a built-in graphics feature called Word Art to create logos or to fashion text that appears to be curved or has a texture to it. If you have some experience with a computer graphics program such as Super Paint, Paint Shop Pro, or even the simple MacPaint and Paint programs that are incorporated into the Macintosh and Windows systems, you can create text-only logos such as the ones shown in Figure 14-3.

14

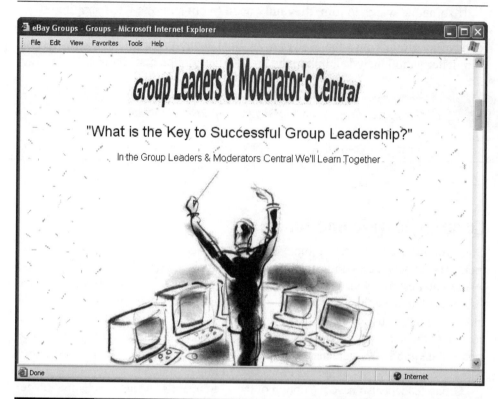

**Group Leaders & Moderator's Central**

"What is the Key to Successful Group Leadership?"

In the Group Leaders & Moderators Central We'll Learn Together

Done                                                    Internet

**FIGURE 14-2**    Creating a welcome image will attract more members to join up.

**WATCH OUT!**    *When you create an image for your group, be sure not to incorporate eBay's own image into it. You can mention the name eBay, but don't copy or try to duplicate eBay's logo, which is trademarked and which eBay prohibits anyone else from using.*

Besides creating a welcome page, you need to create and edit a home page for your group. A home page provides members with links to such standard features as:

■ **Announcements**    These are announcements and other messages posted by a group leader or moderator in chronological order, with the most recent at the top.

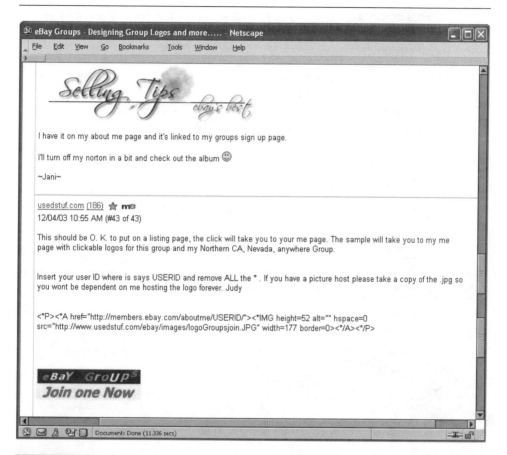

Selling Tips ebay's best

I have it on my about me page and it's linked to my groups sign up page.

I'll turn off my norton in a bit and check out the album 😊

~Jani~

usedstuf.com (186) ⭐ me
12/04/03 10:55 AM (#43 of 43)

This should be O. K. to put on a listing page, the click will take you to your me page. The sample will take you to my me page with clickable logos for this group and my Northern CA, Nevada, anywhere Group.

Insert your user ID where is says USERID and remove ALL the * . If you have a picture host please take a copy of the .jpg so you wont be dependent on me hosting the logo forever. Judy

<*P><*A href="http://members.ebay.com/aboutme/USERID/"><*IMG height=52 alt="" hspace=0 src="http://www.usedstuf.com/ebay/images/logoGroupsjoin.JPG" width=177 border=0><*/A><*/P>

eBaY GroUPs
Join one Now

| FIGURE 14-3 | Group logos don't have to use images, but they can be enlivened with well-arranged text. |

**14**

■ **Discussions**  These are the lists of topics and discussions that have been posted to the group.

■ **Photo albums**  A photo album is a set of images and accompanying captions. Each album has its own title and description, and contains many individual photos. A photo album must be created before you can add a photo. Click on Photo Albums in the left-hand column, and then click the Add Photo Album link. Whenever you want to add a photo, first click the appropriate album, and then click the Add to This Album link. The system allots each member 2MB of space on eBay servers to host photos.

- **Events calendar**   The Events Calendar function allows any member of an eBay group to publicize a future event and control many of the event attributes.

- **Polls**   A *poll*, as the name implies, is a sort of online survey. You ask a question and solicit opinions from your members. Each question can have up to five possible answers, such as the question from the Antiques Anonymous eBay group shown in Figure 14-4.

COLLECTOR'S NOTE   *Any image that has already been added to a group photo album can also be included in the welcome page. If an image is available, first select the desired album title in the Select an Album pull-down menu. Then select the desired image title from the Select Image menu.*

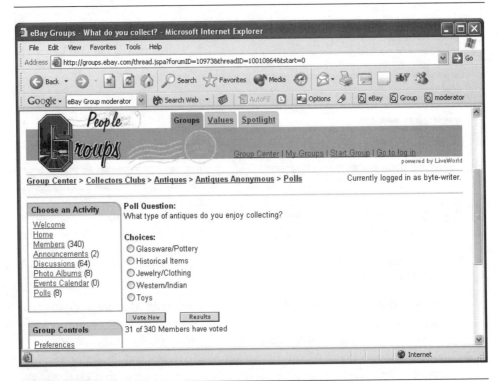

**FIGURE 14-4**   Polls let you find out about your members and increase their level of involvement.

# Serving as Moderator

A good moderator can make an eBay group work. Moderators are unsung heroes as far as groups go: they don't run the group, and they don't necessarily have to have started the group, but they do a lot of the day-to-day work that keeps the discussion flowing smoothly and productively. Responsibilities of a typical moderator include:

- Screening all message postings to make sure they aren't profane or abusive and don't contain unsolicited advertising

- Being present on the message boards to suggest topics, post replies, and answer questions

- Being available to iron out disputes or conflicts that may arise between members

- Reviewing photos that are posted to photo albums to make sure they are not offensive in some way

- Explaining to members why a photo or message was deleted

- Banning members who create ongoing problems

- Helping organize eBay parties, create poll questions, or organize other events

If you encounter a thread in which someone gets profane and abusive, when you are the moderator, you need to get involved. Step in and tell members that this is unacceptable behavior. You may even have to delete an individual post if it someone gets abusive and accuses people unfairly. If you encounter a dispute between members, you may need to refer to your group's charter.

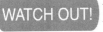 *Before you agree to be a moderator, you might want to review the list of Restricted Group Activities at http://pages.ebay.com/help/welcome/group-restricted-activities.html so you are aware of all the different situations you might have to deal with.*

## Getting Nonparticipating Members to Be Active

Perhaps the biggest problem faced by eBay group moderators and leaders is that of nonparticipating members: members who join but rarely, if ever, post. There isn't a

14

penalty from eBay if you have members who join but don't participate in discussions. When you're trying to get a group off the ground and help nurture it, it's a source of frustration more than anything. It's something practically every group leader faces at one time or another, and something you just have to work through. Based on what I read on the groups themselves, if you can get half your members to participate, you are doing well—anything more than that and you are doing *really* well.

One problem is that you can't really remove nonparticipating members. You can ban someone from participating in a group, but if they are not participating to begin with, this only spreads ill will and does not help your group at all. Perhaps the best solution is to approach your nonparticipating members individually, through eBay's communication system. Send a letter to each one, asking them to be more active members and, if they are not interested in the group, to remove themselves.

If you don't want to take this "interventionist" approach, try to increase members' interest by putting them in charge, allowing them to suggest topics, and giving them attention in some way. Consider the following:

- **Conduct polls**    Get members to spout off and complain or comment about topics of common interest.

- **Create photo albums**    A photo album is a set of images of eBay members. If you rotate the images every few days, so that every member is on the "cover" of the album at one time or another, people will be encouraged to post more images.

- **Involve members**    Get other members (not just moderators) to help you with the day-to-day tasks involved in running the group. One can function as a sort of virtual welcome wagon to greet new members. Another can run events such as Share-Your-Wares, in which members post links to their sales, especially those that fit into a particular "theme."

You might also suggest to members that they put some emotion and playfulness into their postings. In case they aren't aware of it already (they may not be), you can remind them that if they enter one of the standard keyboard combinations for emoticons, such as the smiley face :-), eBay groups will automatically insert a brightly colored icon. The emoticons that are available are listed in the eBay Groups Information Center's Frequently Asked Questions page (http://groups.ebay.com/ forum.jspa?forumID=1255), shown in Figure 14-5. (You have to be a member of the group to read the FAQ page, however.)

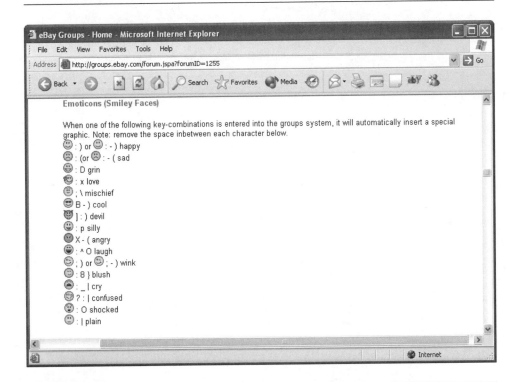

FIGURE 14-5    Encourage members to be playful and put some emotion into their postings.

14

## Links for Collectors

| Web Site | Address | What's There |
|---|---|---|
| eBay Group Center page | http://groups.ebay.com/ index.jspa | List of current eBay groups, a search box for finding groups by keyword, and a link to start your own group |
| eBay Groups Guidelines | http://pages.ebay.com/ help/policies/group- guidelines.html | Rules and procedures for creating a group or participating in one |
| Restricted Group Activities | http://pages.ebay.com/ help/welcome/group- restricted-activities.html | A set of situations to be avoided and actions that are not allowed in any eBay group |

# Chapter 15

# Collecting Your Financial and Tax Data

## In This Chapter You'll Learn...

■ How to avoid potential legal pitfalls

■ Simple options for managing inventory and keeping track of sales

■ How to account for tax you need to pay and deductions you can take

■ How to account for expenses and income so you can streamline your finances

Financial and legal considerations play a bigger role in everyday collecting than you probably think. You're continually calculating the value of various objects and trying to determine whether something is a good buy, or whether you can sell something at a profit. When you have developed a system, as described in Chapter 13, and begun to sell in quantity, you need to keep close watch on your available inventory. At tax time, you have to report your income from eBay, but at the same time, you get to report many new business-related deductions that can result in substantial savings.

This chapter examines the side of selling on eBay that individuals only think about when they have to—when April 15th's "tax day" approaches, for instance. Rather than putting off accounting and tax requirements, I encourage you to embrace them, or at least find an accountant or tax expert to help you deal with them. You'll not only be better organized and avoid running into legal trouble, but you'll come up with some new deductions that can save you money, too.

# Steering Clear of Legal Issues

You don't have to be a lawyer, a paralegal, or a legal buff to keep your eBay business out of trouble. You just need to be aware of what the pitfalls are and take some commonsense steps to avoid them. For instance, you need to make sure you have all the necessary permits. If you run an eBay business or a collectibles business out of your home, you might technically have to obtain a permit or business license to do so. It's true, your city authorities might never find out about what you're doing. But do you really want to take the chance? This is just one of the legal considerations you have to keep in mind when you start selling collectibles in quantity on eBay. Other potential legal pitfalls you need to avoid are described in the sections that follow.

# Avoiding Trademark Violations

*Trademark* is a legal concept that enables a business to protect the use of distinctive words, symbols, slogans, or other things that identify its products or services in the marketplace. A business is involved in *trade,* and to remain unique and recognizable to its customers, it develops and uses its *trade name.* eBay, itself, has trademarked its name, as you can tell by the ® (for *registered*) mark on the cover of the book you are reading right now. Trademarking a name doesn't mean that you or another entity, like this book's publisher, can't mention the name in print. It's the use of the trademarked name that matters: reproducing eBay's distinctive logo is a potential infringement, as is using the eBay logo to advertise one of your own auction listings.

As someone who sells collectibles, many of which bear a trade name and a logo, you need to be careful when you sell and describe those items. A company can trademark any visual element that accompanies a particular tangible product or line of goods and serves to identify and distinguish it from products sold by other sources. In other words, a trademark is not necessarily just for a business's trade name. In fact, you can trademark names, phrases, slogans, symbols, designs, or shapes. Just look at the bottom of eBay's home page in Figure 15-1. You see a group of other companies' trademarked logos, and a notice from eBay reminding visitors that it reserves all rights to use its trademark.

Company names are important on eBay. You might want to give your business a name, and use that name on your web site; in that case, you have to make sure you aren't infringing on someone else's trademarked ownership of that name. You also have to be careful about using trademarked images and phrases when you prepare sales descriptions for your own collectibles. Remember the following:

- You can't use a trademarked phrase or name in a sales description unless you are actually selling something that bears the trademark.

- You can't use a trademarked logo or image in a sales description *as a design element* in that description.

- You can take photos of objects that have trademarks on them as put there by the manufacturer.

In early 2004, messages circulated on a discussion board run by a well-known eBay seller with the user ID tabberone, stating that eBay had pulled sales listings that used the words *shabby* and *chic* in the titles. Apparently eBay decided that the use of the terms potentially infringed on the trademark of the well-known Shabby Chic line of products.

**15**

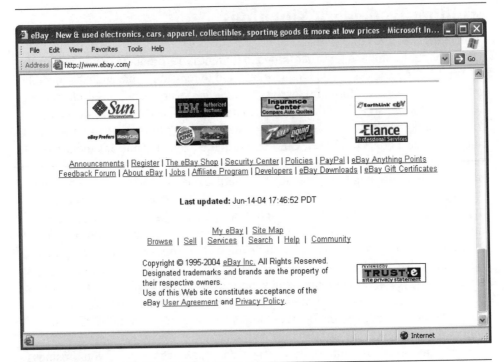

**FIGURE 15-1**    eBay and other businesses protect their trademarks, so be careful when you sell a trademarked item.

## Trade Talk

eBay can't be everywhere. Its staff cannot possibly check every one of the millions of items sold on its site for copyright or trademark infringement. But that doesn't mean people can get away with anything. The Verified Rights Owner (VeRO) program enlists the help of eBay members themselves who report sales that infringe upon the copyright, trademark, or other rights of third parties. VeRO program participants and other rights owners can report infringing items and have such items removed. You can become a member of the VeRO program yourself by creating an About Me page, then sending a message to eBay by following the e-mail link at http://pages.ebay.com/help/confidence/vero-rights-owner.html. The members listed are companies and individuals who are concerned about protecting their trademarks and copyrighted items; you should be careful about trying to sell anything associated with anyone on the list.

**COLLECTOR'S NOTE** *You can determine yourself whether someone has already trademarked the name you want to use. Just go to the United States Patent and Trademark Office home page (http://www.uspto.gov), and click Search under the heading Trademarks on the left-hand side of the page. When the Trademark Electronic Search System (TESS) page appears, choose the type of search you want to conduct, then enter the search terms. This approach can be time-consuming, but the price is right (it doesn't cost anything). If you are serious about using a phrase or image that might be protected, you'll probably want to hire an intellectual property lawyer to do a more in-depth search and to file the necessary paperwork when you decide to trademark a name.*

## Trying Not to Step on Someone Else's Copyright

*Copyright* is a legal term that describes the right of the creator of a creative work (or a person or entity to whom the creator has transferred the copyright) to control how it is copied. If someone uses material covered by copyright without asking the copyright owner, the copyright owner can sue and be compensated for any losses that have been suffered. The owner can even obtain a court order (called an *injunction*) that forces the infringing party to stop. For example, you can sell a *Batman* issue on eBay, but if you decide to draw and print your own homemade comic book about a character that looks very much like Batman, you are likely to receive a letter from an attorney for DC Comics, which holds the copyright to the Batman character. This happened to one eBay seller; he was forced to destroy the remaining copies and agreed to pay a settlement to DC Comics.

The most common way to infringe on someone's copyright on eBay is to copy auction material. Both text and images are covered by copyright. But text descriptions are to some extent "disposable." The truth is that most eBay sellers come up with descriptions by reading someone else's work and "adapting" it to suit their own items. I've never heard of a complaint about "borrowed" auction description text, but I've heard plenty of complaints about stolen images. It's easy to copy images, though many sellers protect theirs with a *watermark*: a word or image that is embedded in the body of the image (see the words "NYC Designs for Less" in Figure 15-2) and cannot be removed without seriously damaging the image. Images take time to capture and edit, and sellers are understandably miffed when they see their images being used in someone else's auction listing. Not only is it a copyright violation, but it's also misleading to bidders and buyers.

15

**FIGURE 15-2**    Many sellers protect their images by inserting digital watermarks that identify ownership.

## eBay's Potentially Infringing, Questionable, and Prohibited Items

People collect anything and everything. That, of course, doesn't mean you can put just anything up for sale. The folks who attempted to sell pieces of the space shuttle *Columbia* wreckage on eBay in February 2003 found that out the hard way when they were arrested and the sales listings were immediately pulled off the auction site. That's only one of the most notorious examples. Some more mundane items that fall under the category of "collectible" might also fall into one of eBay's "prohibited," "questionable," or "potentially infringing" designations.

### Avoiding Potentially Infringing Items

Items that eBay describes as "potentially infringing" are ones that can be held to be in violation of the owner's trademark or copyright. These include software, illegal movie or audio recordings, and video game enhancers. They also include items that include the signature or photo of a famous individual who did not authorize his or her depiction. It's OK to sell movie memorabilia that an actor has authorized. But stay away from recent movie or music memorabilia that bears the images of people who may not have authorized the item. If someone offers you $8 \times 10$ movie photos, be wary if you see that there are multiple copies of the same item being sold on eBay. They could easily be unauthorized reprints.

## Avoiding Questionable Items

Objects designated as "questionable items" are ones that can't be sold under certain conditions. On the other hand, you can sell them under other conditions. For example, you can't sell any burial items or grave-related items that relate to Native Americans. You cannot sell historical graves or tombstones. But you can sell new grave markers and grave sites. You can't sell electronics equipment that transmits radio signals or that can monitor cellular communications. But you can sell cell phones, stereos, DVD players, and the like.

TIP   *Your best option for understanding these distinctions is checking eBay's up-to-date lists of prohibited, questionable, and potentially infringing items at http://pages.ebay.com/help/sell/questions/prohibited-items.html.*

## Avoiding Prohibited Items

There aren't any gray areas with regard to things that eBay designates as "prohibited items." They violate eBay's rules, and they may also violate trade laws in the United States or in other countries. Here are some examples:

- **Alcohol**   You can sell collectible beer cans or wine bottles. But don't try to sell something that contains alcohol if the container is not especially collectible. (However, a small group of pre-approved sellers is allowed to sell wine on the site "under controlled conditions.")

- **Animals**   You can sell depictions of animals or figurines of them. But don't try to purchase or sell animals on eBay (other than tropical fish or snails, feeder insects, or worms, that is).

- **Firearms**   Even if an old gun or rifle is considered a valuable antique, you can't sell it on eBay.

15

■ **Tobacco**    eBay is very strict about prohibiting the sale of tobacco. It allows the sale of collectible tobacco-related items, including packages that contain tobacco, if the value of the item is in the packaging and not the tobacco. For instance, the classic Prince Albert in a Tin listing shown in Figure 15-3 is allowed because of the container's antique value.

Sometimes, the difference between something that is prohibited and something that is questionable is not always clear. When in doubt, refer to eBay's descriptions, and save the items that can get you into trouble for other marketplaces.

## Observing Collecting Best Practices

The corporate-sounding phrase *best practices* is used to describe practices that aren't laws, necessarily, but common sense everyone needs to follow in order to do business well and avoid trouble of one sort or another. Many collectors' organizations have

**FIGURE 15-3**    Some substances that are prohibited can be sold if they are in collectible containers.

their own code of ethics or a set of guidelines that members are asked to follow when pursuing their hobby. You should be aware of such requirements and follow them as closely as you can.

For instance, butterfly collecting is a time-honored activity that has both environmental and legal implications. If you catch a butterfly in one country, taking it home with you might violate customs or other laws. And some species are rare enough that catching and mounting them may actually make them more endangered. Accordingly, the Lepidopterists' Society has published a statement on collecting *Lepidoptera* (butterflies and moths, in other words). The statement's guidelines say that collecting needs to be pursued in a way that does not damage the environment. (Anyone who pursues butterfly collecting should be familiar with the statement; see http://alpha.furman.edu/~snyder/snyder/lep/coll.htm.) Here are some other activities that carry legal ramifications:

- **Gun collecting**    There are obvious considerations with selling guns to minors, even if they are antiques.

- **Knife collecting**    Guns aren't the only weapons that are covered by regulations. So are knives and swords. The British Knife Collectors Guild lists a variety of laws that cover the possession and carrying of knives at http://www.bkcg.co.uk/guide/cpslinks.html. In general, restrictions on knives are even more stringent than in the U.S.

- **Spiders and insects**    The Young Entomologists' Society (YES) has guidelines (see http://members.aol.com/YESedu/collpoli.html) that cover damage to the environment, protection of species, and preservation of endangered species.

In your zeal to excel in eBay's trading community, don't lose sight of the community of collectors that you already belong to.

# Managing Your Inventory

A collector who doesn't have a way to keep track of what he or she has can easily misplace or forget about some valuable items. If your collection stretches into several hundred or even thousands of pieces, you have to start thinking about insurance. Even if you only have a few objects but they are especially valuable, such as fine art works, you have to have a list as well as photos for insurance purposes. That way, if disaster or thieves strike, you have some money to start over with. It's important to document your collection and keep track of the inventory you have for sale. Once you come up with a system, you only have to use it every time you make an addition to your collection.

## Keeping Track of What's on Hand

The word *inventory* seems formal and businesslike when it comes to a collection. For collectors, an inventory need only consist of a list that you keep on paper or on your computer. For each item in your collection, record the following:

■ The name of the item

■ The date you purchased it

■ Where you bought it

■ A brief description of the item

■ The purchase price

For tax purposes, be sure to keep a file of any receipts you receive, in case you are called upon to document your purchases. Beyond this basic, must-have information, you can add optional data such as:

■ The estimated value of the item. This can be useful for insurance, especially if the value is dramatically higher than what you paid.

■ Significant features that might affect the value: signed by the artist, purchased from the artist's wife, and so on.

■ Any flaws or blemishes, or an official grading if you have received one.

If your collection stretches into hundreds of separate pieces, it's advisable to number your objects. Keep the numbering simple: use a three-digit system that starts at 001 and goes to 999, or a four-digit system if you need to get into the thousands. If your collection is really valuable, you'll benefit by taking photos of your collection or panning across it with a video camera as well.

*The Antique and Art Information Network puts out several products related to inventory tracking and accounting for collectors and antiques dealers. Find out more about their products at http://www.aain.com/ aainproductmenu.html.*

## Finding Storage Space

One aspect of keeping a collection organized is finding space to store it. Some collectors put their treasures all over the walls, if they are easily mounted. Others put toys, radios, and trains on shelves in a basement or rec room. Be sure your storage area is equipped with a dehumidifier, because humidity can damage many collectibles. Other environmental controls like sprinklers or air conditioning are important.

# Making Your Business Less Taxing

The truth is simple: income from your eBay business is subject to tax just like income from any other type of business activity. It doesn't matter whether eBay sales are your sole source of income or just a sideline. You have to report money you make from auctions just as you would any other income.

The good news is that because you have income from your eBay business, you can deduct the expenses associated with that business. That includes the camera you use to photograph the items you sell, the computer you use to prepare the sales, the fees you pay to eBay, and much more. It's all a matter of keeping appropriate financial records. It can actually be fun to keep track of where your eBay business is at financially and save a few bucks at tax time as well.

WATCH OUT!    *You know how to use a computer, and you can handle accounting and tax software. Does that mean you should actually attempt to do your own taxes? Not unless you are up on the latest changes to tax law. In my opinion, you should hire an accountant to file your taxes for you. Mine continually comes up with new ways to lower the taxes I have to pay.*

## Choosing a Legal Form for Your Business

15

You don't have to be concerned with deciding on a legal form for your business until it really becomes a business: until you start depending on it for all your income, or for a large percentage of it. Then you have to be concerned with the potential for liability, either from disgruntled customers or from companies who feel you have potentially violated their trademark. Such incidents aren't likely to happen, especially if you observe the good business practices described throughout this book. But businesses that have employees, pay license fees, and have significant income might benefit by deciding whether to incorporate or to run the organization as a sole proprietorship.

## Considering Incorporation

The legal form of a business is a designation that is recognized by taxing and licensing agencies. You have a number of options to choose from, and the choice can affect the amount of taxes you pay and your liability in case of loss. Some eBay sellers choose to incorporate in order to reduce liability. It isn't difficult to incorporate, but it's not something I recommend doing yourself. When my brother incorporated to start up an audio restoration business, he hired an attorney well versed in such matters to lead him through the process.

When you incorporate, you separate your company from the people who own and operate it. The company's managers (in other words, you) are shielded from liability in terms of debts and obligations. Once you decide to incorporate, you next have to pick one of two options: a C corporation or an S corporation. The latter is the most likely choice for small businesses, whether they are auction concerns or not. However, there is a third practical alternative: the limited liability company (LLC).

S corporations get liability protection, but they are complex to set up. The filing process can take weeks or even months. The prospect can be daunting for a lone entrepreneur who's just starting out and has only a few dozen sales a month. It's advisable to wait until you have enough income to hire an attorney and pay incorporation fees before you seriously consider incorporating, even as an S corporation.

C corporations are for large-scale businesses, rather than small auction sales operations. Profits are taxed at the corporate level, and C corporations tend to be large and have lots of shareholders. In order to incorporate, all stockholders and shareholders must agree on the name of the company, the choice of the people who will manage it, and many other issues.

The limited liability company combines aspects of both S and C corporations. LLCs have a number of attractive options that make them good candidates for small businesses. Income and losses are shared by the individual investors, who are known as *members*. Members are subject to limited liability for debts and obligations of the LLC. In addition, LLCs receive favorable tax treatment.

> TIP *The Nolo Press web site (http://www.nolo.com) has extensive information on legal terms and is a good place to do some legal self-help.*

## Creating a Sole Proprietorship

If you don't want to choose one of the incorporation options, you can choose to designate your business as a sole proprietorship. In a *sole proprietorship,* you're the only boss. You make all the decisions and you get all the benefits. On the other hand, you take on all the problems that arise, too. This is the simplest and least expensive type of business because you can run it yourself. You don't need an accountant or lawyer to help you form the business (though it helps), and you certainly don't have to answer to partners or stockholders. (However, a sole proprietorship *can be* a corporation or Limited Liability Company.) To declare a sole proprietorship, you may have to file an application; check with your local county clerk.

## Partnerships

On the other hand, if you do all the work of acquiring collectibles and putting them up for sale with one or two other individuals, you might prefer to designate your operation as a formal partnership. In a partnership, all partners are held personally liable for losses. (A partnership can also be a corporation or Limited Liability Company.) The partners share the risk and profit with each other. Ideally, your partners bring skills to the endeavor that complement your own contributions. The rate of taxes that each partner pays is based on his or her percentage of income from the partnership.

## Tackling the Sales Tax Question

The question "Should I charge sales tax?" is one I hear all the time from people who conduct business online.

In order to charge sales tax in the first place, you may need to get a state resale tax ID number. This requirement varies by state, however; check with your state department of revenue to make sure.

**WATCH OUT!** *If you charge sales tax to residents of a certain state, make sure you mention that in your terms of sale. If you don't mention it in the description or terms of sale and then ask for it after the sale is complete, the buyer may object and you'll have a dispute on your hands.*

**15**

Some states have a more complex sales tax system than others. The sales tax in California, for example, varies depending on what county you live in because some counties have their own tax that is charged in addition to the state sales tax. (Of course, if you have a resale number you don't have to pay sales tax on items you buy that you plan to resell.)

## Confronting Employee Tax Considerations

The moment you hire employees, all kinds of new tax and accounting requirements become relevant. If you have a sole proprietorship, for instance, you need to report the income on Schedule C, Profit and Loss from Business. If you hire employees as independent contractors, things are far more simple. You need to get each contractor to fill out a Form 1099, which reports their Social Security and other information to the government.

If you hire someone who is a regular employee, things get much more complicated. You have to deal with additional accounting tasks: payroll, taxes, benefits, and insurance. This is the time when you need professional help. Remember, a salary includes not only the actual amount you pay your employee but as much as 30 percent in additional overhead as well—federal and state withholding, Social Security and Medicare (FICA) taxes, worker's compensation insurance, long-term disability insurance, vacation pay and sick leave, and perhaps other benefits as well. Benefit requirements vary from state to state.

> TIP
>
> *Consider hiring someone for a month-long "probation" period if you aren't sure how they'll work out. When employees are working at your home, you have to make sure they'll get along with your pets and possibly your family members. Try to get someone who has references from a friend or family member, if possible.*

# Accounting 101 for Collectors

You can keep records of your income and expenses in an old-fashioned record book you get from the office supply store. You can gather all your receipts and stuff them in a big envelope. Or you can enter the information in a newfangled accounting program like Quicken (http://www.quicken.com) or QuickBooks (http://www.quickbooks.com). You can rely on eBay to keep records of your previous transactions on your My eBay page. However you do it, it's a good idea to follow some sort of regular and systematic record-keeping procedure. The idea is to be able to print out a list of your sales from eBay as well as your business expenses so you can accurately report what you have sold and what you paid to get the merchandise you sold. It's not that difficult, even for a finance-phobe like me. It's just a matter of keeping receipts and other records, choosing one of the two accounting methods described in the next section, and establishing your accounting period.

## Cash Versus Accrual Basis

*Cash basis* and *accrual basis* sound complicated, but they're just two different ways of describing how you keep track of income and expenses. You don't have to know every last detail about the two methods. But if you know that the options exist and have an idea of how they differ, you'll be able to discuss them with your accountant or tax preparer.

In the cash method, you report income when you actually receive it and write off expenses when you pay them. This is the easy way to report income and expenses, and probably the way most new small businesses do it.

If your eBay business maintains a steady inventory (and some such businesses do), you must use the accrual basis accounting method. For instance, suppose your eBay business sells an inventory of surplus items. You report income when you make the sale (not when you actually receive the payment), and you write down expenses when goods or services are received (even though you may not have made the cash payment yet). For example, suppose 25 of your eBay sales are completed on June 30, and you ask your customers to get their payments to you by July 8. The payments don't all arrive, however, until July 15. You still record the income as having been received on June 30, when the payment was originally due.

Accrual accounting creates a more accurate picture of a business's financial situation. If a company is having cash flow problems and is extending payment on some of its bills, cash-basis accounting provides an unduly rosy financial picture, whereas the accrual-basis method would be more accurate. Because a small eBay collector's business isn't likely to have a steady inventory, chances are the cash-based method is the one to use.

 *When you win an auction on eBay, print the seller's page of the auction complete with description and photos. Keep these pages in a file until the item arrives. You will always be able to tell what is still due to come your way. When it arrives, transfer the page to your inventory/purchases file. This will make life a little simpler at tax time.*

15

## Your Accounting Period

With either the cash or accrual system, you need to pick an accounting period. Many businesses stick to the calendar year: January 1 to December 31. But you don't have to follow these dates. Many corporations and other large businesses pick a date other than December 31 to function as the end of the fiscal year.

COLLECTOR'S NOTE

*If you use the fiscal-year method of accounting, you must file your tax return three-and-a-half months after the end of the fiscal year. If the fiscal year ends on June 30, for example, you must file by October 15.*

## Tracking Sales with a Database

Because collections are continually evolving, and the number of items you have available for sale is constantly changing as you sell on eBay, it's natural to use one of the many office database software packages to set up a database to record sales as well as inventory. Microsoft Access, which comes with the Professional Edition of Microsoft Office, is an obvious choice. If you are adept with spreadsheets like Excel, you can use that as well. A simple example of an Excel inventory is shown in Figure 15-4.

WATCH OUT!

*Be sure to make a copy of your collection's database and store it in a safe location away from your computer. That way, if anything happens to your machine or to your data, you can replace it using the secure copy.*

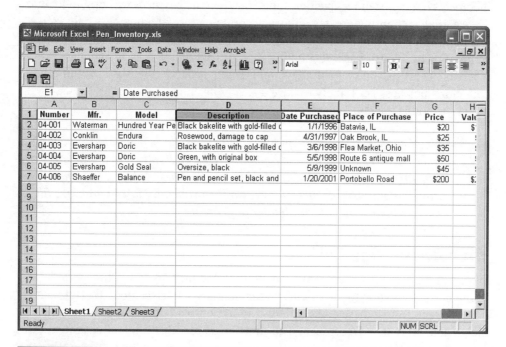

---
**FIGURE 15-4**    Any program that can present data in rows and columns can be used to track sales or inventory.

# Expenses You Should Track

Being meticulous and systematic about the financial records you keep isn't just a good principle to follow. It can have an impact on your bottom line, too. The more accurate your expenses, the more deductions you'll be able to take. Besides that, you'll have a realistic picture of how your business is doing if you can compare your income against the costs that are required to generate it.

You might think of the financial side of your eBay business as consisting of different financial accounts. Every time a financial event occurs, an account's balance either decreases or increases. When someone purchases one of your auction items and you deposit the payment, your bank account increases and the money people owe you decreases. The dual activity—one account goes up while another goes down—is known as *double-entry bookkeeping*.

## Recording Your Income: Your Bank Account

Your bank account is your income from sales—the good stuff. As an eBay businessperson, you're likely to get income in any number of forms: personal checks, PayPal transfers, or direct deposits to your bank account from credit card companies.

The best way to record your income is to be systematic about it: for each item, write down a brief, informal statement. This is a personal record that you may make on the stub that comes with many checks that are issued as payments. Be sure to include the following information:

- The date of the transaction

- The type of payment (PayPal, credit card, or check)

- The amount you were paid

- The name of your high bidder or buyer

This is probably the most enjoyable thing you can record in your accounting software or booklet.

## Your Accounts Receivable: What You Expect to Receive

This is the amount that people owe you and that you expect to receive at some point—those checks that are in the mail, the money in your PayPal account that hasn't yet been transferred to the bank.

**15**

## Your Asset Account

Every business has equipment of one sort or another that it uses to produce its goods or services. Such business equipment goes by the name *assets* in accounting jargon. As an eBay seller, you probably have assets such as:

- Your computer
- Your digital camera and/or scanner
- Modems, hubs, cables, speakers, printers, and other computer-related equipment
- Postage machines

You need to keep records of your assets that include the following information:

- Name, model number, and description
- Purchase date
- Purchase price, including fees
- Date the item went into service
- Amount of time the item is put to personal (as opposed to business) use

File these records in a safe location along with your other tax-related information. You might have to *expense* (in other words, spread out) the original cost of the equipment that is expected to help you generate income over its useful life. Expensing the cost of an asset over its life span is called *depreciation*. In order to depreciate an item, you estimate how many years you're going to use it and then divide the original cost by the number of years. The result is the amount that you report in any given year. For example, if you purchase a digital camera that costs $1000 and you expect to use it in your business for five years, you expense $200 of the cost each year.

## Your Expense Account

If you scour flea markets and estate sales, you pay for the collectibles you sell on eBay. Such payments should be recorded for accounting purposes. In addition you, like any online businessperson, probably need to make regular payments to the company that gives you Internet access, and possibly web page designers and computer technicians. If you hire employees to help you, the payment system becomes more involved.

When you spend the day at the flea market or at an auction, do you chow down at the local burger joint? Be sure to get a receipt for that lunch and file it away in your receipts envelope at the end of the day. Meals, gas and mileage, and postage are all business expenses—costs that you incur in order to produce revenue—and you can deduct them at tax time.

As your business becomes more successful you may decide to advertise to direct collectors to your eBay offerings. This is heavily supported by eBay, and it currently has a co-op advertising program in which it will pay up to 25 percent of your cost for print advertising. Your 75 percent is tax deductible, too.

Pulling together evidence of expenses doesn't have to be a high-tech matter. If you have a handheld PC, great. Otherwise, get a big folder and use it to hold any receipts, canceled checks, and credit card statements. Be sure your records include basic information such as:

- Date the expense occurred

- Name of the person or company that received payment from you

- Type of expense incurred (equipment, utilities, supplies, and so on)

If some of your collectors' items are especially valuable, you should make an effort to insure them. The cost of insurance should be listed as one of your business expenses when your collecting business gains income on eBay. In addition, anything you pay to repair or restore your art, furniture, or other valuable collectibles should be included as well.

TIP

*You can find out more about business expenses that are allowable as deductions by consulting the Internal Revenue Service's Publication 334, Tax Guide for Small Businesses (http://www.irs.gov/pub/irs-pdf/ p334.pdf).*

15

# Links for Collectors

| Web Site | Address | What's There |
|---|---|---|
| Verified Rights Owners program | http://pages.ebay.com/help/ community/vero-aboutme.html | A program in which eBay members monitor listings for copyright infringement |
| Self-service utility for searching trademarks | http://www.uspto.gov, click Search under Trademarks, then click the type of search | List of trademarks already owned |
| Prohibited, Questionable, and Potentially Infringing Items page | http://pages.ebay.com/help/sell/ questions/prohibited-items.html | Lists of items that you cannot list for sale on eBay |
| Internal Revenue Service | http://www.irs.gov | Tax forms you can print out and publications with tips for small businesses |

# Appendix A

# Top 10 eBay Frauds to Avoid

A ny marketplace that attracts a large number of buyers and sellers, many of whom are new to the process or to the marketplace itself, is going to be plagued by scam artists and outright thieves. eBay is no exception. In fact, it's well known for instances of fraud, many of which occur *only* on eBay.

Although some eBay scams are elaborate, many are not. They prey on eBay users' natural desire for safety and the wish to believe that other people are basically good and trustworthy. Half the battle, when it comes to avoiding such trouble, is simply knowing what problems you need to guard against. With that in mind, the following sections list 10 of the most common types of fraud you might encounter on eBay.

**WATCH OUT!** *The number of fraudulent incidents on eBay is, unfortunately, increasing, and they are changing all the time, just like virus attacks. Keep track of new scams on the eBay Trust and Safety discussion board (http://forums.ebay.com/db2/forum.jsp?forum=107).*

# The "Pay Me by Western Union" Fraud

The most popular scam on eBay takes place when you try to buy something from a seller who demands payment by Western Union. A buyer will see a plasma TV, car, motorcycle, or other expensive item available at a Buy It Now price of about 35 to 50 percent of the going price. The deal looks great, but you have to move fast to close the sale. The seller insists on a Western Union payment, and usually wants the deal to be done outside the eBay web site. Often, the seller's stated location will be in the U.S., England, or Italy. However, the place where you are to transfer the funds turns out to be in Nigeria or some other part of Africa. You will never see the merchandise or your money again. There is no recourse when you send money with Western Union. eBay buyers get scammed every week with deals like this. Don't allow yourself to be part of that sad group.

**WATCH OUT!** *Singapore and other Pacific Rim countries are also hotbeds of Internet fraud. If you receive an eBay order from any of these questionable areas, insist that they pay by international money order in U.S. funds. Do not ship until your bank verifies that the payment has cleared. Beware of international buyers who ask you to FedEx something they buy with a credit card. They will want you to ship FedEx so the item arrives before the stolen credit card number is canceled.*

# The "Update Your Account" Scam

In this scam, you receive an e-mail from eBay or PayPal—at least, it looks like a legitimate e-mail message from one of those companies. The message asks you to update your account information. Some messages request the information politely, in the guise of routine updating. Other messages try to instill fear: there has been a security breach and someone is impersonating you, or you need to verify your data to keep people from using your eBay account fraudulently.

Whatever the pretense, you are asked to supply every bit of personal info you can imagine: passwords, Social Security numbers, bank account numbers, credit card numbers, your address, and often, anything else the sender can think of. Sometimes, the e-mail asks only for your eBay user ID and password. If you are gullible enough to send along even this minimal amount of information, the thief/hacker/con man is able to "hijack" your account. In other words, he or she is able to offer items for sale using your account, then collect the money and never ship anything. You get stuck with the negative feedback and the complaints from disgruntled buyers. If you receive such an e-mail message yourself, be sure to forward it to either the eBay or PayPal security departments.

> TIP  *To keep your account from being hijacked, check your About Me page periodically to make sure your description and contact information are as you wrote them and haven't been changed by someone who has taken over your account.*

# The Fake eBay Web Page Variation

Some spoof e-mails don't ask for you to e-mail back your personal information directly to the fraud artist. After all, eBay takes pains to remind its account holders that it will never send e-mails that ask for such information (neither will PayPal). Instead, an even trickier spoof e-mail contains a link that looks like this:

> In order to update your account information, please go to this WEB PAGE.

If you click the highlighted link that's embedded in the body of the e-mail (in this example, the words "web page"), your browser launches and goes to what appears to be one of eBay's or PayPal's real pages. If you look closely, however, you'll see a slight variation in the URL that will tip you off that

A

you're visiting a fake web site—a site that has nothing to do with eBay or PayPal but has been designed to look like them. Instead of a URL beginning with http://pages.ebay.com/aw-cgi, you'll see one beginning with http://pages.ebay.com/ aww-cgi, or ...aw-cji, or something slightly different from the legitimate address.

Fake web sites can be convincing enough to get you to enter your personal information and submit it. You think you are actually improving your security or making it easier to use eBay or PayPal. In reality, you are making it easier for someone to access those sites and take money from other people while using your information.

 *If you receive an "update your account" e-mail message from eBay or PayPal and you suspect that it's fraudulent, forward the message to spoof@eBay.com or spoof@paypal.com so the two organizations can be aware of it and deal with it. Also read eBay's official statement on spoof e-mails at http://pages.ebay.com/help/confidence/spoof-email.html.*

# The Fake Sale Held by an Account "Hijacker"

You already know, from the previous section, that eBay accounts can be hijacked by fraudulent users. It can be difficult to tell whether or not a seller is really offering items for sale or really is who he or she claims to be. But there are some tell-tale signs you can look for that indicate a sale may not be legitimate:

- The items for sale look like they have been copied out of a printed or online catalog; the seller has not taken photos of them with a digital camera.

- If you win the auction you are directed not to use PayPal or even your credit card, but to send payment via Western Union.

Such frauds are particularly insidious because they take advantage of the positive feedback rating the ostensible seller has already built up. Even if the listing looks like it has been copied from printed material, the seller might have glowing feedback comments that make visitors place bids. As you know from the "pay me by Western Union" fraud mentioned earlier, any time buyers are asked to send payment via Western Union they should refrain from doing so. Use eBay's payment system in order to take advantage of built-in fraud protection systems. If the seller insists that you pay by Western Union, don't give in; report the seller to eBay and ask them to investigate possible account hijacking.

# The "Second Chance" Nonoffer

You didn't win the auction, but suddenly it seems you're in luck: the seller has sent a Second Chance offer to you and to other unsuccessful bidders. The seller gives you a chance to buy that item (typically, an item that is expensive and hard-to-find). The catch: you have to pay not through eBay but via Western Union. To overcome your skepticism, the seller tempts you with an extremely low price. The item that sold for $799 can be yours for only $349, for instance.

Often, the location where you are instructed to wire transfer the money is located in Europe or Asia. Resist the temptation to go for the bargain; if you do, you'll never see your money again.

COLLECTOR'S NOTE  *In some cases, when buyers or sellers rightly ask what kind of protection they will have if they conduct a transaction off of eBay using Western Union, con artists have sent official-looking e-mails that appear to come from eBay and that offer as much as $40,000 in insurance protection. In fact, eBay offers $250 in fraud insurance, but only for transactions that are completed through eBay.*

# The "If You Just Make Up the Difference…" Fraud

Your high bidder should send you payment for the amount you specify and in one of the forms you specify. *You* should never end up sending a check to one of your own buyers, no matter how tempting it might be.

It sounds implausible, but it happens: A con artist wins an item on eBay. In this example, assume the winning bid was $1000. The buyer lives outside the United States. The buyer explains to you that he or she knows someone in the U.S. who owes him or her a larger sum, such as $3000, and will instruct the debtor to send a cashier's check to you for the full amount owed—$3000. All you have to do is deposit a cashier's check for the balance (in this example, $2000). Not only that, but your check must be sent by FedEx overnight. You do receive the cashier's check for $3000, and you deposit it and send the buyer the balance, as requested.

Later, your bank informs you that the cashier's check was fake. It was made on a high-quality color copier. The bank demands that you reimburse them for the total of $3000. Not only that, but you have lost the merchandise you sold.

When you try to locate the con artist, don't be surprised to find that the person was using a hijacked eBay account to make the purchase and you have no way to find them.

A

# The Plain and Simple Credit Card Con

This one isn't as complicated as the preceding example, but it's effective: You accept credit card purchases, and you sell something to a high bidder or buyer who wants to pay not through PayPal but directly with the credit card. The buyer, however, asks that you ship the item FedEx to an overseas location (for example, Singapore). Not long after you do so, your bank informs you that the charges are being reversed and presented to you because the credit card was stolen.

Moral of the story: If you accept credit cards, check the address of the card's owner and compare it to the shipping address. If the two addresses do not match, phone the owner and verify that the purchase is legitimate. (Some eBay sellers go to the extra length of restricting sales to countries that are prone to such instances of fraud, such as Singapore and Malaysia.)

# The "I Demand a Refund" Cheat

You ship something to a buyer, and the buyer demands a refund for some reason. The reasons vary. Often the buyer complains that the item was not in the condition you mentioned in your original eBay description. Perhaps a piece was missing from the item; perhaps the item was damaged in transit, or so the buyer claims. When the item is returned, you discover that a piece has been removed and replaced; the buyer is a collector who took the piece from your item in good condition and replaced it with a piece of his or her item, which was not in such good condition. In the world of comic books and magazines, collectors have been known to take a ripped and yellowed page from their valuable publication, exchange it for the better page from the item they just bought, and demand a refund.

# The "Lost in the Mail" Liar

If you don't get delivery confirmation from a buyer, you can never know for certain that your item was lost in transit. For your piece of mind, it's better to go through the extra expense of obtaining delivery confirmation as well as insurance. The insurance can provide you with some compensation in case the item is really lost or damaged by the shipper (although it can take a while to get reimbursed). The delivery confirmation gives you evidence that your item reached its destination.

Some disreputable buyers claim that they never received something and demand a refund when, in fact, they did receive the item in question. Sellers occasionally adjust their terms of sale to prevent this: they prohibit refunds under any circumstances, for instance. But you need to take into account the relatively few times when items really do get lost or stolen in transit and really don't reach their destination: delivery confirmation will tell you whether or not your buyer is telling the truth.

# The Company Check Calamity

After you successfully sell an item, the winning bidder or buyer contacts you with a problem. The buyer doesn't have personal checks for some reason, but does have a check issued by his or employer. The check is for more than the purchase price, but if you will just refund the difference by sending a check or money order, everything will be fine.

Smelling trouble, you inform the buyer that you'll take the company check as long as you can wait a week or more for the check to clear before you send out the difference. The buyer agrees. When the check arrives, you hurry it to the bank, and when the check appears to clear (it shows up in your bank account, which you can check online) you send out the item and the check or money order for the difference, thinking everything went smoothly. Not long after, your bank informs you that the check was forged, and the bank has not been paid by the company in question. The problem is that there's a difference between when a check clears and when the check is paid. A check can seem to clear and still end up bouncing when the bank is not reimbursed. Make sure you ask your bank whether the check has been "paid" rather than "cleared" before you ship what you've sold.

> TIP
>
> *To find out more about the latest scams afflicting eBay buyers and sellers, check eBay's Trust and Safety (SafeHarbor) discussion group (http:// forums.ebay.com/db2/forum.jsp?forum=107): click Community in the eBay navigation bar, click Discussion Boards (under Talk), and then click Trust and Safety (SafeHarbor).*

A

# Appendix B

## eBay Collectors' Lingo

***About Me***    A page that you can create on eBay's web site that provides some brief personal information about you and collects your current sales on the same page.

***active listing***    A sale that is currently happening.

***artifacts***    Historical items of interest to collectors, grave markings, Native American items, or other objects the sale of which is restricted on eBay. See http://pages.ebay.com/help/policies/artifacts.html.

***as is***    Indicates that an item is being sold in its advertised condition and with no other warranty, either implied or stated.

***authentication***    The process of certifying that an autograph or other object is what the owner claims it to be—in other words, that it is original or genuine and not a fake.

***bid increment***    A predetermined amount by which bids increase as they are placed. The increment varies depending on the current high bid.

***bid retraction***    The process of canceling a bid that has already been made. Retractions are allowed only in exceptional circumstances, such as the entry of the wrong bid amount or if the description of the item changes "significantly." See http://pages.ebay.com/help/buy/bid-retract.html.

***bid shielding***    A process in which two bidders conspire to defraud a seller out of a high bid. The high bidder retracts the bid at the last minute, so the partner's lower bid can win.

***Big Ticket Items***    A category made up of items that are currently for sale on eBay and that have a starting bid or current high bid of $5000 or more.

***BIN killer***    Someone who places a bid early in an auction that has a Buy It Now price and no reserve price. As soon as the first bid is placed, the Buy It Now price goes away.

***blocked bidder***    Someone who has specifically been excluded from bidding on an item, usually because of problems with previous transactions.

***Buy It Now***    A way to sell your item on eBay for a fixed price.

***certificate of authenticity (COA)***    A statement by an appraiser, historical expert, or other authority certifying that a collectible object is genuine.

***certification***    The process of evaluating the authenticity and condition of a collectible by a third-party grading service.

*chargeback*    A fee charged to a seller by a credit card company for accepting a credit card number for a purchase that turns out to be fraudulent.

*chat*    Normally used as a shorthand term for Internet Relay Chat, a real-time communications method on the Internet. eBay regularly uses *chat* to describe its Community Boards, which are really message boards.

*checkout*    A way of streamlining the end of a transaction in which the seller specifies how much to pay for shipping, insurance, and sales tax when the item is listed. The buyer then receives an e-mail at the end of the auction that automatically lists the total and where the item should be shipped.

*consignment*    The process of selling something for someone else. The seller who offers the merchandise and conducts the sale usually collects a fee for his or her services.

*cookie*    A small bit of information that is placed on a visitor's computer by a web site and that provides the site (such as eBay) with information when you revisit, so you don't have to log in again.

*counter*    A utility that tracks the number of visits that have been made to a web page.

*Dutch auction*    An auction format that enables a group of identical items to be sold to a group of bidders at once rather than in separate sales.

*eBay Stores*    A feature that enables sellers to sell a group of items at a fixed price on their own web page.

*feedback*    A system of communication that enables eBay users who have been involved in transactions with other users to leave comments that describe their level of responsiveness, the quality of the transaction, or related (and sometimes unrelated) issues.

*final value fee*    The fee charged to a seller by eBay for selling something either to the highest bidder or on a Buy It Now basis.

*fink*    Someone who turns out to be a fraudulent buyer or seller.

*gallery*    An eBay feature that enables sellers to post photos of their items that buyers can then browse.

*grading*    A system for describing the condition of an item.

*HTF*    Hard to Find, a descriptor used frequently by participants in eBay's message board or in auction listings.

B

*HTML*    HyperText Markup Language, the set of instructions that is used to present text and images on web pages, including eBay auction descriptions.

*ID Verify*    A program in which sellers or buyers have their personal information verified against consumer and business databases so that others can trust that they are who they say they are.

*keyword spamming*    The practice of including brand names or other keywords that aren't related to the item being sold in an effort to get extra attention for the item.

*live auction*    An auction held in real time. See http://pages.liveauctions.ebay.com/help/welcome/overview.html.

*maker's mark*    A trademark or other identifying stamp or mark printed on an object to identify its manufacturer and sometimes its date and model number.

*MIB*    Mint in Box. This abbreviation is frequently used in auction listings titles. The item in the box is in mint condition; however, the box may not be.

*MIMB*    Mint in Mint Box. The item in the box is in mint condition, and the box is, too.

*My eBay*    A page you can configure to include the items you have sold and the items you have obtained recently or on which you have bid.

*NARU*    Not a Registered User. This term is used to describe someone who has been suspended from eBay.

*new old stock*    An item that is not new but has never been sold and is still in its original packaging.

*nonpaying bidder*    Someone who qualifies to obtain an item by being the high bidder but then fails to complete the transaction by not paying for the item.

*NR*    No Reserve. Used to describe a sale for which a reserve amount has not been specified. The high bidder will win the item.

*NRFB*    Never Removed from Box.

*OO*    Original Outfit. The clothing in which a doll or figurine was originally dressed and sold.

*pink*    Someone who works at eBay. When they post on message boards, their name is highlighted with a pink background. Whenever they post, you also see the eBay logo next to their name.

***proxy bid***   A bid that eBay places for you automatically based on the maximum amount you are willing to pay for an item. If someone outbids you, eBay automatically places proxy bids up to your maximum amount.

***relist***   To put an item up for sale again after a sale has ended.

***reserve price***   An amount specified by a seller as the minimum price he or she is willing to accept for an item. The reserve price is kept secret until a bidder meets it. The seller is not obligated to sell an item if the reserve price has not been met.

***shill bidding***   An illegal practice involving the use of family members or friends to drive up the bidding on an item (sometimes called *bid padding*).

***shooting star***   Someone who has earned a feedback rating of 10,000 or more.

***snipe***   A bid placed in the closing seconds of an auction in an attempt to prevent any higher bids from being placed before the sale ends.

***star chart***   A system for visually representing someone's feedback rating. A yellow star next to the member's user ID means that person has a feedback rating of 10 to 49 points, for instance. See http://pages.ebay.com/help/feedback/reputation-stars.html.

***trademark***   See *maker's mark*.

***Verified Rights Owner (VeRO) program***   A program in which owners of brand names, copyrights, or trademarks, or their authorized representatives, work to make sure that eBay sales do not infringe upon those intellectual property rights.

B

# Appendix C

## Collectors' Resources on the Web

Collectors love to search and discover things on their own. The Web is the perfect place to do research—about the objects you love, the items you buy and sell on eBay, and other types of merchandise you might want to trade. The "Links for Collectors" lists at the end of this book's chapters direct you to resources that are of interest primarily within eBay itself, although other web sites are included too. This appendix focuses on online resources that make you a more knowledgeable and competent collector.

# Online Price Guides

As a collector, you're undoubtedly familiar with printed price guides. These guides will probably never go completely out of style. They contain photos of collectibles along with general historical information and data about grading and condition. But as an eBay user, you're also aware that online auctions are giving printed price guides some serious competition. You can enjoy the best of both the online and traditional information resources by researching the databases listed here.

## Kovels' Online Antiques and Collectibles Price Guides

### http://www.tias.com/stores/kovels

Ralph and Terry Kovel, who have published dozens of price guides over the years, have gathered the contents of 12 of their books and made them available online in a searchable database. An estimated 450,000 items are included, and it's free to search the database. It's not always easy to uncover exactly what you're looking for though.

## Artprice.com

### http://web.artprice.com/start.aspx

This site provides you with an extensive database of auction results. The auction results are taken from auction houses around the world—not apparently from eBay, however. You can use a free demo to search the database of 4 million auction results. Other services require a subscription; for frequent users, the cost is $8.95 per month, but other payment arrangements are also available on a pay-as-you-go basis.

# Collect.com

## http://www.collect.com

Krause Publications, a publisher of price guides for many types of collectibles, provides an online database for sports cards and antiques. You need to register to access these databases, but registration is free. At this writing, online pricing information for coins, comics, and records were being planned as well.

# Maine Antique Digest

## http://www.maineantiquedigest.com

This publication contains a searchable database of 7500 works of art and antiques. The catch is that, to access it, you need to subscribe to the *Maine Antique Digest*, which costs $43 per year. The magazine has interesting news about upcoming auctions and high-ticket sales, however.

# GPAnalysis.com

## http://www.gpanalysis.com

This site is set up to look and feel like one that tracks the stock market. Instead, the site tracks up-to-the-minute sales of CGC-graded comic books. GPAnalysis.com charges an $8.95 per month membership fee. Discounts are given if you subscribe on a yearly basis.

# Auction Services

Online auctions are among the most popular of all resources on the Internet—so popular that a group of web sites have sprung up that are especially designed to provide services to both buyers and sellers. Most of the services are designed to help eBay sellers get their sales online, design sales, and research the value of what they sell. Five of the most popular of these services are listed here.

C

# Andale

## http://www.andale.com

Andale is widely known among auction service providers for its free search utilities. A search box that appears on the site's home page lets you search eBay's database of completed auctions. The search results you receive recommend the best categories in which you should place items for sale. Another search option on the Price Finder page gives you detailed reports on the prices sellers have received for items in the past. Other products function as hit counters, sales analyzers, and listing tools. All Andale's products except the free search utilities require monthly subscriptions.

# HammerTap

## http://www.hammertap.com

All HammerTap's products are designed to work with eBay, and all are available either free or on a free-trial basis: you try out the product for 30 days, and then pay a fee if you decide to keep it. One tool, HammerSnipe, is an online service that lets you place snipe bids in the last few seconds of an auction. DeepAnalysis is market research software that recommends the best categories and products to sell on eBay. Other software lets you research bidders or even block particular bidders from participating in your sales.

# Marketworks

## http://www.marketworks.com

This site became well known as Auctionworks before it changed its name. Marketworks provides services for high-volume eBay sellers and PowerSellers. It offers time-controlled listing services, automated feedback, auction tracking, and relisting. You can also indefinitely maintain your inventory in a web store you create for your account without incurring a listing fee—you pay a fee only when an item sells.

## SpareDollar

### http://www.sparedollar.com

This site is popular with many eBay sellers, who are attracted to its competitive rates for 50MB of image hosting space as well as software that helps you list your sales on eBay. For $4.95 per month, you gain access to all the site's hit counters, sales listing uploaders, image editors, and tools for automatically leaving feedback.

## Vendio

### http://www.vendio.com

You'll see the Vendio logo at the bottom of many eBay sales descriptions. That means the seller has used the company's Sales Manager service to prepare listings. You can try the online service for free; if you want to keep using it, you pay $12.95 to $39.95 per month.

# Online Appraisals

Real-world appraisers charge $50 to $100 or even more per hour. But online appraisers can provide you with an estimate for less than $20. Here are some suggestions.

## Ask the Appraiser

### http://www.collectingchannel.com/ata

This online appraisal service, provided by CollectingChannel.com, is the one eBay sends you to when you click the Get an Appraisal link on one of its pages. (This doesn't mean that it's better or different than the other services listed in this section.) You submit a description of your item and some photos and pay a $19.95 appraisal fee. In return, you get an online version of your appraisal as well as one that is sent to you by e-mail. The appraisal provides you with the market value of the object; other online appraisals also estimate the replacement value.

C

 *Posting the appraisal online gives you the ability to direct prospective buyers to the report.*

## About.com's eBay Experts Page

### http://experts.about.com/q/2160/index.htm

About.com has a series of "Experts" pages, where knowledgeable people are made available to ask questions about a wide variety of topics. This particular page covers buying and selling on eBay. Occasionally, sellers ask for an appraisal on an item they want to sell, and often, experts respond with an opinion.

## WhatsItWorthToYou.com

### http://www.wiw2u.com

This site has an unusual program called Second Opinion in which its experts review an item you want to purchase online (such as an eBay auction listing) and tell you if it's worth your bids. This will cost you $9.95. A "Classic Appraisal" costs $9.95, too.

## Instappraisal

### http://www.instappraisal.com/antique_appraisals.asp

This site's experts will review your auction description and the photos you send and provide you with an appraisal for $17.95. The report tells you the "fair market value" of the item (the price a buyer might reasonably pay) as well as the "replacement value" (the cost to replace the item with a comparable one).

## Antique Appraisals Online

### http://www.antique-appraise.com

The offline version of this appraisal company, Wilcox & Hall, has been in operation since 1959. This site charges $18.95 for an appraisal, but the resulting report includes extensive historical information about what you have as well as details about similar items that have sold at real-world auctions. Also available are online tutorials that teach you how to do your own online appraisals; they cost only $2.95 each.

# Index

# INTERNATIONAL CONTACT INFORMATION

**AUSTRALIA**
McGraw-Hill Book Company
Australia Pty. Ltd.
TEL +61-2-9900-1800
FAX +61-2-9878-8881
http://www.mcgraw-hill.com.au
books-it_sydney@mcgraw-hill.com

**CANADA**
McGraw-Hill Ryerson Ltd.
TEL +905-430-5000
FAX +905-430-5020
http://www.mcgraw-hill.ca

**GREECE, MIDDLE EAST, & AFRICA
(Excluding South Africa)**
McGraw-Hill Hellas
TEL +30-210-6560-990
TEL +30-210-6560-993
TEL +30-210-6560-994
FAX +30-210-6545-525

**MEXICO (Also serving Latin America)**
McGraw-Hill Interamericana Editores
S.A. de C.V.
TEL +525-1500-5108
FAX +525-117-1589
http://www.mcgraw-hill.com.mx
carlos_ruiz@mcgraw-hill.com

**SINGAPORE (Serving Asia)**
McGraw-Hill Book Company
TEL +65-6863-1580
FAX +65-6862-3354
http://www.mcgraw-hill.com.sg
mghasia@mcgraw-hill.com

**SOUTH AFRICA**
McGraw-Hill South Africa
TEL +27-11-622-7512
FAX +27-11-622-9045
robyn_swanepoel@mcgraw-hill.com

**SPAIN**
McGraw-Hill/
Interamericana de España, S.A.U.
TEL +34-91-180-3000
FAX +34-91-372-8513
http://www.mcgraw-hill.es
professional@mcgraw-hill.es

**UNITED KINGDOM, NORTHERN,
EASTERN, & CENTRAL EUROPE**
McGraw-Hill Education Europe
TEL +44-1-628-502500
FAX +44-1-628-770224
http://www.mcgraw-hill.co.uk
emea_queries@mcgraw-hill.com

**ALL OTHER INQUIRIES Contact:**
McGraw-Hill/Osborne
TEL +1-510-420-7700
FAX +1-510-420-7703
http://www.osborne.com
omg_international@mcgraw-hill.com

# Sound Off!

Visit us at **www.osborne.com/bookregistration** and let us know what you thought of this book. While you're online you'll have the opportunity to register for newsletters and special offers from McGraw-Hill/Osborne.

*We want to hear from you!*

# Sneak Peek

Visit us today at **www.betabooks.com** and see what's coming from McGraw-Hill/Osborne tomorrow!

Based on the successful software paradigm, Bet@Books™ allows computing professionals to view partial and sometimes complete text versions of selected titles online. Bet@Books™ viewing is free, invites comments and feedback, and allows you to "test drive" books in progress on the subjects that interest you the most.

# eBay Your Way to Success

**eBay Your Business:
Maximize Profits and
Get Results**
0072257113

**How to Do Everything
with eBay**
0072254262

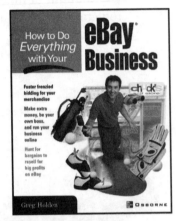

**How to Do Everything
with Your eBay Business**
007222948-9

**eBay PowerSeller Secrets**
0072258691

## Available at bookstores everywhere